English Fiction of the Eighteenth Century 1700–1789

Clive T. Probyn

Longman

London and New York

Longman Group Limited
Longman House, Burnt Mill, Harlow,
Essex CM20 2JE, England
and Associated Companies throughout the world

*Published in the United States of America
by Longman Inc., New York*

First published 1987
Fourth impression 1994

BRITISH LIBRARY CATALOGUING IN PUBLICATION DATA
Probyn, Clive T.
 English fiction of the eighteenth century,
 1700–1789.
 1. English fiction – 18th century –
 History and criticism
 I. Title
 823'.5'09   PR851

ISBN 0-582-49370-6 CSD
ISBN 0-582-49369-2 PPR

LIBRARY OF CONGRESS CATALOGING IN PUBLICATION DATA
Probyn, Clive T.
 English fiction of the eighteenth century,
1700–1789.

 (Longman literature in English series)
 Bibliographic: p.
 Includes index.
 1. English fiction — 18th century — History and
criticism. I. Title.   II. Series.
PR851.P76 1988   823'.5'09   86–30536
ISBN 0–582–49370–6
ISBN 0–582–49369–2 (pbk.)

Set in Linotron 202 9½/11pt Bembo
Produced by Longman Singapore Publishers (Pte) Ltd.
Printed in Singapore

Contents

Editors' Preface

The multi-volume Longman Literature in English Series provides students of literature with a critical introduction to the major genres in their historical and cultural context. Each volume gives a coherent account of a clearly defined area, and the series, when complete, will offer a practical and comprehensive guide to literature written in English from Anglo-Saxon times to the present. The aim of the series as a whole is to show that the most valuable and stimulating approach to the study of literature is that based upon an awareness of the relations between literary forms and their historical contexts. Thus the areas covered by most of the separate volumes are defined by period and genre. Each volume offers new and informed ways of reading literary works, and provides guidance for further reading in an extensive reference section.

In recent years, the nature of English studies has been questioned in a number of increasingly radical ways. The very terms employed to define a series of this kind – period, genre, history, context, canon – have become the focus of extensive critical debate, which has necessarily influenced in varying degrees the successive volumes published since 1985. But however fierce the debate, it rages around the traditional terms and concepts.

As well as studies on all periods of English and American literature, the series includes books on criticism and literary theory, and on the intellectual and cultural context. A comprehensive series of this kind must of course include other literatures written in English, and therefore a group of volumes deals with Irish and Scottish literature, and the literatures of India, Africa, the Caribbean, Australia and Canada. The forty-seven volumes of the series cover the following areas: Pre-Renaissance English Literature, English Poetry, English Drama, English Fiction, English Prose, Criticism and Literary Theory, Intellectual and Cultural Context, American Literature, Other Literatures in English.

David Carroll
Michael Wheeler

Longman Literature in English Series
General Editors: David Carroll and Michael Wheeler
Lancaster University

Pre-Renaissance English Literature

* ★ English Literature before Chaucer *Michael Swanton*
* English Literature in the Age of Chaucer
* ★ English Medieval Romance *W. R. J. Barron*

English Poetry

* ★ English Poetry of the Sixteenth Century (Second Edition) *Gary Waller*
* ★ English Poetry of the Seventeenth Century (Second Edition) *George Parfitt*
* English Poetry of the Eighteenth Century, 1700–1789
* ★ English Poetry of the Romantic Period, 1789–1830 (Second Edition) *J. R. Watson*
* ★ English Poetry of the Victorian Period, 1830–1890 *Bernard Richards*
* English Poetry of the Early Modern Period, 1890–1940
* ★ English Poetry since 1940 *Neil Corcoran*

English Drama

* English Drama before Shakespeare
* ★ English Drama: Shakespeare to the Restoration, 1590–1660 *Alexander Leggatt*
* ★ English Drama: Restoration and Eighteenth Century, 1660–1789 *Richard W. Bevis*
* English Drama: Romantic and Victorian, 1789–1890
* English Drama of the Early Modern Period, 1890–1940
* English Drama since 1940

English Fiction

* ★ English Fiction of the Eighteenth Century, 1700–1789 *Clive T. Probyn*
* ★ English Fiction of the Romantic Period, 1789–1830 *Gary Kelly*
* ★ English Fiction of the Victorian Period, 1830–1890 (Second Edition) *Michael Wheeler*
* ★ English Fiction of the Early Modern Period, 1890–1940 *Douglas Hewitt*
* English Fiction since 1940

English Prose

★ English Prose of the Seventeenth Century, 1590–1700 *Roger Pooley*
English Prose of the Eighteenth Century
English Prose of the Nineteenth Century

Criticism and Literary Theory

Criticism and Literary Theory from Sidney to Johnson
Criticism and Literary Theory from Wordsworth to Arnold
Criticism and Literary Theory from 1890 to the Present

The Intellectual and Cultural Context

The Sixteenth Century
★ The Seventeenth Century, 1603–1700 *Graham Parry*
★ The Eighteenth Century, 1700–1789 (Second Edition) *James Sambrook*
The Romantic Period, 1789–1830
★ The Victorian Period, 1830–1890 *Robin Gilmour*
The Twentieth Century: 1890 to the Present

American Literature

American Literature before 1880
★ American Poetry of the Twentieth Century *Richard Gray*
★ American Drama of the Twentieth Century *Gerald M. Berkowitz*
★ American Fiction 1865–1940 *Brian Lee*
★ American Fiction since 1940 *Tony Hilfer*
★ Twentieth-Century America *Douglas Tallack*

Other Literatures

Irish Literature since 1800
Scottish Literature since 1700

Australian Literature
★ Indian Literature in English *William Walsh*
African Literature in English: East and West
Southern African Literature in English
Caribbean Literature in English
★ Canadian Literature in English *W. J. Keith*

★ *Already published*

Author's Preface

Anyone who might doubt the extraordinary range of the eighteenth-century novel need only imagine Moll Flanders and Evelina, Pamela and Fanny Hill, Ferdinand Count Fathom and Harley, Tristram Shandy and Manfred, all meeting together in the same room, with Robinson Crusoe and Sir Charles Grandison kicking their heels in the lobby. One wonders what they might have in common. As for a single and comprehensive literary theory of the novel, even between the years 1700 and 1789, one would need the combined talents of a Linnaeus and a Procrustes. The salient feature of the novel in these years is its diversity, its formal instability, its mixing of modes and techniques. By 1767 the early novelists had established all of the techniques of narrative prose fiction, but this was not achieved by a monocular concentration on the novel form itself. There are poems in *Pamela* and *The Man of Feeling*, pages of theatrical dialogue in *Grandison*, political and historical essays in the novels of Defoe and Fielding, autobiography in *Amelia* and *Tristram Shandy*, diary and allegory in *Robinson Crusoe*, as well as novels in letter-form, fragmentary novels, and novels exhibiting what seems to us now a consummate literary shape. The task of defining the novel was first encountered in this period, and the range of responses was as wide as the number of its major practitioners.

Northrop Frye rightly pointed out in *Anatomy of Criticism* (1957): 'The literary historian who identifies fiction with the novel is greatly embarrassed by the length of time that the world managed to get along without the novel, and until his great deliverance in Defoe, his perspective is intolerably cramped.' But equally, it is beyond dispute that what we now recognize as the first major, and astonishingly rapid, developmental stage in the evolution of the novel occurred between the years 1719 (the date of *Robinson Crusoe*) and 1767 (the ninth and final volume of *Tristram Shandy*): a period of less than fifty years, a single lifetime. Some of the decisions forced on the present study may seem like those enunciated by Thwackum in *Tom Jones*: 'When I mention Religion, I mean the Christian Religion; and not only the Christian Religion, but the Protestant Religion; and not only the Protestant

Religion, but the Church of England.' Prose fiction here means the novel. Except for purposes of illustration and contrast, there is no detailed discussion in this book of travel literature, philosophical fable, occasional journalism, or political allegory. Although *Gulliver's Travels* and Johnson's *Rasselas* are prose fictions, and share some of the characteristics of the novel, the first is primarily a complex mixture of forms and purposes inside a parodic traveller's tale, and the second a philosophical argument, essentially an argument pinned to an inessential oriental setting. None of their characteristics is absent from texts which we would indisputably call novels but, equally, many of the essentially novelistic elements are absent in them.

There are five dominant 'strong' voices in the novel during the eighteenth century: Defoe, Richardson, Fielding, Smollett, and Sterne. These are the canonical figures who engross critical attention, not through any conspiracy of literary history but because they are by any standards the writers who best combine socially significant interests with artistic skills of a high order. However new and illuminating the insights of modern criticism may be, particularly those of feminist criticism, their *artistic* pre-eminence goes unchallenged. The distinction to be made between these five major writers and others, apart from their intrinsic quality, is a matter for literary sociology. And here, it seems, we reach another difficulty. Pat Rogers has remarked, with reference to Ian Watt's classic *The Rise of the Novel* (1957), that we are still in a 'neo-Wattian' position regarding the sociology of the emergent novel. Watt's study has been recently criticized for its notion that the middle-class reader was both the instrument and the beneficiary of the novel's 'rise', and for its assumption that 'formal realism' is the purpose and the yardstick of the novel's development in this period. My own view is that the question of whether the early novel develops 'formal realism' by opposing itself to romance, or whether 'formal realism' was simply an episode within a continuing but changing romance tradition, remains a permanent artistic option during this period. Smollett, for example, never seems to have resolved the contrary impulses of romance and realism until 1771, and from the 1760s romance was being revaluated as a literary means of expressing imaginative experience deemed inappropriate to, and in some ways directly opposed to, the methods of Defoe and Richardson. Such stresses and tensions are more obvious in the 'minor' writers of any period, and some attention is paid to a very select few in what follows.

After one chapter on each of the five major novelists, Chapter 7 looks at some 'transitional' novels. The term 'transitional' does not imply that the novel up to 1765 had proceeded in a smooth evolutionary curve in an upward qualitative direction, nor does it imply that by 1765 the novel's characteristics had been fixed. Signs of a continuing struggle to find an appropriate form for a different kind of experience are just as remarkable in these later novels, but at the same time they do lead our attention to a changing literary and moral climate. One major turning-point is *Tristram Shandy*, which has been seen (persuasively in both cases) as a parody of the novel and as the quintessential European example of the novel form. *Tristram Shandy* proved to be an unrepeatable experiment, but to a lesser extent each of the five major novelists produces works which are more remarkable for what they do *not* have in common with their contemporaries rather than for their generic similarities.

A note on texts used

As far as possible I have chosen editions of novels which are both textually reliable and readily available. In most cases this means the recent World's Classics series of novels published by Oxford University Press. These are textually of a high standard, though often underannotated. The first textual reference identifies the edition used by a chapter-end note, and all subsequent references are to that edition and to its page references (none of Defoe's novels has formal divisions, and Richardson's proceed by numbered letters). In certain cases there are standard scholarly editions with substantial editorial commentary and notes. For ease of reference, volume and/or book and chapter references are also included, where appropriate, together with page references (as in the case of *Tom Jones* and *Sir Charles Grandison*, for example). In the case of Richardson's *Clarissa* I have used the one-volume edition edited by Angus Ross, Harmondsworth, 1985. Unfortunately this edition (as in the case of the four-volume Everyman edition, 1932, reprinted London, 1962) obliterates Richardson's careful structuring of each of the eight volumes (though the last two were published as one volume), and where there is need to refer to the *original* format, the volume references in the text are to the original 1748–49 edition.

I would like to thank Geoffrey Hiller for commenting on parts of this book; Andrew Milner for a conversation and a memo; Geoffrey Dobbs for a box of books; Jocelyn Harris for hunting down a quotation; Gail Ward for so ably converting a manuscript into a process of words; and Meg, Zoë, Andrew, and Fiona for the gift of temporary neglect.

CTP
Monash
November 1985

List of Abbreviations

The following common abbreviations have been used in the text:

JELH   Journal of English Literary History
MP   Modern Philology
NCBEL   New Cambridge Bibliography of English Literature
PBSA   Publications of the Bibliographical Society of America
PMLA   Publications of the Modern Language Association of
          America
RES   Review of English Studies
SB   Studies in Bibliography
TSLL   Texas Studies in Language and Literature

For Martin and Ruthe Battestin

Chapter 1
The Unstable Genre: Novels and Readers, 1692–1785

In 1752 Samuel Richardson wrote: 'Twenty years ago I was the most obscure man in Great Britain, and now I am admitted to the company of the first characters of the Kingdom.' Samuel Johnson remarked of Laurence Sterne in 1773: 'any man who has a name, or who has the power of pleasing, will be very generally invited in London. The man, Sterne, I have been told, has had engagements for three months.' Literary forms have a social history as well as their authors, and in these two examples it was the novel which provided Richardson and Sterne with their rapid upward mobility into the most fashionable circles. One of Richardson's female correspondents in London regretfully informed him in 1761 that 'we are obliged to read every foolish book that fashion renders prevalent in conversation . . . even the bishops admire [*Tristram Shandy*]'.

The 'eighteenth-century novel' is an almost meaningless label, given the extraordinary variety of approaches to fictional prose narrative in the period 1700–89. Although historians of the form can trace its origins to earlier prose fiction of the seventeenth century, Defoe, generally regarded as the first pioneer of the novel as we have come to understand it, strenuously maintained that his novels were not invented but discovered, not fictions but ready-made history and therefore in need of neither formal parentage nor pedigree. Imagined as a social event, we might say that the novel, like its hero or heroine, began life as a foundling, was identified as a bastard, became an adopted outsider, then a parvenu, and then eventually in our own time displaced all other literary genres. Within its first development phase in the eighteenth century its rise was phenomenal: it came second only to the sermon in terms of its domination of the printed word.

Although, as we shall see, definition of the novel's genealogy perplexed its authors, everyone else seemed to be content to dispense with such critical enquiries. Two exceptions are worth noting, however. In William Congreve's *Incognita; or, Love and Duty Reconcil'd: A Novel* (1692), changes in the nature and subject of prose fiction are foreshadowed (a generation before Defoe's novels began to appear), based on an oppositional relationship with romance. The defining characteristic of the modern novel is now a recognizable, familiar, and contemporary reality:

> Romances are generally composed of the Constant Loves and invincible Courages of Hero's, Heroines, Kings and Queens, Mortals of the first Rank, and so forth; where lofty Language, miraculous Contingencies and impossible Performances, elevate and surprize the Reader into a giddy Delight, which leaves him flat upon the Ground wherever he gives of, and vexes him to think how he has suffer'd himself to be pleased and transported, concerned and afflicted at the several Passages which he hath Read, viz. these Knights success to their Damosels Misfortunes, and such like, when he is forced to be very well convinced that 'tis all a lye. Novels are of a more familiar nature; Come near us, and represent to us Intrigues in practice . . . not such as are wholly unusual or unpresidented. (ii–iii)

Both sexes read novels, but in this period the numerical (if not qualitative) majority were actually written by women. A female readership is overtly assumed by Richardson, Fielding, and Fanny Burney, and among the 350 occasions on which Sterne addresses his readership in *Tristram Shandy* he directs specific remarks to 'Jenny', 'Madam', and 'Julia'.

Congreve's comment in *Incognita* seems to have defined the characteristics of the novel form in advance of its 'genesis' in Defoe, if we regard social realism as the only distinguishing criterion of the new novel. In fact, anxieties about the relationship between the novel and romance persisted throughout this period. In 1749 Henry Fielding articulated a standard objection to the use and to the motives of earlier fiction in a disparaging reference to the prolific and inflaming fictions of Aphra Behn:

> This young Fellow lay in Bed reading one of Mrs. *Behn's* Novels; for he had been instructed by a Friend, that he would find no more effectual Method of recommending himself to the Ladies than the improving his Understanding, and filling his Mind with good Literature.[1]

Clearly, the young Tom Jones has been misinformed. 'Good literature' certainly improves the understanding, but Mrs Behn's novels are neither 'good' in Fielding's sense nor worthy of the label 'literature', and the association of the term 'novel' with such writers as Mrs Behn meant that 'serious' novelists avoided using the term to describe their own prose fiction. The problem confronting the first wave of novelists in the early eighteenth century was thus of disassociation and re-definition of the form itself. Clara Reeve's *The Progress of Romance* (2 vols, 1785), the first critical study of the novel in book form, offers the same definition as Congreve, almost a century later, and after the appearance of all of the novels discussed in this present book:

> The Romance is an heroic fable, which treats of fabulous persons and things. – The Novel is a picture of real life and manners, and of the times in which it is written. The Romance in lofty and elevated language, describes what never happened nor is likely to happen. – The Novel gives a familiar relation of such things, as pass every day before our eyes, such as may happen to our friend, or to ourselves; and the perfection of it, is to represent every scene, in so easy and natural a manner, and to make them appear so probable, as to deceive us into a persuasion (at least while we are reading) that all is real, until we are affected by the joys or distresses, of the persons in the story, as if they were our own. (I, 111)[2]

Clara Reeve's 1785 list of novels includes all the authors (though not all of their novels) which we now regard as *the* eighteenth-century tradition, even though there is a generic vagueness about what a novel actually is. After brief mention of Cervantes, Bunyan, Swift (*Gulliver's Travels* and *A Tale of a Tub* are cited as novels), she discusses Defoe's *Robinson Crusoe*, Richardson's *Pamela*, *Clarissa*, and *Grandison* ('to praise the works of *Mr. Richardson* is to hold a candle to the Sun', I, 134), Fielding's *Joseph Andrews* and *Tom Jones*, all the novels of Smollett, Sterne's *Tristram Shandy* ('not a woman's book', II, 30), and *A Sentimental Journey*. The interest of this list is that a reader twenty years younger than Clara Reeve (who was born in 1729), could have read every one of these novels as they came off the press. All were published in a period of little more than fifty years (1719–71), and such a reader would therefore be familiar with the entire development of the new genre in all its modes and methods: Defoe's fictional autobio-graphies, Richardson's epistolary novels, Fielding's parodic novel *Shamela*, his 'comic epic poem in prose' (*Joseph Andrews* and *Tom Jones*), the arch-parodic novel *Tristram Shandy*, and the picaresque fiction of Smollett (*Roderick Random* and *Humphry Clinker*). Such an imagined reader would, of course, already be familiar with Bunyan's *Pilgrim's Progress* (1684: 160 editions by 1792), and might also have read the philosophic pseudo-novels of Samuel Johnson (*Rasselas*, 1759) and perhaps also Voltaire's *Candide* (1759).

Such a reader would have read only a fraction of the total number of novels published between 1700 and 1780. In the 1730s alone, almost two hundred new or reprinted works of fiction appeared, and between 1660 and 1800 over a thousand works of epistolary fiction.[3] Writing became a boom industry. In Ian Watt's words, ' there is perhaps no other period where so many of the acknowledged masterpieces received such immediate and handsome monetary reward'.[4] Fielding earned £700 for the first edition of *Tom Jones* and an additional £100 for the second edition; Sterne's *A Sentimental Journey* earned him £1000; Gibbon's *Decline and Fall of the Roman Empire* netted £6000 for its author; Swift asked for and got £200 for *Gulliver's Travels*; Pope earned about £5000 for his ten years' labour on a translation of Homer's *Iliad*, and not much less again for his *Odyssey* – each providing about £500 per annum, £100 less than Johnson thought adequate for a life of 'splendour'. Nobody knew more than Defoe about the economics of the book trade. 'Writing', he said in 1725, 'is become a very considerable Branch of the English Commerce. The Booksellers are the master Manufacturers or Employers. The several Writers, Authors, Copyers, Sub-writers, and all other Operators with Pen and Ink are the workmen employed by the said Master Manufacturers'; and it is characteristic of the indefatigable and commercially-minded Defoe that his *Essay upon Literature* (1726) deals not with the art of writing but with the technology of book production.

Reading is a promiscuous activity. We read different kinds of 'literature' and at different levels. In the early eighteenth century the extension of readership is a sub-category of much broader educational and social ideologies. As Richard Altick has remarked in *The English Common Reader*, literacy in an industrial and increasingly democratic society was 'a revolutionary social concept: that of the democracy of print'.[5] This does not mean that there was a social equality among the early readers of literature. Altick goes on to indicate that for the lower professional classes, an usher in a school, for example, the choice could lie between buying a

> newly published quarto volume and a good pair of
> breeches (each cost from 10s. to 12s.), or between a
> volume of essays and a month's supply of tea and sugar
> for his family of six (2s. 6d.) . . . A woman in one of the
> London trades during the 1770's could have bought a
> three-volume novel in paper covers only with the proceeds
> of a week's work. To purchase the *Spectator* in a dozen
> little 12mo volumes (16s.) would have cost an Oxfordshire

carpenter eight days' toil; to acquire the 1743 version of the *Dunciad* at 7s. 6d. would have taken almost a full two weeks' salary of a ten-pound-a-year school usher.

Some readers, however, put intellectual satisfaction above primary needs. In 1734 an anonymous commentator in *The Gentleman's Magazine* remarked on the proliferation of morally instructive works pouring from the presses in instalments cheap enough to compete with life's necessities:

> You have Bayle's *Dictionary*, and Rapin's *History* from two places. The Bible can't escape, I bought the other Day, three Pennyworth of the Gospel, made easy and familiar to Porters, Carmen, and Chimney-Sweepers . . . What an Age of Wit and Learning is this! In which so many Persons in the lowest Stations of Life, are more intent upon cultivating their Minds, than upon feeding and cloathing their Bodies.

The novel is the most spectacular product of a rapidly increasing middle-class readership, but it is a latecomer in the context of an increasing literacy. It rides on a wave already set in motion by early and organized attempts to propagate Christian belief and social orthodoxy through the teaching of reading skills. The Society for Promoting Christian Knowledge was established in 1699 and taught through a network of charity schools and parochial libraries (eighty by the year 1730), with a clear and functional purpose. In 1745 Joseph Butler, Bishop of Bristol, preached a sermon including these words: 'It is most manifest that a Christian and useful Education to the children of the Poor is very necessary to their Piety, Virtue, and honest Livelihood.' James Nelson, a London apothecary, added what had already become a commonplace moral objection to secular fiction: in 1756 he attacked 'the swarms of lewd Plays, Poems and Romances, calculated to inflame the Minds and corrupt the Hearts of the Reader'. As the squads of moral censors moved across the literary landscape, it is interesting to note that not until 1886 did the publication of novels outstrip the publication of religious books.[6] The moral climate of Defoe's time necessitated a careful tempering of imaginative pleasure and overt moral instruction based on a simple distinction between literature as a platform for moral self-improvement within a Christian context and reading for the as yet undefined purpose of vicarious imaginative pleasure. The anonymous author of *The History of Genesis* (1708) exhorted his readers to 'throw away all fond and amorous Romances,

and fabulous Histories of Giants, the bombast Atchievements of
Knight Errantry, and the like'.

A similar contrast is drawn by Mrs Shirley in Richardson's *Sir
Charles Grandison* almost fifty years later: 'The reading in fashion when
I was young was Romances. You, my children, have in that respect
fallen into happier days. The present age is greatly obliged to the
authors of the *Spectator*.' It is true that Addison and Steele's series of
271 weekly articles on topics of the day (including essays on Locke,
Milton, critical theory, as well as fashions in manners) proved an enormous success. Allowing for each issue being read by 20 persons
Addison generously calculated that he was reaching 60,000 readers each
day in the cities of London and Westminster alone (*Spectator* 10, 12
March 1711). The first collected edition of the *Spectator* (9000 copies)
reached its ninth edition in 1729. From 1700 to 1760 more than half
the booksellers were in London. Production of works of fiction rose
from 7 per annum (1700–40) to 20 per annum after 1740, to 40 per
annum in the period 1770–1800. The world's first newspaper, *The
Daily Courant*, appeared in 1702 and by 1724 London had 3 daily newspapers, 7 published three times a week, and 6 weekly journals. Edward
Cave established *The Gentleman's Magazine* in 1731, and its circulation
rose to 10,000 copies in an eight-year period. In 1724 there were 75
printers active in London. By 1785 there were 124. Fielding's
publisher, Andrew Millar, left an immense fortune of nearly £100,000,
as did William Strahan. Jacob Tonson spent more than £20,000 on a
country estate. Thomas Guy, another London bookseller, was rich
enough to endow Guy's hospital. The founding publisher of the
present book, Thomas Longman, opened his shop in 1724. Griffiths
started his *Monthly Review* in 1749, followed by Smollett's *Critical
Review* in 1756. Richardson's *Pamela* appeared in the same year as the
first London circulating library, established by a dissenting minister,
the Rev. Samuel Fancourt, at a membership fee of one guinea a year.
Literature had become a commodity like any other manufactured
article, its entrepreneurs and financiers being the booksellers.

Once beyond the patronage of well-intentioned but socially
conservative religious censors, the possibility of self-education through
books became a reality for the modestly well-to-do. Ephraim Chambers published his *Cyclopaedia* in 1728 (a fifth edition came out in 1746),
and Samuel Johnson himself wrote the Preface to Robert Dodsley's
The Preceptor (1748), a collection of articles rather like a Home
University manual on reading, speaking, writing letters, geometry,
geography, astronomy, history, rhetoric, poetry, drawing, logic,
natural philosophy, ethics, morality, trade, laws and government,
human life and manners. The whole was described as 'a General
Course of Education'. For those of slender means, John Wesley

produced many simplified versions of textbooks on grammar, logic, and mathematics. Wesley's Book Room (established in 1741) produced works of biography, poetry, travel, conduct-books, twenty-three editions of the 'home doctor' *Primitive Physic* (1747) by 1791, school-books, the select works of Locke, Shakespeare, and Malebranche, not to mention religious works such as collections of prayers and hymns. The disincentives to joining the ranks of the literate were economic, i.e. the purchase- or borrowing-price, the cost of acquiring literacy itself, and leisure. Pirated editions, large print-runs in small formats, and second-hand bookstalls, together with the circulating library itself, could and did meet the demand. When Swift addressed his *Drapier's Letters* to the whole people of Ireland in 1724 he took control of the means of production in order to surmount the twin problems of cost and illiteracy. Letters I and IV are addressed to the 'Tradesmen, Shop-keepers, Farmers, and Country-People in General', and he instructs them to 'read this Paper with the utmost Attention, or *get it read to you by others*; which that you may do at the less Expence, I have ordered the Printer to sell it at the lowest Rate'. In the later ferment of the French Revolution, and as a response to Burke's *Reflections on the French Revolution* (1790), Tom Paine published the second part of his *Rights of Man* in two formats, one at three shillings (the same price as Burke's book), and another at sixpence as a direct response to popular demand. The second part sold 32,000 copies in a month, and possibly 200,000 copies were in circulation by 1793. The figures derived from the stamp tax indicate that the average daily sale of newspapers in the period from 1753 to 1775 rose from 23,673 to 41,615. In 1780 the figure is 45,422.

The most difficult question to determine is not the rise of a literate audience in the period 1700 to 1780, nor the identification of the instru-mental agents of the rapid demand for, and development of, prose fiction in particular, but the relationship between the producers and the consumers. There seems no reason to doubt that from the 1760s onwards novels were being specifically produced for a middle-class and perhaps predominantly female readership. But in the early stages, and in common with all new literary forms, the novelist had two major tasks: to create a specific readership from within the ranks of the already literate, and to communicate the literary rules by which the novel was to be understood as different from other and cognate genres of prose fiction. Fielding, a classically-educated member of the patrician class, relied for some of his comic–epic effects on parallels drawn with a literary culture unfamiliar to some of his readers. Accordingly, he quotes neither in Latin nor Greek, but in the English translations of Dryden (among others). In *Joseph Andrews* he points out the novelty of his formal invention, substituting the pedigree of the highbrow comic epic in prose for the 'expected' ingredients of the popular

'Romance'. His reader, therefore, may 'expect a kind of Entertainment, not to be found, nor which was even intended, in the following Pages'. Such remarks are designed to rearrange and control the expectations of the anonymous reader, to establish a new wavelength in the space between the new voice and the conventional messages from long-established literary forms. By such means the novel is arranged on a new shelf in the reader's literary imagination: the old books are pushed to one side, to remain as fenced-off neighbours.

Less than forty years later, a more immediate choice of literary diet is available. As Mrs Malaprop and Sir Anthony Absolute enter in Act I of Sheridan's *The Rivals* (1775), the romantic heroine Lydia Languish hurriedly conceals her library of preferred reading in order to display what she thinks she ought to be seen studying. Her preference is for amorous and sentimental fiction: Smollett's *Peregrine Pickle* (which includes the Memoirs of a Lady of Quality) and *Roderick Random* disappear; a translation of Scarron's *L'Adultère Innocente* (1722) is concealed between the covers of Richard Allestree's devotional classic *The Whole Duty of Man* (1659); the three-volume epistolary novel *The History of Lord Aimworth* (1773) goes under the sofa; Ovid (probably *Metamorphoses*) goes behind a cushion; Mackenzie's *The Man of Feeling* (1771) is slipped into her friend Julia's pocket; and the morally improving works of Hester Chapone (*Letters on the Improvement of the Mind. Addressed to a Young Lady* (1773), James Fordyce's *Sermons to Young Women* (1765), and Lord Chesterfield's *Letters . . . to his Son* (1774, described by Johnson as teaching 'the morals of a whore, and the manners of a dancing master'), are arranged to be seen. Lydia's character is clearly at risk. She goes to the circulating library in search of a translation of D'Arnaud's *The Tears of Sensibility* (1773) and Sterne's *A Sentimental Journey*. Sir Anthony informs Mrs Malaprop of the deleterious consequences of reading such fiction: 'Madam, a circulating library in a town is, as an evergreen tree, of diabolical knowledge! It blossoms through the year! And depend on it, Mrs Malaprop, that they who are so fond of handling the leaves will long for the fruit at last' (I. 2).[7]

The links between literacy, literature, and social ideology are inseparable. What the circulating library offered was the possibility of some degree of unsupervised choice, a limited freedom to exercise personal taste, and the chance to indulge in imaginative fantasies free from oppressive social duties. Lydia, already a familiar type of female reader addicted to romantic fiction, knows full well that what she is expected to read is not what she chooses to read. The ancient moral argument about female vanity is now couched in terms of literary choice. In 1696 Mary Astell's *A Serious Proposal to the Ladies* had recommended instructive reading as the lesser of two evils: 'Were not a Morning more advantageously spent at a Book than at a Looking-Glass, and an Evening in Meditations than in Gaming.' By 1761, *The Annual Register* commented, 'the reading female hires her novel from some County Circulating Library, which consists of about a hundred volumes'. A large female readership exacted demands on authors to meet a known public taste. *The Adventures of a Bank-Note* by Thomas Bridges (4 vols, 1770) responds to the new arbiters of the mass market: 'Now, will I, my learned friend, Mr. Circulating Librarian, indulge you with a chapter of true tragical light reading, to please your taste' (IV, 71). Q. D. Leavis noted in her *Fiction and the Reading Public* that the reader now begins to determine the nature of the literary product: she points to 'a narrowing down process', the effect of a mid-century demand for literary censorship during which Sterne is replaced by Mrs Radcliffe and others, 'whereas the response of the reader of the 'fifties had been a complex one, it now became a simple response to the extremely unskilful and clumsy call for tears, pity, shudders, and so forth'.[8] It was to ridicule and redirect such popular taste that Jane Austen wrote *Northanger Abbey* (1797–98). Austen's point about the Gothic horror novels of Mrs Radcliffe and her imitators is that they were as exotic, fantastic, and alien from common experience as the French heroic romances had seemed to Richardson and Fielding. In Chapter 25 she writes:

> it was not in them perhaps that human nature, at least in the midland counties of England was to be looked for . . . in the central part of England there was surely some security for the existence even of a wife not beloved, in the laws of the land, and the manners of the age. Murder was not tolerated, servants were not slaves, and neither poison nor sleeping potions to be procured, like rhubarb from every druggist.

In reacting against the escapist fantasies of the romance, of course, the new novel was offering a mirror of a different kind, a reflection and a social analysis of low life (Defoe), of feminine social mobility (Richardson), of the social hierarchy itself (Fielding), and individual anatomies of feeling (Mackenzie and Sterne), in a form which was intellectually more accessible than any previous literary genre. James Lackington, the London bookseller, recorded his own fictional preferences in the 1790s, making clear that there was no necessary distinction between English and French or Spanish novels, and made the point about the value of fiction for utilitarian self-education:

by the *best*, I mean those written by Cervantes, Fielding, Smollett, Richardson, Miss Burney, Voltaire, Marmontel, Sterne, Le Sage, Goldsmith, Mackenzie, Dr. Moor, Green, C. Smith, Gunning, Lee, Reeves, Lennox, Radcliff, and some others. Indeed I have often thought with Fielding, that some of those publications have given us a more genuine history of Man, in what are called Romances, than is sometimes to be found under the more respectable titles of History, Biography, εc.⁹

James Lackington's Temple of the Muses made him a fortune from second-hand and remainder bookselling. His first catalogue contained 1200 titles, appearing in 1779, and in 1791 he estimated his profits at £4000. In 1792 it was £5000, and 'I now sell more than one hundred thousand volumes annually' (261, 268). His *Memoirs* are full of amusing and specific details of the London book trade, the circulating library, methodism, and reading habits. In a trip from London to Edinburgh in 1787, via York, Newcastle, Glasgow, Carlisle, Leeds, Lancaster, Preston, and Manchester, he found 'very few works of the most esteemed authors'. Apart from York and Leeds there was 'nothing but trash to be found'. He reached the same conclusion in 1790: 'London, as in all other articles of commerce, is likewise the grand emporium of Great-Britain for books' (276). Feeding his bibliomania on tea, bread, and 'Wesley's Gospel-shops' as a young man he had accumulated a library which is perhaps some indication of contemporary taste:

> Fletcher's Checks to Antinomianism, εc. 5 volumes; Watts' Improvement of the Mind; Young's Night Thoughts; Wake's Translation of the Apostolickal Epistles; Fleetwood's Life of Christ; the first twenty Numbers of Hinton's Dictionary of the Arts and Sciences; some of Mr. Wesley's Journals, and some of the pious lives published by him; and about a dozen other volumes of the latter sort, besides old magazines. (128)

This private library became the stock for his first shop in 1774, and it is clear that divinity and moral philosophy come first in importance and (presumably) sales, followed by English poetry, the English translations of Greek, Latin, and French poets, then English translations of Greek and Latin prose ('History, Voyages, Travels, Natural History, Biography, εc'), then plays. Novels come last in this list before astronomy, geography, electricity, pneumatics, and other useful sciences. Lackington makes two comments on his trading methods which have broad cultural implications. The first is in relation to his lucrative (and, strictly, illegal) method of remaindering books at half-price. The second indicates a specific female clientele for fiction:

> it affords me the most pleasing satisfaction, independent of
> the emoluments which have accrued to me from this plan,
> when I reflect what prodigious numbers in inferior or
> *reduced* situations of life, have been essentially benefited in
> consequence of being thus enabled to indulge their natural
> propensity for the acquisition of knowledge, on easy
> terms: nay, I could almost be vain enough to assert, that I
> have thereby been highly instrumental in diffusing that
> general desire for READING, now so prevalent among
> the inferior orders of society. (218)

> Ladies now in general read, not only novels, although
> many of that class are excellent productions, and tend to
> polish both the heart and head; but they also read the best
> works in various languages; and there are some thousands
> of ladies, who frequent my shop, that know as well what
> books to choose, and are as well acquainted with works of
> taste and genius, as any gentleman in the kingdom,
> notwithstanding they sneer against novel readers. (251)

Lackington's entrepreneurial skills no doubt conditioned both his rhetoric and his argument, and caution is necessary when reading his accounts (240–41 and 243) of *Tom Jones* and *Roderick Random* on every rural bacon-rack, of farmers going to town with strict instructions to buy *Peregrine Pickle*, and of their wives trading eggs for *The History of Pamela Andrews*. When Lackington states that 'all ranks and degrees now READ' (243) he no doubt believed that in the previous forty years a revolution in book-buying had taken place. Indeed it had, but there is no proof that the ability to buy and read novels had swept the entire country and at all levels of literacy. On the other hand, the instrumental agency of the bookseller in this literary revolution is beyond question. In his *Ode to the Hero of Finsbury Square* (1795), Peter Pindar (i.e. Robert Wolcot) mocked Lackington's rise to gentrification through bookselling. As the bookseller steps into his coach outside his 'Temple of the Muses', clutching his *Memoirs* and a volume of 'Puffs and Lies for my book', a legend points sardonically to easy money gained by exploitation of the new reading public:

> Approach, good People and the Chariot view
> Who dares presume to say, 'tis all a Bubble.
> Trace the proud Scroll–'tis wonderful, but true,
> *Small Profits do great Things* with little Trouble.

It was an entrepreneurial decision of two booksellers, Charles Rivington and John Osborne, which prompted the novel-writing career of the printer Samuel Richardson. Their request for a manual on letter-writing led directly to the composition of *Pamela*. Twelve years later Samuel Johnson wrote in *The Adventurer* (no. 115, 11 December 1753) that his age was characterized as 'The Age of Authors'. What he termed an 'epidemical conspiracy for the destruction of paper' had turned 'our nobles and our peasants, our soldiers and traders, our men and women, all into wits, philosophers and writers'. Most notable of all, for Johnson, was the rise of the woman writer, 'a generation of Amazons of the pen, who with the spirit of their predecessors have set masculine tyranny at defiance, asserted their claim to the regions of science, and seem resolved to contest the usurpations of virility'.[10] Beneath Johnson's sarcasm lay a profound and revolutionary truth: women were not only writing in greater numbers than ever before, they were not only reading more than ever before; some of their male counterparts were also questioning the patriarchal values of society itself, women's gender roles, and their economic status. Those who feared that unsupervised reading of fiction could disturb the social hierarchies were right. The new novel brought new ways of thinking into the public arena. There is a clear connection between Defoe's dissenting background and his radical social vision in *Moll Flanders* and *Roxana*. All his people are outsiders (by choice or necessity), just as Richardson's heroines in *Pamela* and *Clarissa* are resistant to social orthodoxies. The author, the bookseller, and the book-buying public formed a new entrepreneurial nexus against the traditional custodians of cultural ideology, the patron, the patrician, and the priest (see, for example, John Wesley's opinion on the moral relationship between novels and history books, Ch. 7, note 10, below).

And yet the novel is the most recalcitrant of literary forms, resisting all attempts to force any single development. Any attempt to classify the bewildering variety of types and subspecies in this period is doomed to failure. We cannot speak of 'the political novel' or 'the social problem novel' or 'the novel of manners' in this period, although such labels may be applicable to other periods. One recent critic has rightly remarked that 'the novels of Defoe, Richardson, and Fielding are all so different that the three authors appear to be producing works which virtually belong to separate genres', even though their traditional roots in seventeenth-century prose fiction may be traced back to spiritual biography, the picaresque, and French heroic romance.[11] Even in the case of Richardson's novels, 'the most drastically "new" development in fiction in the eighteenth century', it needs to be pointed out that there were between fifty and a hundred epistolary novels and short stories published before *Pamela* appeared in 1741.[12]

The difference between Defoe and Richardson is as great as that between Richardson and Fielding, whereas Sterne's *Tristram Shandy* has been seen both as the quintessential novel and as utterly eccentric. The arrangement adopted in this present book recognizes the fact that Defoe, Richardson, Fielding, Sterne, and Smollett are the major writers of this period: they are each discussed in separate chapters. What this conceals is not only the vast range and number of novels written by less significant authors, but also their extraordinary cross-referencing both in terms of content and forms. Some indication of this context, though inevitably superficial, is necessary in order to show that the novel-reading public of the time was not always served by masters in the form.

In an age when imitation of classical writers was a fundamental and respectable mode of literary expression, copying the example of contemporary masters was both inevitable and lucrative. However dubiously motivated, imitation is also an index of popular taste and literary influence. Some examples will indicate this. Richard Cumberland copied the style of *Tristram Shandy* in *Flim-Flams: or the Life of my Uncle* (1797–1805); an anonymous author claiming to be the natural daughter of Fielding, and taking her name from Tom Jones's father, published *The History of Charlotte Summers* (1749). William Combe wrote an (obviously) spurious continuation of Sterne's *A Sentimental Journey* called *Letters supposed to have been written by Yorick and Eliza* (1779); Francis Gentleman's *A Trip to the Moon* (1764–65) imitated both Swift and Sterne; another anonymous work, *The Peregrination of Jeremiah Grant* (1763) includes chapters in imitation of Fielding, Smollett, and Sterne. Unlike so many of these derivative works, a few are still perfectly readable in their own right, such as Francis Coventry's Fieldingesque biography of a Bologna lap-dog, *The History of Pompey the Little* (1751: ten editions by 1824). John Dunton's much earlier *A Voyage Round the World* (1691) reverses the obligation of imitation to model. Its digressive teasing of the reader's expectations anticipated *Tristram Shandy*, and the latter's popularity prompted a retitled reprint of the former in 1762, as *The Life, Travels, and Adventures of Christopher Wagstaff, Gentleman, Grandfather to Tristram Shandy*. Fielding's *Tom Jones* provoked the anonymous offspring entitled *The History of Tom Jones the Foundling: in his Married State* (1750). The point of this proliferation is clear: the major novelists, whatever else they had achieved, had established a recognizable and marketable style which was seen to be their own distinct stylistic trademark. Contemporary readers and imitators, as well as subsequent literary historians, coincide in their views that there is a qualitative difference between the five major novelists and everybody else.

Even so, the diversity of eighteenth-century fiction *not* represented by the major novelists is remarkable. Under this heading we might mention the following: Utopian fiction (Robert Paltock's *Life and Adventures of Peter Wilkins*, 1751, for example); didactic conduct-books (Sarah Fielding's *The Governess, or the Little Female Academy*, 1749); the fictional historical novel (Sarah Fielding's *The Lives of Cleopatra and Octavia*, 1759); pretended translations of exotic manuscript tales (James Ridley's *Tales of the Genii*, 1764); scandal novels (*The Precipitate Choice: or the History of Lord Ossory and Miss Rivers*, 1772); early feminist novels (Harriet Lee, *The Errors of Innocence*, 1786, and Mary Wollstonecraft Godwin's *The Wrongs of Woman: or Maria*, 1798); secret or sensational history (a genre virtually monopolized by Mary Manley – see, for example, her account of the Duchess of Marlborough, *The Secret History of Queen Zarah and the Zarzarians*, 1705); rogue biographies (Alexander Smith, *The History of the Lives and Robberies of the most noted Highway-Men*, 1713: pre-dating Defoe's own works in this genre); erotic memoirs (John Cleland's *Memoirs of a Woman of Pleasure*, 1748–49: better known as *Fanny Hill*, the one-volume abridgement of 1750); early Gothic fiction (Walpole's *The Castle of Otranto*, 1765); early science fiction (the anonymous *Aerostatic Spy: or Adventures with an Air Balloon*, 1785) – and various permutations of virtually any of these subspecies of prose fiction.[13]

With the exception of Richardson, the eighteenth-century novelist's inheritance of a generically varied background of prose fiction continued to find expression in mixed modes of narrative discourse. The inherent generic instability of the novel at this time, or its refusal to accommodate any single narrative mode, is exemplified in Smollett's *Humphry Clinker* (1771). Within its formal epistolary structure it also contains elements of the travel book, topographical guide, occasional essay, character-sketch, spiritual biography, and the picaresque. Interpolated narratives in Fielding's novels (Leonora's story in *Joseph Andrews*, the Man of the Hill's biography in *Tom Jones*, for example) are small-scale parables of major themes in each novel, but taken out of context are virtually indistinguishable from countless short romances and the kind of moral fables from which Johnson's *Rasselas* is constructed. At the end of this period the epistolary mode still served the purposes of Fanny Burney's *Evelina* (1778) and (in an early version) Jane Austen's *Sense and Sensibility* (1811). *Gulliver's Travels* (1726) is not a novel, but Swift's *A Tale of a Tub* (1704) has been interpreted as a parody of the novel form before the novel as we know it even emerged.[14] There was no shortage of narrative methods available to the eighteenth-century novelist. Indeed, one critic has suggested that 'as a serious artistic endeavour', the English novel 'might have got started more quickly if there had been *no* prose fiction about, rather than the medley of semi-literary genres which existed in 1700'.[15] The seventeenth century offered English translations of the vast French heroic romances – some of which are mentioned by Fielding in his Preface to *Joseph Andrews*. Gautier de Coste de la Calprenède *Cassandre* (1642–45) is, at 1400 folio pages, an average-sized work in its genre, and Madeleine de Scudéry's *Artamenes or The Grand Cyrus* (1653–54) is longer than Richardson's *Clarissa*. Spanish picaresque novels, such as *Lazarillo de Tormes* (translated in 1576) and Aleman's *Guzman de Alfarache* (translated in 1622) are part of the parentage of Defoe's *Captain Singleton* and *Moll Flanders* (1722). Bunyan's spiritual biographies in *The Pilgrim's Progress, Mr Badman*, and *The Holy War* dimly foreshadow the early eighteenth-century deployment of spiritual allegories in Richardson and Defoe. Romance and anti-romance modes were provided by Cervantes's *Don Quixote* (translated in 1612, and the model for Fielding's 'Manner' in *Joseph Andrews*); and there were the thirteen novels of Aphra Behn (*Oroonoko: Or, The Royal Slave*, 1688, is her best-known novel), a pioneer woman writer who showed in Virginia Woolf's words, that 'money could be made by writing'.[16]

A glance at the prefaces written by Defoe, Richardson, and Fielding indicates their anxiety about literary influence and an urgent need to define their own approaches to prose fiction both in relation to the previous seventeenth-century context and to assumptions about the nature of fictional truth. Defoe reacts against the fashion for 'novels and romances' in *Moll Flanders* by constructing a 'private history' which pre-exists his 'editorial' shaping. Richardson similarly posed as the mere editor of Pamela's letters, 'which have their foundation both in *Truth* and *Nature*' (1741 Preface). Fielding is the first English novelist *not* to pretend that his novels are anything but art, i.e. 'comic–epic poems in prose' with a distinguished imputed ancestry stemming from Homer himself, but nevertheless insists that his novels are also 'true' to life (see Ch. 4 below). Resistance to *literary* influence thus leads, ostensibly, to an elevation of authentic private memoir (*Moll Flanders, Colonel Jack, Roxana, Pamela, Clarissa*, etc.) or to an emblematic or allegorical mode of writing which concerns itself with universal and timeless truth (*Joseph Andrews* and *Tom Jones*).

The novelty of the eighteenth-century novel is more than a matter of its form. It examines, for the first time, radical questions of a social, economic, and sexual nature. Some modern readers of Richardson's novels see his work as a reaction to, as well as an examination of, the patriarchal society of which it is a product. In addition to its analysis of social class, sexual mores, and the marriage market, *Clarissa* has recently been called the first work of fiction to exalt woman, offering 'an extended study of the evolution of the single person in a society apparently inimical to the development of individuals, but ultimately deeply dependent on the ideology of individualism'.[17] The same novel also demands new ways of reading. Richardson distances himself from the 'art' of fiction in the very act of creating it, thus *Clarissa* has no 'author' and no 'reader'. It is presented as an autonomous series of letters from various correspondents (Clarissa, Lovelace, Anna Howe), and everything in the novel is created by writing it down in letters. In John Preston's words, 'The only action [*Clarissa*] can tolerate is the act of writing. In this novel the only activity rendered with immediacy is that of letter-writing. The characters exist within the limits of the letters. The book is made up of documents, and the documents are what the book is about'.[18] Although Fielding drops all pretence to such authorial absenteeism, ostentatiously inviting the reader to witness his skilful creation of a self-consciously literary artefact, he also depends for his success on a subtle nurturing of the reader's response and a complex play of sympathy. Sterne, similarly, teases the reader, even harangues his reader, for his false 'novelistic' expectations about a continuous and 'coherent' plot. In so doing, he exposes the essential artifice of all autobiographical writing, and of the complexities in the act of reading itself. Defoe may be technically the weakest of the early novelists, but his novels are the most revolutionary of all, and in some ways the most challenging to critical interpretation.

Ronald Paulson has remarked that 'the early novel was created in an age when moral justification was still necessary and the description of everyday life for its own sake was considered frivolous'.[19] Defoe's lust for verisimilitude, 'life', the actuality of things, places, and objects, overwhelms that aspect of 'significant form' which we come to expect from masters of the novel form: his novels rarely finish, they simply stop, sometimes to restart in a sequel (as in *Robinson Crusoe*). Nevertheless, Defoe insists on his novels having a clear moral shape and function. He displays the necessary distinction between literal events and their moral, figurative, or allegorical significance in the Preface to *Moll Flanders*:

> as this work [*Moll Flanders*] is chiefly recommended to those who know how to read it, and how to make good the uses of it which the story all along recommends to them; so it is hop'd that such readers will be much more pleas'd with the moral than the fable, with the application than with the relation, and with the end of the writer than with the life of the person written of.

If this is more than lip-service to the conventional demand for moral education through literature, it is not at all clear what precisely 'the moral' of this novel is. A blunt statement of a moral intention is, as we shall see, no guarantee that the novel is significant simply and only because it preaches a lesson. Similarly, Richardson instructed readers of *Clarissa* that 'the author at his first setting out, apprised the reader, that the story was to be looked upon as the vehicle only to the instruction' (1499).

In his earlier novel, *Pamela*, the roots of the novel in Puritan conduct-books appear to have become the supporting trunk: the novel is to teach 'religion and morality . . . the parental, the filial, and social duties . . . to paint VICE in its proper colours . . . to set VIRTUE in its own amiable light, to make it look lovely . . . to give practical examples, worthy to be followed in the most critical and affecting cases, by the virgin, the bride, and the wife'. Fielding's apologia is the classical satirist's defence: 'I describe not Men, but Manners; not an Individual but a Species . . . not to expose one pitiful Wretch, to the small and contemptible Circle of his Acquaintance; but to hold the Glass to thousands in their Closets, that they may contemplate their Deformity, and endeavour to reduce it, and thus by suffering private Mortification may avoid public Shame' (*Joseph Andrews*, III, 1).[20] Whereas Richardson's Preface implies that moral truth is exemplified in and may be learned from his novel, Fielding implies that the reader is already familiar with moral truth and needs only to be reminded, not instructed. Sterne's didactic intentions are closer to Fielding, given the former's statement that the author–reader relationship is an extension into literary terms of 'conversation', but as in so many ways Sterne simply escapes from this conventional distinction between 'Story' and 'Instruction' and exploits every available narrative method in order to break down distinctions between life and art. Within the allegedly autobiographical structure of *Tristram Shandy* we find all of Northrop Frye's forms of narrative discourse – the novel, the confession, the anatomy, and the romance – from each of which Sterne triumphantly escapes.[21]

Each of the major novelists approaches the novel from a different angle: Defoe by way of fictional biography, Richardson through epistolary narrative (both indicating in different ways the limitations of a first-person narrative), Fielding (in *Joseph Andrews* and *Tom Jones* at least) through the comic epic in prose, and Sterne through a parody of autobiography (reprocessing the known fictional modes of narrative presentation of the self in order to explode the notion that individual experience can be 'contained' and transmitted through public forms). Each is prone to repeat rather than change a successfully established method. Defoe's repetition directly correlates with atrophy of the imagination and a hyperdevelopment of didacticism: the fictional goldmine of *Robinson Crusoe* (1719), brilliantly combining (in Watt's phrase) circumstantial realism and moral pattern, eventually degenerates to a leaden preaching in *Further Adventures* (1719) and *Serious Reflexions*

(1720). Elsewhere, in Defoe's criminal biographies, quality is maintained by switching social levels – from low life in *Moll Flanders* to high life in *Roxana*. Richardson's two-volume *Pamela* of 1740–41 (four revised editions appeared) was followed by a two-volume sequel (December 1741), and few if any readers see anything but a falling away in quality in the third and fourth volumes. By contrast, Fielding's first novel, *Joseph Andrews*, grows out of a parody of *Shamela*. This is not repeated in *Tom Jones*, described by one Fielding scholar as 'at once the last and the consummate literary achievement of England's Augustan Age'.[22] *Amelia* was a critical failure: it failed to reconfirm the achievement and style of Fielding's previous novels. Sterne's tiny novel, *A Sentimental Journey*, actually arises from Volume VII, Chapters 42 and 43 of *Tristram Shandy*, repeating and elaborating its apparently shapeless comic wandering, the child and emblem of its parent novel.

The distinction between a major and a minor novelist lies neither in numerical output nor popularity, nor even exclusively in innovation of form, but in the degree to which artistic excellence supports a significant point of view. What distinguishes Defoe, Richardson, Fielding, and Sterne from their less able contemporaries is their imaginative domination of a particular form. Minor novelists of the period are often dominated *by* a given form and fail to imprint their own artistic personalities on it. The form passes through their hands, as it were, unmarked and unchanged. For example, the major novelists' relative clarity, organization, and psychological control over character are in marked contrast to the clotted plots and bewildering digressions of Eliza Haywood's fiction, in which the *significance* of the novel's often fortuitous and helter-skelter series of incidents is simply tacked on as a form of ending. Whereas mysterious births, accidental meetings, and heroic sentiments in Fielding's *Tom Jones: A Foundling* (1749) carry a particular significance (as signs of a Providential pattern in human life, or simply stylistic games to exhibit human self-delusion), in Haywood's *The Fortunate Foundlings* (1744) there is no such control. With its double-foundling plot (Horatio and Louisa), its conflict between Love and Duty, its peripatetic locations (in London, Aix-La-Chapelle, Vienna, the Danube during Marlborough's wars, St Germain, the court of Louis de Bourbon in Paris), and its reliance on masquerades, last-minute rescues from attempted rape, imprisonment in both jail and monastery, its audience with the King of Sweden, the reuniting of 'lost' parents, its marriage ending, to mention only a few incidents, it is hardly a disappointment to find that the significance of all this frantic action is consigned to the final (and inscrutable) sentence: 'By these examples we may learn, that to sustain with fortitude and patience whatever ills we are preordained to suffer, entitles us to relief, while by impatient struggling we should but augment the score, and provoke fate to shew us the vanity of all attempts to frustrate its decrees' (352). Such novels arise from and essentially remain within the inherited traditions of French heroic romances.[23]

Charlotte Lennox's satire of romance, *The Female Quixote* (nine books in two volumes, 1752) triggers a rather more Augustan reaction to the absurdities of romance, anticipating Jane Austen's *Northanger Abbey*, through the heroine Arabella. She is a characterological cliché enclosed within a romantic parody, a type of the leisured and unworldly female who recurs throughout eighteenth-century fiction (Leonora in *Joseph Andrews*, Lydia in *Humphry Clinker*, Euphelia in Johnson's *Rambler*, nos 42 and 46, 1751). Her reading of romances induces in her a literary image of life, her head is full of knight errantry, 'courtesie', swords and honour. Her admirer, Mr Glanville, is (like Henry Tilney) more common-sensical and finds her romantic obsessions unintelligible. Such literary preconceptions are not always restricted to the female sex: the classical learning of Parson Adams in *Joseph Andrews* and Walter Shandy's philosophical obsessions in *Tristram Shandy* both induce myopia. Arabella, however, is the chief casualty of this literary fashion – 'She could not separate her Ideas of Glory, Virtue, Courage, Generosity, and Honour, from the false Representations of them in the Actions of Oroondates, Juba, Artaxerxes, and the rest of the imaginary Heroes' (Book VIII, Ch. 7, p. 240). But in a later discussion of the literary theory of the novel (Book IX, Ch. 11) Arabella is interrogated by a doctor of theology, who informs both Arabella and the reader that 'the great Use of Books, is that of participating without Labour or Hazard [in] the Experience of others', and that the value of fiction depends upon a recognition of its fictionality. 'Nothing is more different from a Human Being, than Heroes or Heroines', says the doctor (318). This becomes a common motif in Fielding. Similarly, in Goldsmith's single novel, it is a signal of Primrose's self-delusion that he gives two of his daughters names associated with romance (Olivia and Sophia: Ch. 1 of *The Vicar of Wakefield*). whereas in Defoe's *Roxana* the romantic name given to the titular heroine at a masked ball signals a fine irony. Roxana's hard-headed and mercantile attitude towards her sexual identity is grotesquely parodied by her naming. Finally, Mrs Lennox directs her reader's attention to the best contemporary examples of prose fiction, whose method unites the pleasures of fiction with useful moral truths:

> An admirable Writer of our own Time, has found the
> Way to convey the most solid Instructions, the noblest
> Sentiments, and the most exalted Piety, in the pleasing

> Dress of a Novel, and, to use the Words of the greatest
> Genius in the present Age, 'Has taught the Passions to
> move the Command of Virtue'.

A footnote indicates that Arabella should abandon romance for Richardson's *Clarissa* and take Johnson's *Rambler*, no. 97 as her critical guide. Rather less tactfully, a Dr Edward Wilmot published his translation, from the French, of *Nymphomania; or a Dissertation Concerning Furor Uterinus* (1775), in which reading novels was cited as a cause of female sexual disorders. He also cited Johnson's remark: 'I have often wished, (since novels *will* be read,) that . . . this species of composition, no longer perverted to the worst purposes, by an abandoned race of scribblers, might be monopolized by men [*sic*] of genius who have abilities, and inclinations to *make . . . the passions move at the command of virtue.*'[24]

This subject, the alleged feminization of the novel, will be discussed in later chapters, but it would be a mistake to assume that readers of romantic novels were either all naive females or readers incapable of reading 'serious' literature at the same time. Just as the sophisticated Dorothy Osborne read and enjoyed the fictional romances of the seventeenth century alongside devotional literature such as Jeremy Taylor's *Holy Living* (a Puritan conduct-book), so almost a century later Sarah Fielding could write a 'Moral Romance' (*The Adventures of David Simple*, 1744) for one readership and, in 1762, publish her translation of *Xenophon's Memoir of Socrates* for another.

In spite of Henry Fielding's editorial hand, Sarah Fielding's *David Simple* betrays more than a few weaknesses of the 'minor' novel of the time. It also reflects some of the better novels' determination to disclaim romance in favour of psychological probability. In Book IV, Chapter 9, in a paragraph which Henry Fielding himself might have written, there is this somewhat sardonic remark:

> Perhaps it may here be expected I should give some
> Description of the Persons of my favourite Characters; but
> as the Writers of Novels and Romances have already
> exhausted all the Beauties of Nature to adorn their Heroes
> and Heroines, I shall leave it to my Readers Imagination
> to form them just as they like best: It is their Minds I
> have taken most pains to bring them acquainted with.[25]

David Simple is, as his name makes clear, a naive hero, a good man betrayed by a corrupt society. The novel's structure is based on a favourite narrative device of romance, the *récit*, an interpolated narrative in which characters are persuaded to give their life histories. Time thus loops backwards and the present is to be understood only in terms of the past (examples are the history of Cynthia in II, iv, on the torment of an intelligent woman forced to adopt the conventional inanities of a passive feminine role; the history of Camilla and Valentine in II, 5–III, 6, on the trial of innocence confronted by poverty and social predators). To the reader familiar with romance conventions, much can be inferred about subsequent events from the opening sentence of Isabella's story: 'I was bred up from five Years of Age in a Nunnery' (196). Henry Fielding also uses the *récit* formula, especially in the first few books of *Amelia*. The romantic episode in *Joseph Andrews*, 'The History of Leonard and Paul', functions much like Sarah Fielding's story of Camilla and Valentine. But whereas Henry Fielding always subjects an individual episode to an overall design (most notably in the Man of the Hill *récit* in *Tom Jones*) a lesser novelist is trapped by simple accumulation. In fact, the narrative principle of *David Simple* is not far from Francis Coventry's *History of Pompey the Little* (1751), a picaresque social satire deriving its comic style from *Tom Jones*, but entirely lacking any *significant* form. This novel follows the ups and downs of a lap-dog, born in the house of an Italian courtesan, sinking through the social levels, rising to high society, dropping to the world of Grub Street, and eventually reuniting with his owner Lady Tempest. The plot principle of this, and of many other minor novels, is the best friend of the despairing novelist, Fortune. It is precisely this cliché of the second-rate novel that Henry Fielding transforms into a sub-textual and transcendent determinant of human action through the idea of Providential ordering.

External and apparently arbitrary effects of chance, if allowed to determine character and structure, reduce characters to ciphers (about whom no questions of motive are asked) and formal significance is sacrificed to variety of incident, to a randomness which may prove a disabling weakness in an artistically serious work of fiction. Captain Booth, in Henry Fielding's *Amelia*, is criticized for his passive fatalism. What he learns is the necessity for positive moral action and thus to enact in his own life the pattern of the author's world-view. As Martin Battestin has shown, 'Design . . . implies an artificer. The assertion of Order and Harmony in the Creation entails the correlative belief in God's superintending Providence: as Pope has it, Nature is Art; Chance, Direction'.[26]

If the romance (and, in Fielding's case, via *Don Quixote*, the anti-romance) provided models for the narrative shape of eighteenth-century fiction, another legacy of the seventeenth century provided a distinct moral and spiritual shape. In 1741 Richardson wrote to his friend Aaron Hill that *Pamela* 'might possibly introduce a new species of writing', which would 'turn young people into a course of reading different from the pomp and parade of romance-writing, and dismissing the improbable and marvellous, with which novels generally abound, might tend to promote the cause of religion and virtue'.[27] For his most celebrated supporter, Samuel Johnson, Richardson's work accomplished exactly this, as Charlotte Lennox's comment above indicates. Johnson's full conservative authority is placed behind this notion of the novel's function as a vehicle for popular instruction. It is a view of art which imposes upon the artist a duty to pre-select those subjects most conducive to a moral programme. As the most democratic of all literary forms the novel's very accessibility carried dangers for the untutored mind. In *The Rambler*, no. 4, 1751, Johnson probably had in mind Smollett's *Roderick Random* (1748) and Fielding's *Tom Jones* (1749), but his remarks on the novel are indiscriminate:

> These books are written chiefly to the young, the
> ignorant, and the idle, to whom they serve as lectures of
> conduct, and introductions into life. They are the
> entertainment of minds unfurnished with ideas, and
> therefore easily susceptible of impressions; not fixed by
> principles, and therefore easily following the current of
> fancy; not informed by experience, and consequently open
> to every false suggestion and partial account.

It is not surprising, in view of this, that Johnson should regard *Tom Jones* as a 'vicious book', since its whole comic method requires a maturity of character in the reader which Johnson evidently cannot associate with the novel as a genre.[28] But this demand for responsible moral instruction pre-dated Johnson. One strand of the eighteenth-century novel's genesis can be traced to the Puritan conduct-books of the seventeenth century. Not all of these guides to moral and spiritual self-analysis were written by Puritans, but the best-known included Bayly's *Practice of Piety* (1613) and Richard Allestree's frequently reprinted *The Whole Duty of Man* (1658–60), manifestations of a patriarchal society in which the spiritual message is conveyed in mercantile and political images, like profit and loss accounts on the road to spiritual solvency, and in which worldly success is attributed to signs of God's favour. The reader of such conduct-books, the reader of novels, and the imprisoned characters of some novels (Robinson Crusoe, Moll Flanders, Pamela, Clarissa) have much in common – each is a single isolated individual with only a text between him- or herself and a mysterious universe, reckoning up the state of his moral being in relation to immanent laws. *Pamela*, it has been recently claimed, is 'probably the first novel which attempted to give a really detailed account of a character's inmost thoughts and feelings'.[29] Richardson's close friend Edward Young interpreted *Pamela* as 'The Whole Duty of WOMAN'. When the silent individual reader of a conduct-book is enfolded within the pages of a novel, *Pamela* and *Clarissa* are the result. The reader becomes the external witness to a private self-analysis and confession. Richardson and Defoe, through letters and 'private history', ostensibly provide no authorial screen between individual experience and the reader's direct access to innermost truths. Letters are the most informal though not necessarily the most honest method of literary self-expression. An autobiography is by definition a life seen through one pair of eyes. The single most significant literary revolution brought about by the eighteenth-century novel is not the fact of its concentration on an individual life but the unprecedented claim it makes to the importance, and the questions it raises about the validity and significance, of the individual experience in oppositional relationships with society.

Notes

1. *The History of Tom Jones A Foundling*, edited by Fredson Bowers, with an Introduction and Commentary by Martin C. Battestin, 2 vols, Oxford, 1974, II, 530. For a discussion of the various types of novels and related genres in the previous century (including those of Aphra Behn), see Paul Salzman, *English Prose Fiction 1558–1700: A Critical History*, Oxford, 1985, particularly pp. 265–337.

2. Clare Reeve, *The Progress of Romance*, 2 vols (1785), I, 7, points out that 'it was not till I had completed my design, that I read either Dr Beattie's *Dissertation on Fable and Romance*, or Mr Warton's *History of English Poetry*'. James Beattie's *Dissertations Moral and Critical* was published in 1783 in Dublin, and in London in 1786. His discussion of fable and romance, a historical sketch of fiction, may be found on pp. 501–74. Thomas Warton's *History of English Poetry*, 3 vols (1774–81), contains a prefatory account of the origin of romantic fiction in Europe.

3. For a detailed list, see *New Cambridge Bibliography of English Literature*, Volume II, *1660–1800*, edited by George Watson (Cambridge, 1971), columns 975–1014; Robert A. Day, *Told in Letters: Epistolary Fiction Before Richardson* (Ann Arbor, 1966); Robert D. Mayo, *The English Novel in Magazines, 1740–1815* (Evanston and London, 1962), which provides a bibliography of all narrative works in excess of 5000 words published in non-newspaper British magazines in alphabetical order of title (pp. 439–620). Charlotte E. Morgan, *The Rise of the Novel of Manners: A Study of English Prose Fiction between 1600 and 1740* (1911; reprinted New York, 1963), includes a chronological list of 653 prose narratives printed between 1600 and 1740. See also W. H. McBurney, *A Checklist of English Prose Fiction, 1700–1739* (Cambridge, Mass., 1960).

4. Ian Watt, *The Rise of the Novel: Studies in Defoe, Richardson and Fielding* (London, 1957), p. 11. The following very rough figures are taken from Watt, p. 290. Much more needs to be known about the economics of novel production before any accurate generalizations may be made; but it is significant that Fanny Burney received only thirty pounds in total for the three editions of her enormously popular novel *Evelina* (1778). Ian Watt's book remains the classic introduction to its subject, although some of its assumptions have been challenged in, for example, Diana Spearman, *The Novel and Society* (London, 1966), which redirects attention to the development of the novel from earlier romance narratives; and more recently in Lennard C. Davis, *Factual Fictions: The Origins of the English Novel* (New York, 1983). Diana Laurenson and Alan Swingewood, in *The Sociology of Literature* (London, 1972) contest Watt's assumption of a causal link between the emergence of the novel and a 'specifically middle class public consisting of wealthy shopkeepers, tradesmen, administrative and clerical workers' (pp. 184–85: and see Ch. 7, note 3 below).

5. Richard Altick, *The English Common Reader: A Social History of the Mass Reading Public 1800–1900* (Chicago and London, 1957), p. 1. Material in this and following paragraphs is drawn from A. S. Collins, 'The Growth of the Reading Public during the Eighteenth Century', *RES*, 2, no. 7 (July 1926), 284–94, and no. 8 (October), 428–38; Altick, pp. 30–77; Watt, pp. 35–59; Victor E. Neuberg, *Popular Education in Eighteenth-Century England* (London, 1971).

   The indicator of literacy adopted by David Cressy in *Literacy and the Social Order: Reading and Writing in Tudor and Stuart England* (Cambridge, 1980), is of little aid to students of the novel-reading public: the ability to write one's name is the determinant in his statistics. However, he points out that 'the period from the fifteenth to the nineteenth century saw, in most parts of the western world, a general transition from restricted to mass literacy. Skills which were once the preserve of a small clerical and specialist elite became laicized, generalized and widely available' (p. 175). In support of this he suggests that by 1714 'signature illiteracy' was confined to 55 per cent of males and 75 per cent of women. After 1754, the date of Lord Harwicke's act requiring all brides and grooms (except Quakers, Jews, and the royal family) to sign or mark the marriage register, the figures are 40 per cent of men and 60 per cent of women. Literacy remained 'highly stratified' (p. 177), and remained at 40 per cent for males with only a marginal improvement for women until the early nineteenth century. The graph of female illiteracy on p. 145 (London and East Anglia from 1580 to 1730) indicates that in London in 1580–89 female illiteracy was up to 90 per cent, but that by 1720–29 it had dropped to an estimated 45 per cent. As he remarks on p. 189, 'Literacy unlocked a variety of doors, but it did not necessarily secure admission.'

6. V. Colby, *The Singular Approach: Women Novelists in the Nineteenth Century* (New York, 1970), p. 7.

7. Commercial circulating libraries were established by booksellers. Edinburgh may have had one as early as 1725, and by 1800 most of the larger towns in Britain had a circulating rental library. Subscription libraries grew out of 'book clubs' (Dumfries Society Library began in 1745, Liverpool Lycaeum about 1758) and by 1800 were common. The best known, the London Library (1841) is extant. 'Mechanics' Institutes', for workers and small tradesmen, which included fiction, came later, in the 1790s. See E. D. Johnson and Michael H. Harris, *History of Libraries in the Western World*, third edition (New Jersey, 1976), pp. 164–66.

8. Q. D. Leavis, *Fiction and the Reading Public* (London, 1939), pp. 131, 133–34. By the 1770s, it seemed to Smollett, the business of writing novels had become a 'branch of business . . . now so engrossed by female authors, who publish merely for the propagation of virtue, with so much ease and spirit, and delicacy, and knowledge of the human heart, and all in the serene tranquillity of high life, that the reader is not only enchanted by their genius, but reformed by their morality': *Humphry Clinker*, edited by Lewis M. Knapp (London, 1966), p. 127. Laurenson and Swingewood, cited above, suggest that the very existence of women novelists was itself a cause of the novel's decline (p. 184). No evidence is given in support of this claim.

9. James Lackington, *Memoirs of the Forty-Five First Years of the Life of James Lackington*, seventh edition (1794), p. 232. On pp. 240–41 Lackington includes the following composite list of readers and their literary preferences (only three of which are novels) available in his bookshop:

> – Here you may find an old *bawd* enquiring for 'The Countess of Huntingdon's Hymn-book;' an old worn-out *rake*, for 'Harris's List of Covent-garden Ladies;' simple *Simon*, for 'The Art of writing Love-letters;' and Dolly for a Dream-book, or a Book about Moles; the lady of true taste and delicacy wants Louisa Matthews; and my lady's *maid*, 'Ovid's Art of Love;' a *doubting* Christian, calls for 'The Crumbs of Comfort;' and a practical *Antinomian*, for 'Eton's Honey-comb of Free Justification;' the pious *Churchwoman*, for 'The Week's Preparation;' and the *Atheist*, for 'Hammond's Letter to Dr. Priestley; Toulmin's Eternity of the World, and Hume's Dialogues on Natural Religion;' the *Mathematician*, for 'Sanderson's Fluxions;' and the *Beau*, for 'The Toilet of Flora;' the *Courtier*, for 'Machiavel's Prince,' or 'Burke on the Revolution in France;' and a *Republican*, for 'Paine's Rights of Man;' the tap-room *Politician*, wants 'The History of Wat Tyler,' or of 'The Fisherman of Naples;' and an old Chelsea *Pensioner*, calls for 'The History of the Wars of glorious Queen Anne;' the *Critic* calls for 'Bayle's Historical Dictionary–Blair's Lectures–Johnson's Lives of the Poets, and the last month's Reviews': and my *Barber* wants 'The Sessions Paper,' or 'The Trial of John the Painter;' the *Freethinker* asks for 'Hume's Essays,' and the young *Student*, for 'Leland's View of Deistical Writers;' the *Fortune-teller* wants 'Sibley's Translation of Placidus de Titus,' or 'Sanderson's Secrets of Palmistry;' and the *Sceptic* wants 'Cornelius Agrippa's Vanity of the Arts and Sciences;' an *old hardened sinner*, wants 'Bunyan's Good News for the vilest of Men;' and a *moral Christian wants* 'The Whole Duty of Man;' the *Roman Catholic* wants 'The Lives of the Saints;' the *Protestant* wants 'Fox's Book of Martyrs;' one asks for 'An Account of Animal Magnetism;' another for 'The Victorious Philosopher's Stone discovered;' one wants 'The Death of Abel;' another desires to have 'The Spanish Rogue;' one wants an 'Ecclesiastical History;' another, 'The Tyburn Chronicle;' one wants 'Johnson's Lives of the Highwaymen;' another wants 'Gibbons's Lives of pious Women;' Miss W——h calls for 'Euclid in *Greek*;' and a young *divine* for 'Juliet Grenville, a novel;' and the *philosopher* dips into books on every subject.

10. Compare Henry Mackenzie's remark to his cousin, Elizabeth Rose, 26 January 1771: 'your Sex is certainly very high in the Republic of Letters at this very Aera. Mrs. McAulay in History, Mrs. Montague in Criticism, Mrs. Brooke in Novel . . . are inferior to few': *Henry Mackenzie's Letters to Elizabeth Rose of Kilravock: On Literary Events and People, 1768–1815*, edited by Horst W. Drescher (Edinburgh, 1967), p. 70. Catherine Macaulay

(1731–91) wrote a popular *History of England,* 8 vols (London, 1763–83); Mrs Elizabeth Montagu (1720–1800) wrote an anonymous reply to Voltaire's hostile remarks on Shakespeare, *Essay on the Writings and Genius of Shakespeare* (1769); Frances Brooke (1724–89) was a periodical journalist (*The Old Maid* ran from 1755 to 1756) and novelist (*History of Lady Julia Mandeville,* 1763; *History of Emily Montague,* 1769, etc.).

11. Paul Salzman, *English Prose Fiction 1558–1700: A Critical History* (Oxford, 1985), p. 339. This is a lucid and useful account of the prose genres before Defoe, i.e. the novella, the courtly prose fiction of Nashe and Lyly, Sidney's *Arcadia,* the various types of romance, picaresque fiction, travel literature, Bunyan's spiritual biographies, and the Restoration novels of Aphra Behn and Congreve.

12. See Natascha Würtzbach, *The Novel in Letters: Epistolary Fiction in the English Novel 1678–1740* (London, 1969), which reprints nine early epistolary novels. The imprecise figure recognizes the problem of defining an epistolary novel.

13. For the earlier period, see John B. Richetti, *Popular Fiction before Richardson: Narrative Patterns 1700–1739* (Oxford, 1969).

14. Gabriel Josipovici, *The World and the Book: A Study of Modern Fiction* (London, 1971), p. 154. See also pp. 146–49 for some critical remarks on Watt's *The Rise of the Novel,* which 'demonstrates perfectly how impossible it is to say anything meaningful about the novel so long as one is operating within its own categories'.

15. Pat Rogers, *Robinson Crusoe,* Unwin Critical Library (London, 1979), p. 92.

16. Virginia Woolf, *A Room of One's Own* (1929; reprinted London, 1979), p. 62. More modern perspectives may be found in Patricia Stubbs, *Women and Fiction: Feminism and the Novel, 1880–1920* (Brighton, 1979), which, although mainly concerned with the nineteenth-century novel, makes a case for the view that sexual inequality is the central theme in the English novel.

17. Rita Goldberg, *Sex and Enlightenment: Women in Richardson and Diderot* (Cambridge, 1984), pp. 205, 207.

18. John Preston, *The Created Self: The Reader's Role in Eighteenth-Century Fiction* (London, 1970), p. 53.

19. Ronald Paulson, *Satire and the Novel in Eighteenth-Century England* (New Haven, 1967), p. 18.

20. *The History of the Adventures of Joseph Andrews,* edited by Douglas Brooks (Oxford, 1980), pp. 168–69.

21. Northrop Frye, *The Anatomy of Criticism: Four Essays* (Princeton, 1957), p. 312. Frye sees Sterne's greatest success in *Tristram Shandy* as the merging of the novel with the anatomy (the greatest anatomy being Burton's *Anatomy of Melancholy,* 1621, 'the most comprehensive survey of human life in one book that English literature had seen since Chaucer', p. 311).

22. Martin Battestin, *The Providence of Wit: Aspects of Form in Augustan Literature and the Arts* (Oxford, 1974), p. 141.

23. Some of the most frequently cited romances come from Calprenède's *La Cléopâtre* (1646–57: translated 1652–63), a twenty-three volume collection of short stories. For a discussion relating to Fielding, see Henry Knight Miller, *Henry Fielding's Tom Jones and the Romance Tradition* (Victoria, British

Columbia, 1976) and Homer Goldberg, *The Art of Joseph Andrews* (Chicago, 1969), pp. 27–62. Dr Johnson's definition of romance in his *Dictionary* (1751) is: 'A military fable of the middle ages; a tale of wild adventures in war and love. A lie; a fiction.' In *Rambler* 4 (31 March 1750), he remarked: 'almost all the fictions of the last age will vanish, if you deprive them of a hermit and a wood, a battle and a shipwreck.' Johnson underestimated the imaginative potency of such machinery.

24. Quoted in Michael Shinagel, 'Memoirs of a Woman of Pleasure: Pornography and the Mid-Eighteenth-Century Novel', in *Studies in Change and Revolution: Aspects of English Intellectual History, 1640–1800*, edited by Paul Korshin (Menston, 1972), p. 231.

25. *The Adventures of David Simple*, edited by Malcolm Kelsall (London, 1969), p. 303. The precise extent of her brother's assistance in writing this novel remains a matter for speculation.

26. Battestin, p. 150.

27. *Selected Letters of Samuel Richardson*, edited by John Carroll (Oxford, 1964), p. 41.

28. For a discussion of Johnson's somewhat surprising condemnation of Fielding's novel, and his preference for the works of Richardson, see Bernard Harrison, *Henry Fielding's Tom Jones: The Novelist as Moral Philosopher* (London, 1975), pp. 11–27, an excellent evaluation of Fielding's moral seriousness in the novel form.

29. Goldberg, *Sex and Enlightenment*. pp. 24–65, has a detailed discussion of this point.

Chapter 2
Fictional Lives and Realist Fiction: Daniel Defoe

Defoe was fascinated by processes. In his first book, *An Essay on Projects* (1697), he proposed schemes for improving a range of contemporary social systems: banking, insurance, lotteries, bankruptcy and debtor schemes, education (particularly for women), commercial law, and the recruitment of seamen both for peaceful trade and in time of war. The common link between all of these interests is not simply money, 'the great Hinge upon which the World turns', as he put it, but the mysterious social dynamics of which money is simply the transactional symbol. Defoe's eyes were on the contracts which both bind together and demarcate social groups, and on the relationships between individuals and groups. Defoe's knowledge of his own society was intimate and broad-ranging, so much so that, in the words of Peter Earle, 'It is possible to base a study of English society in the early eighteenth century almost entirely on the writings of Daniel Defoe'.[1] As a Dissenter and a journalist, he could stand back from society in order to record and anticipate its rapidly changing character. Historians of the period have used his *Tour thro' England and Wales* (1724) as a major documentary source.

His first novel contains a confession: artistically, it illustrates Defoe's deepest convictions about the primacy of individualism, its social and spiritual cost, and the inevitability of an anxious, dynamic restlessness in the human personality: 'I have been in all my Circumstances a *Memento* to those who are touch'd with the general Plague of Mankind, whence, for aught I know, one half of their Miseries flow; I mean, that of not being satisfy'd with the Station wherein God and Nature has plac'd them'.[2]

This Rousseau-like confession of social restlessness at odds with a fixed and apparently divinely ordained hierarchy could well stand as Defoe's own testament. There is nothing self-pitying about the dynamism which energizes Defoe's characters: they are not afraid of worldly failure because they never linger on temporary setbacks. They are self-motivating before being self-analytical; they are driven by irresistible needs for domination and self-definition, either spurning or denied benefits or constraints of inherited social place and ambition-constraining wealth; they hoist themselves up the social and spiritual scales by their own bootstraps, initially abandoning (or never belonging to) a hierarchical society, in order to re-enter it several levels further up by their own self-reliance. If conventional morality and the law stand in their way, then a short-term trespass will be repented of by a deferred act of contrition. The body precedes the soul in Defoe's work, just as the first challenge is control by the individual of his or her physical environment. When conventional pieties obstruct the individual in a state of necessity – where the choice is starvation or criminality – then spiritual accommodation can, and does, wait. The nervous anxiety which characterizes Defoe's heroes and heroines is this: will it be too late to reconcile their material wealth, the result of their self-dependence and self-definition, with the irresistible demands of religious justice exacted from the sinner?

Defoe turned to the novel at the end of an extraordinary life of variety. The first part of *Robinson Crusoe* appeared in his fifty-ninth year, only one of sixteen publications in 1719, and only the best known from a total of between five hundred and six hundred books, pamphlets, and journals. It was perhaps his 412th work to date.[3] Most of Defoe's life remains, paradoxically, a closed book. To Swift, and to many contemporaries, he was 'that fellow whose name I forgot', a member of that class of writers whom Swift had pilloried in *Gulliver's Travels* (1726) and *A Modest Proposal* (1729), the economic projector. To Pope, he was a mere Grub Street hack writer. Defoe seems irrecoverable except as an emblem of his fictional characters,[4] and such was his range of interests, his obsession for facts, his close scrutiny of social change, his readiness to write upon almost every conceivable topic, that a superficial reader may easily mistake his craft of fiction for the crudest sort of accumulative reportage. One cowers before the sheer bulk of his published work, but even the most hostile reader of his novels must admit that their craggy, monumental energy brought to the English novel a radically new concern for how life was lived, as opposed to how the writer might imagine, or wish, life was to be lived, and in social environments which demand elemental powers of self-preservation. Defoe was a pioneer in every sense of the word, driving an individual through a social environment like a drill bit through a rock face until the precious metal of social/material/spiritual success is reached. In so doing, everything is sacrificed, especially the critics' demand that the content and shape of the novel should be integrated. In Ian Watt's words, 'Defoe flouts the orderliness of litera-ture to demonstrate his total devotion to the disorderliness of life'[5]: but through Defoe's sometimes blundering efforts, the novel came to a precarious deliverance.

His novels commonly begin with an act of self-assertion, of rebellion, or exclusion. Robinson Crusoe and Moll Flanders flout the demands of society either by an act of will or through a deterministic necessity: both must be finally accommodated within the society which has failed, initially, to find them a place. Crusoe's 'original sin' is disobeying his earthly father's advice to stay at home and enjoy a safe prosperity, but on his island Crusoe conflates this filial disobedience with Adam's sin against God. There is little difference in Defoe's world between social and spiritual rebellion; they are almost synonymous, except that God cannot be as easily gulled as human society. Defoe's keen sense of process is, perhaps inevitably, allied to a poor sense of an ending. This is his *least* successful contribution to the development of the novel, but it does show that social roles need not be the same thing as personal identity. Thus, in his second novel (and the first of four criminal autobiographies), *The Life of Captain Singleton* (1720), even a wealthy ex-pirate can settle down to a respectable life in England. Some of the social costs may be trivial, but others (psychological and familial) are enormous:

> Why first, says I, you shall not disclose your self to one of your Relations in *England*, but your Sister, no not to one.
>
> Secondly, we will not shave off our Mustachoes or Beards, (for we had all along worn our Beards after the *Grecian* Manner) nor leave off our long Vests, that we may pass for *Grecians* and Foreigners.
>
> Thirdly, That we shall never speak *English* in publick before any body, your Sister excepted.
>
> Fourthly, That we will always live together, and pass for Brothers.[6]

Robinson Crusoe

Charles Gildon, Defoe's first substantive critic, interpreted *Robinson Crusoe* as an allegory of Defoe's own life[7]; Ian Watt (after Marx's mention in *Das Kapital*, 1867), endorses the economic theorists' view of the novel as illustrating *homo economicus* and the rise of economic individualism.[8] Not everyone insisted on seeing this novel as a metaphor: Leslie Stephen's essay of 1868 reported that *Crusoe* was 'a book for boys rather than men', falling 'short of any high intellectual interest'. . . . one of the most charming of books'. It is essentially, of course, a superb adventure story charged with the primary appeal of all narrative fiction: suspense, individual resourcefulness, threatening disasters, and eventual triumph. Even Dr Johnson wished it had been longer. Robinson, like Gulliver after him, and like the fortunate inhabitants of Johnson's Happy Valley in *Rasselas*, is not initially driven to leave England by economic imperatives (as Watt suggests), but by a barely conscious realization of a deep restlessness of spirit. His father's sermon on the benefits and protection offered by middle-class membership (fourth and fifth paragraphs) is no antidote and even at the age of sixty-one it is his 'native Propensity to rambling' (*Farther Adventures of Robinson Crusoe*, opening paragraph), not at all his need for money, which again sets him off on his travels round three-quarters of the globe. The reader of today will almost certainly cheer Crusoe's rebellion against his father's sound but complacent advice and applaud his determination to strike out for himself, even though at the expense of filial duty. In breaking with his father, Crusoe commits (in his own mind) an act of 'Original Sin' which (as in Milton's version of the same story in *Paradise Lost*) is the first step towards loneliness. But it is *also* the first step towards self-realization. Throughout the novel Crusoe's omen-ridden conscience conquers its inhibitions, and on each occasion he takes a giant step towards a lonely self-determination. As in all of Defoe's novels, the shape of this book is determined by the shape of an individual life. But there are additional patterns here. There is surely *some* irony in these elegantly phrased and deliberately balanced paragraphs, which carry such a stultifying complacency. Nevertheless, here is the world to which all of Defoe's characters dream of belonging, an inactive state of calm, all passion spent. In all of his novels, Defoe writes about the struggle to gain such stability. Crusoe, Moll, Colonel Jacque, and Roxana all arrive eventually here:

> the middle Station of Life was calculated for all kind of
> Vertues and all kinds of Enjoyments; that Peace and Plenty
> were the Hand-maids of a middle Fortune; that
> Temperance, Moderation, Quietness, Health, Society, all
> agreeable Diversions, and all desirable Pleasures, were the
> Blessings attending the middle Station of Life; that this
> Way Man went silently and smoothly thro' the World,
> and comfortably out of it . . . in easy Circumstances
> sliding gently thro' the World, and sensibly tasting the
> Sweets of living, without the bitter, feeling that they are
> happy, and learning by every Day's Experience to know it
> more sensibly. (4)

Robinson, like his deceased elder brother before him, rejects his father's advice. An eighteen-year-old is unlikely to see the world through the eyes of a parent in late middle age, particularly if (as here) the world on offer is so patently dull. Defoe's God rewards not the stay-at-home but the challenger; luck becomes Providence; Good Fortune becomes money in the bank.

When Robinson is rescued from slavery among the Moors (34), he sells the slave boy Xury, the companion of his adventures, for twice thirty pieces of eight. He later regrets the transaction, not from a sense of having inhumanly betrayed his deliverer into a further period of slavery, but because he is desperately short of labourers on his Brazilian plantation. The economic and spiritual self-determinism of Crusoe, defined here by its reduction of all relationships to a system of value, turns all of Crusoe's human contacts into materialistic terms. However, when Crusoe sees that he has created *precisely* his father's notion of a 'Middle Station, or upper Degree of low Life' on his Brazilian plantation, he feels cheated. Success has come too quickly, in the old way, and without satisfaction. Repeating an already established pattern is not enough. A dynamic restlessness is Crusoe's curse and his glory. It is as though greater self-punishment is needed to realize his full potential: 'I must go and leave the happy View I had of being a rich and thriving Man in my new Plantation, only to pursue a rash and immoderate Desire of rising faster than the Nature of the Thing admitted' (38). Eight years to the day after his rebellion against his father he returns to the sea as his destiny. He embarks for Africa and the slave trade as means towards greater wealth.[9]

The spiritual guilt that shadows Crusoe throughout the novel (often prefigured in dreams) reaches a chilling climax exactly at mid-point in the book (153) when he comes across the *single* footprint in the sand – surely one of the greatest dramatic moments in all fiction. Typically, the discovery triggers Crusoe's dormant egocentric conscience about self-determination. Thinking at first that the footprint has been left by the Devil, he says (157) 'as I could not foresee what the Ends of Divine Wisdom might be in all this, so I was not to dispute his Sovereignty, who, as I was his Creature, had an undoubted Right by Creation to govern and dispose of me absolutely as he thought fit'. Crusoe's consolation is the Bible, salvaged from the shipwreck along with almost everything else Crusoe needs for a re-creation of the social world he has rejected as insufficient: tools, clothes, food, arms, even money (which he at first scorns as useless but which 'upon Second Thoughts' he took away, 57). Money is a token for social transactions and as sole survivor there is no one to exchange with. In fact, Crusoe's material and spiritual transactions are with the island itself, initially barren but to be rendered fruitful by work and by God's providence.

The island is, like John Locke's image of the human mind at birth, a blank sheet on which Crusoe is free to inscribe his own image. It is also like an empty theatre, in which Crusoe plays a series of roles. He needs furniture, so he becomes a carpenter; he needs clothes suited to the tropics, so becomes a tailor; he grows corn (providentially germinated in the first instance, 70), and becomes a baker; his tent is washed away in a flood, so he becomes a civil engineer and builds drains; he needs broth, so he makes clay cooking pots; he thinks of escape, and attempts to build a boat (127). In other words, the technological skills normally used by specialists must all be acquired anew and practised by a solitary individual if his range of needs is to be satisfied. Crusoe admits 'I had never handled a Tool in my Life' (68).

Crusoe is alone on his island for a little over twenty-seven years, but the last two years are transformed from a solitary 'Death of a Life' (199) by the acquisition of Man Friday (205) who is educated in Crusoe's image, taught to speak English, instructed in the Christian religion, wooed away from cannibalism, and given the status of a servant. It is the start of Crusoe's patriarchal colony and the realization of a dream of empire.[10] When a Spanish sailor and Man Friday's own father are then rescued from the cannibals, Crusoe experiences 'Extasy' at the son's filial affection (238) and a rare moment of fanciful joy; he has become responsible for a society which (unlike Defoe's own) unites absolute political power with absolute freedom of conscience:

> My Island was now peopled, and I thought my self
> very rich in Subjects; and it was a merry Reflection which
> I frequently made, How like a King I look'd. First of all,
> the whole Country was my own meer Property; so that I
> had an undoubted Right of Dominion. 2dly, My People
> were perfectly subjected: I was absolute Lord and Law-
> giver; they all owed their Lives to me, and were ready to
> lay down their Lives, *if there had been Occasion of it*, for
> me. It was remarkable too, we had but three Subjects, and
> they were of three different Religions. My Man *Friday* was
> a Protestant, his Father was a *Pagan* and a *Cannibal*, and
> the *Spaniard* was a Papist: However, I allow'd Liberty of
> Conscience throughout my Dominions: But this is by the
> Way. (241)

That last sentence is characteristic. As in *Moll Flanders* and *Colonel Jacque*[11] such phrases tease the reader with the possibility of deeper meanings, hinting at allegory and symbolic pattern but only to dismiss them as incidental. *Robinson Crusoe* may be implicitly designed as a tract for the times: as Crusoe puts it in *Serious Reflexions*, Defoe's series of moral essays, 'just history of a state of forced confinement', i.e. a critique of a rigidified English society based on restricted privilege, religious intolerance, and lacking in scope for individual creative dynamism. But the opposite may also be true. Defoe may be seen to have abstracted from his own world its new energy directed into colonial expansion, its happy mixture of ideologies, its constitutional balance of powers, and re-created them in the laboratory experiment on Crusoe's island, repeating in a microcosmic individual life the macrocosmic processes of society in the England he has left, and to which he will return.

There is only slightly less ambiguity about the Providential pattern in Crusoe's life. Defoe's own aim, in the *Preface* to *Robinson Crusoe*, is 'to justify and honour the Wisdom of Providence in all the Variety of our Circumstances', and in *Serious Reflexions* he defines Providence as 'the operation of the power, wisdom, justice, and goodness of God by which He influences, governs, and directs not only the means, but the events, of all things which concern us in this world' (187). The point is that Crusoe is a dramatic autonomous character whose uncertainties of faith can only be dispelled when he discovers for himself the certainty of this interpretation of the world, a certainty which his creator doubtless already possessed. Here, the 'strange Concurrence of Days, in the various Providences which befel me', as Crusoe puts it (133), are possibly mere superstition. Again, Crusoe hints at a divinely inspired pattern in the same moment as he denies it. Crusoe's bid for freedom (leaving father, family, and friends) takes place on the same date as his capture and the beginning of slavery; he escapes from slavery on the same date as his escape from the Yarmouth shipwreck; his birthday (30 September) is also the day of his 're-birth' or deliverance from the shipwreck (Defoe's miscalculation of Crusoe's age by one year simply elevates significant pattern at the cost of chronology); 'my wicked Life, and my solitary Life began both on a Day' (133). And later in the novel, with Crusoe on the point of rescue, he writes of 'certain Discoveries of an Invisible World, and a Converse of Spirits' as indubitable evidence of a benevolent spiritual influence in the world. It is as if Defoe's extraordinary ability to make the ordinary exceptional and the commonplace challenging (the making of a pot, the baking of bread) has itself led his mind to pondering social and spiritual themes. Certainly, Crusoe's self-scrutiny is underpinned by his creator's almost anthropological view of religion born out of Crusoe's fear.

Crusoe leaves his colony in the possession of English mutineers, returns to England to find his family 'extinct', takes possession of the wealth generated by his Brazilian estates, experiences a nasty encounter with wolves in Spain and a comic encounter with a bear, marries, and after waiting for almost seven years returns to the island to supervise its development, his wife having died. From Brazil he sends to the island more colonists, including 'seven women, being such as I found proper for Service, or for Wives to such as could take them' (306). This rapid burst of incidents, none of which is treated at any length, serves two purposes. The first is to accelerate the actions of the novel into some kind of final narrative climax, a kind of appetizer for the second purpose, which is to signal a sequel, i.e. the story of Crusoe's next ten years of 'very surprising Incidents'. Most readers, even if they are aware of the two sequels, have chosen to finish with Crusoe at this point, however. The reasons are clear. The third part, Serious Reflexions (1720), is a collection of essays only vaguely connected to Part One, although the parabolic implications of the first part are filled out with overt discussions of Providence (a whole chapter), isolation, and religion. Farther Adventures (1719) is connected with Part One, and contains an account of Crusoe's failure as a governor of his colony, his wanderings around Asia (Persia, Bengal, Siam, China, India, and Siberia) and not much else. The formal coherence of the autobiography is not quite lost, however. True, Crusoe does not struggle for survival, and that elemental conflict of experience rebounding off a single consciousness has been replaced here by an apparently shapeless wanderlust. But there is more here than a commercial exploitation of Part One's immense popularity.[12] Crusoe and Defoe may have turned fiction into a commodity solely dependent on public demand, and Crusoe will play the author again, in Serious Reflexions. But the sensitive reader will also feel the pathos of Crusoe's aimless wanderings. His Asiatic ramblings provide no new worlds for a seventy-two-year-old man to conquer, the island experience is unrepeatable (and he knows this); and one might also discern Defoe's own exasperation in forcing his inventive genius to spread itself geographically so widely but artistically so thinly. A quarter of the way through Farther Adventures there is this admission:

> I have now done with my Island, and all Manner of Discourse about it; and whoever reads the rest of my Memorandums, wou'd do well to turn his Thoughts entirely from it, and expect to read of the Follies of an old Man. . . .
> I was possest with a wandering Spirit, scorn'd all Advantages, I pleased my self with being the Patron of those People I placed there, and doing for them in a kind of haughty Majestick Way, like an old Patriarchal Monarch.[13]

During his brief, twenty-five-day return visit to the island colony Crusoe has played God, bringing new supplies, converting the heathen wives, arranging marriages, making land grants to the colonists. But he also sees the signs of the colony's decay and realizes that he has failed. If there were any doubt in the reader's mind as to the centrality of spiritual and psychological tensions in Part One, Part Two rapidly dispels it. Very little in Part Two catches Crusoe's feelings at all, nothing so revealingly as this passage above. After Man Friday is killed by savages, the whole Prospero-like vision collapses into self-mockery and self-recrimination. There are no more roles left for Crusoe to play, except that of a creature dependent on God's providence.

Captain Singleton and Moll Flanders

Defoe's critics have found it rather odd that sex plays no significant part in Crusoe's self-analysis of his twenty-seven-year isolation. The case of *Moll Flanders* is even more surprising to twentieth-century readers. Moll is born in Newgate prison, twelve years a whore, five times a wife, once to her own brother, twelve years a thief, eight years a transported felon in Virginia, at last rich, honest, and penitent. In *Crusoe* and *Captain Singleton* the mass of details may be different in each case, but the psychological and intellectual structure remains the same: sin (filial rebellion, indifference towards religion, criminality) is followed by repentance and forgiveness.[14] The novel itself serves as both record and testament, exploration and warning.

Defoe's second novel, *Captain Singleton* (1720), repeats the pattern of *Robinson Crusoe*, but in this case the protagonist's retrospective autobiography describes a state of spiritual guilt founded not simply on filial disobedience but on a life of crime: 'I had no Sense of Virtue or Religion upon me' and was in 'a State of Original Wickedness' (6, 7). Abducted as an infant and denied all family connections, Singleton is the classic example, before Moll, of the amoral individual who accumulates great wealth at the price of spiritual and human desolation. Exactly half of the novel is devoted to his epic journey from Madagascar across the burning deserts and inland seas of Africa. His physical resilience is rewarded with gold and ivory, but the moral vacuum within him[15] determines that after only two years in England his wealth is squandered. 'Thus ended my first Harvest of *Wild Oats*, the rest was not sowed to so much advantage', he remarks, using one of many platitudes throughout the novel. Singleton is only too bitterly aware of the exemplary pattern created: 'so this Scene of my Life may be said to have begun in Theft, and ended in Luxury; a sad Setting out, as worse a Coming home' (277).

His adventures as a pirate, which occupy the second half of the book, repeat and deepen the cycle of morally heedless acquisition of wealth, but this time his untutored conscience stirs into life, largely through the agency of William the Quaker. On several occasions Defoe reinforces the (usually *mis*quoted) platitude that the love of money is the root of all evils: 'As to the Wealth I had, which was immensely great, it was all like Dirt under my Feet; I had no Value for it, no Peace in the Possession of it, no great Concern about me for the leaving of it' (265), and the structural weakness of this novel is not only its hasty rounding off but also its moral arbitrariness: Singleton, like Crusoe and Moll, returns to England, but the geographical cycle and the final spiritual repentance are not meshed together.[16] Singleton's self-interested act of charity towards William's sister (whom he marries as his 'Protectress') provides a factitious 'ending' which merely camouflages Singleton's spiritual *Angst*. He merely goes into social hiding. Defoe is unable to analyse, or unwilling to recognize that the transition between a criminal amorality and the spiritual demands made by a respectable settlement in England poses both a psychological and a fictional problem. The problem is essentially a structural one: Defoe's object (Crusoe, Singleton, Moll, Colonel Jacque, Roxana) is also the subject. The single perspective of the first person confession creates problems of narrative reliability: bluntly put, the reader's problem is not only to trace Defoe's didactic intentions through the novel, and to reconcile them with conflicting fictional interests, but also to discriminate authorial ironies (textual or interpolated) for muddles and/or inconsistencies.

The central problem is raised by *Moll Flanders*, the one novel of Defoe's to which the twentieth century has particularly attended.[17] For example, one dilemma faced by all of Defoe's criminal autobiographies is 'Necessity'. In his non-fictional writing there is plenty of evidence to confirm us in believing that to Defoe this was the 'cause' of many criminal careers. Given the choice of starvation or crime, then self-preservation demands the latter. But when Moll, Singleton, and Roxana cease to be in a state of necessity – that is, when they have gained from crime wealth enough to reform – persistence in a life of crime is only justified if there is thought to be no relationship between economics and morality. None of Defoe's criminals retires from crime when they have a mere sufficiency of wealth: the fact is that they go on stealing and prostituting their bodies because the initial and permissible 'survival ethic' has been transformed into and subsumed by an equally powerful professional skill, the acquisition of wealth and social position. It is not the criminal psychology that interests Defoe but the development of entrepreneurial skills. His most significant achievement in literary sociology is to have examined the deployment of these skills in the hands of two remarkable women. Crusoe is sexless: we know as much about his sexual instinct as about his aesthetic sense. But Moll and Roxana trade their physical bodies, the former on the black market, the latter on the open market, and utterly dominate their world by sheer will.

For Moll the connection between her sex and money is made early on. Her first lover throws a purse of guineas into her lap at the moment he expresses his love for her. Moll is more excited by the money, which thereafter becomes the motive and the erotic product of her sexual relationships: 'I was more confounded with the Money than I was before with the Love; and began to be so elevated, that I scarse knew the Ground I stood on.'[18]

Moll's self-perception is not a wholly reliable index to Defoe's stated intentions. The reverse is also true, for we are warned in Defoe's Preface that though her memoirs are authentic their literary production has necessitated editorial shaping: 'as the whole Relation is carefully garbl'd of all the Levity, and Looseness that was in it: So it is all applied, and with the utmost care to vertuous and religious Uses.' What Defoe may mean by this is perhaps indicated by Moll's frequent attempts to turn 'her' narrative into a moral exemplum – 'Thus I gave up myself to a readiness of being ruined without the least concern, and am a fair *Memento* to all young Women, whose Vanity prevails over their Vertue' (25).[19] The difficulty here is that by the end of the novel Moll's moral sense is, at the very least, opportunistic and ambivalent. At worst, it is a form of hypocrisy, a camouflage for a ruthless self-centredness. Her life of crime might have ended when she was arrested and sent to Newgate prison. After confessing her sins to the ordinary of Newgate she feels no peace; 'it was repenting after the Power of farther Sinning was taken away', she admits (274). Defoe had promised that the 'penitent part' of the novel would be 'certainly the best and brightest, if related with equal spirit and life', but the result is this passage, concluding with one of the most awkward sentences Defoe ever wrote:

> All my terrifying Thoughts were past, the Horrors of
> the Place, were become Familiar, and I felt no more
> uneasinesses at the Noise and Clamours of the Prison, than
> they did who made that Noise; in a Word, I was become
> a meer *Newgate-Bird*, as Wicked and as Outragious as any
> of them; nay, I scarce retain'd the Habit and Custom of
> good Breeding, and Manners, which all along till now run

thro' my Conversation; so thoro' a Degeneracy had
possess'd me, that I was no more the same thing that I
had been, than if I had never been otherwise than what I
was now. (279)

Moll is sentenced to transportation to Virginia. But the New World
has its roots in the Old. She is joined on board the ship by her
Lancashire husband, Jemy, and in Virginia hears of the existence of her
brother/husband and their son. Similarly, Moll's pre-Newgate moral
ambivalence shapes her present. After her first meeting with her son
(nephew?) she makes this astonishing remark:

and thus I was as if I had been in a new World, and began
secretly now to wish that I had not brought my *Lancashire*
Husband from *England* at all.
   However, that wish was not hearty neither, for I lov'd
my *Lancashire* Husband entirely, as indeed I had ever done
from the beginning; and he merited from me as much as it
was possible for a Man to do, but that by the way. (335)

Moll inherits land and money from her deceased grandmother. The
son is the instrument of this Providential reward for her repentance,
and Moll rewards him with a gold watch. But in doing so, she again
reveals a nasty moral muddle, a psychological black hole in her personality: 'I told him, I had nothing of any value to bestow but that, and
I desir'd he would now and then kiss it for my sake; *I did not indeed
tell him* that I had stole it from a Gentlewomans side, at a Meeting-
House in *London*, that's by the way' (338). Moll's husband is propelled
along the road to repentance by a similar act of material munificence;
both prosper and in old age return to England, 'where we resolve to
spend the Remainder of our Years in sincere Penitence, for the wicked
Lives we have lived'. Moll has achieved the conventions of social
respectability which had always been her driving ambition, and which
always kept her aloof from the criminal world which sustained her,
but which she has consistently parodied. The cost of this is a permanent neurosis caused by the manner of its achievement.
   The novel is the story of the younger Moll, related by the sexually
superannuated, almost seventy-year-old and penitent old Moll, and
editorially shaped by Defoe. Episodes of brilliantly clear reportage (the
stealing of the child's necklace and her subsequent escape through the
London streets, for example) are immediate, dramatic, and precise. But
there are two, sometimes conflicting, moral purposes. Moll confesses
and repents by writing a pseudonymous memoir, at times playing the
role of social critic (as when she excuses her theft of the child's necklace

by blaming the parents for giving such a valuable object to a child in the first place), imputing motives and suppressing emotional feelings in retrospect which she did not experience at the time, just as she suppresses the names and personalities of nearly all of her husbands and children. She blames the Devil for her corruption. But Defoe blames Moll, and *his* shaky moral purpose is emblematic. Moll's story and her interpretation of it within the commonplace equation of sin, repentance, and forgiveness, is to be seen by the reader as a desperate and even pathetic act of self-deliverance from a life of social ostracism, dehumanized sexuality, and moral contortion.

Just as the old Moll's written memoir follows actual experience, so Moll's spiritual reckoning comes after a much more pragmatic reckoning. After each relationship (first with the elder brother, then in marriage to the younger, then with a gentlemanly tradesman, then a moneyed husband who turns out to be her brother, then with a man at Bath, then marriage to Jemy the highwayman, whom she deserts because he is impoverished, then with a bank clerk, whose death ends her financial security again), Moll assesses her assets with profit and loss accounts. At Bath she realizes that 'this way of Living sunk me exceedingly, and that as I had no settl'd Income, so spending upon the main Stock was but a certain kind of *bleeding to Death*' (106). Defoe never justified prostitution as a social necessity, but the novel does suggest that Moll operates in a world entirely defined by materialism, and that the functioning of a moral conscience is an indulgence affordable only by those with a full stomach and a roof over their heads. As he states in *A Review*:

> Let the honestest Man in this Town tell me when he is sinking, when he sees his Family's Destruction in such an Arrest, or such a Seizure, and has his Friends Money by him, or has his Employers Effects in his Hand; Can he refrain making use of it – ? Can he forbear any more than a Starving Man will forbear his Neighbours Loaf? Will the honestest Man of you all, if ye were drowning in the *Thames*, refuse to lay hold of your Neighbour who is in the same Condition, for fear he drown with you? Nay, will you not pull him down by the Hair of his Head, tread on him with your Feet, tho' you sink him to the Bottom, to get yourself out? – What shall we say? – *Give me not Poverty, lest I Steal*, says the *Wiseman, that is*, if I am poor I shall be a Thief; I tell you all, Gentlemen, in your Poverty, the best of you all will rob your Neighbour; nay go farther, *as I said once on the like Occasion*, you will not only rob your Neighbour, but if in distress, you will EAT

your Neighbour, *ay*, and say Grace to your Meat too –
Distress removes from the Soul, all Relation, Affection,
Sense of Justice, and all the Obligations, either Moral or
Religious, that secure one Man against another.

Not that I say or suggest the Distress makes the
Violence Lawful; but I say it is a Tryal beyond the
Ordinary Power of Humane Nature to withstand; and
therefore that Excellent Petition of the Lord's Prayer,
which I believe is most wanted, and the least thought of,
ought to be every Moment in our Thoughts, *Lead us not
into Temptation.*[20]

Roxana

For Defoe's less sophisticated readers, doubtless, the criminal confession of Moll Flanders provided a vicarious excitement, a tour through
the darker but in no way remote corners of London life. But for the
more sophisticated reader, *Moll Flanders* poses an almost endless series
of questions about the relationship between character and motive,
intention and action, body and spirit, society and the individual. That
Defoe was *also* concerned in this novel with the economic and moral
dilemma of women in contemporary society we can be confident. Two
years after *Moll* he published another novel, *Roxana*, in which some
of the incipient but finally muddled social and sexual themes of *Moll
Flanders* are discussed with an almost electrifying clarity. It is in this
novel that Defoe separates, almost perfectly, the muddle of Moll's (and
his own) imposition of an external, socially conditioned, and utterly
conventional social morality upon an inner, self-wrought, and rigor-
ously feminist perspective on the question of personal identity.

Roxana knows herself better than any other of Defoe's people. After
her first husband, a brewer, goes bankrupt, Roxana acidly remarks:
'Never, Ladies, marry a Fool; any Husband rather than a Fool . . . the
only work (perhaps) that Fools are good for' is breeding children.[21]
The practical necessity of self-preservation is soon made clear by
Roxana's servant Amy, who urges that she should accept her landlord's
sexual advances 'for Bread'. As to Honesty, she adds, 'I think Honesty
is out of the Question, when starving is the Case; are not we almost
starv'd to Death?' (28). Roxana is amazed at the foolish generosity and
the concupiscence of men (74) and astonished by male manoeuvrings
in pursuit of such a commonplace matter as sexual intercourse (141).

The prospect of remarrying, even to the Prince, appals her, since her material wealth has given her a rare freedom from such bondage. She offers only a sexual contract for financial satisfaction, and is always sexually passive: 'I let him lye with me whenever he desir'd it' (145). At the novel's centre there is a discussion of marriage between Roxana and her financial consultant Sir Robert Clayton, who has arrived with an advantageous offer of marriage from a merchant. Both agree that 'a true-bred Merchant is the best Gentleman in the Nation . . . an Estate is a Pond; but . . . a Trade was a Spring . . . the Merchant had his Estate continually flowing' (170). But Roxana's response to this is unequivocal:

> I told him, I knew no State of Matrimony, but what was, at best, a State of Inferiority, if not of Bondage; that I had no Notion of it; that I liv'd a Life of absolute Liberty now; was free as I was born, and having a plentiful Fortune, I did not understand what Coherence the Words *Honour* and *Obey* had with the Liberty of a *Free Woman*; that I knew no Reason the Men had to engross the whole Liberty of the Race, and make the Women, notwithstanding any desparity of Fortune, be subject to the Laws of Marriage, of their own making; that it was my Misfortune to be a Woman, but I was resolv'd it shou'd not be made worse by the Sex; and seeing Liberty seem'd to be the Men's Property, I wou'd be a *Man-Woman*; for as I was born free, I wou'd die so. (171)

Although Roxana's views on marriage are regarded as unnatural (Sir Robert thinks of her language as Amazonian), they constitute Roxana's own almost heroic manifesto of female emancipation. She no longer externalizes her moral conscience by displacement (i.e. blaming the Devil's promptings); and she has risen from the dreaded state of poverty ('my Grave', as she calls it, 39) by her own efforts. But it is also clear that this strenuous and successful attempt at self-definition is purchased at the cost of social and psychological alienation. Poverty and Necessity had determined her cohabitation with the jeweller, but it is Avarice, Pride and Vanity that steer her into the Prince's bed (64); having become, in her own words, a 'She-Merchant' (131) and a 'Man-Woman' (171) she has become androgynous. Her greatest fear, therefore, is to be 'reduced' to the status of a mere woman by marriage. She rejects the Prince's offer, and the only other claim on her female identity is her twelve children. As in *Moll Flanders* the extreme individualism (and in Roxana's case the proud economic feminism) is to be cut down by human imperatives which can be concealed for a time but never finally denied. Her only surviving son is rescued from manual work and set up as a merchant, and he prospers. But, with a painful irony, Roxana's Nemesis is personified by her own daughter: Roxana has conquered the public world of sex and trade, but she is *cannot ignore them* to be racked by unpredictable filial claims on her. After the brilliant social comedy of the scene in which Roxana and her wealthy Dutch merchant play a kind of strip-poker with mortgages, bonds, jewels – her money gained from 'Whoredom and Adultery', his from 'the honest well-gotten Estate of [an] innocent Gentleman' (256–59) – we are led to expect an accommodation of vice with respectability (as in *Moll* and *Singleton*). But the final eighty pages of the novel deal with a terrible inevitability: 'there was a Dart struck into the Liver; there was a secret Hell within, even all the while, when our Joy was at the highest' (260).

Knowing her end from the outset, Roxana's retrospective narrative interpolates ominous moments of moral crisis: her conscience stirs, at first through melodramatic images of 'Devils and Monsters; falling into Gulphs, and off from steep and high Precipices, *and the like*' (264), but also through the ordinary human agency of one of her two daughters. This 'young Slut', as Roxana calls her, unites Roxana's early, secret, and immoral life with her present, discreet, and overtly respectable prosperity. Roxana confronts her guilt, and heaps recriminations upon herself in private: she rejects her earlier sexless freedom as mere 'Platonicks' (232) and sees herself as a 'She-Devil' (301). It is Amy who first thinks of ridding her mistress of her daughter, who tracks Roxana down and confronts her on board a ship bound for Rotterdam. Stylistic evasions such as 'But of that hereafter' (301) do not conceal Roxana's moral duplicity, and although it is Amy who is blamed for having murdered the child, Defoe's analysis of moral guilt is entirely focused on Roxana. The murder is not described, nor is there any certainty it ever takes place, since Amy also disappears. Unlike every one of Defoe's other novels the narrating character is left in a state of excruciating guilt, creating horrifying images of an indeterminable reality too painful to be investigated. The novel ends *without* enclosing its disturbing narrative with the commonplace repentance and prosperity theme. It transcends such moral imperatives by a vision of a continuous private hell: 'the Blast of Heaven seem'd to follow the Injury done to the poor Girl, by us both; and I was brought so low again, that my Repentance seem'd to be only the Consequence of my Misery, as my Misery was of my Crime' (330). For Roxana, the act of writing her Memoirs has not transformed her life, but made it virtually unbearable.

The lure of upward social mobility is irresistible for both Defoe and his heroines, and is the source of that tension in his novels between a dynamic individualism and a static social hierarchy. Moll's ambition to be a gentlewoman and Roxana's to be a princess (234) are both realized, but both exact several kinds of adjustment. In a hierarchical, conservative, and patriarchal society Defoe's heroines refuse to be marginal or repressed. The common feminine roles of virgin, mother, and whore are swept aside. Their struggles for independence, defined neither by family nor land, produce an independence and a self-definition at odds with conventional female roles, and the sign of this transgression is the obsessive *spiritual* pattern which punishes their individualism by final guilt. The new power of money is a profoundly revolutionary theme in Defoe's novels not only because it is the key to social mobility, but precisely because it is not sex-linked. The social possibilities are infinite, even though the spiritual world of Defoe is deterministic. As he aptly put it in *A Review*, money is the 'Mighty Neuter! Thou great *Jack-a-both sides* of the World'. As well as restraining his heroines' sexual and economic rebellion by finally endorsing the *spiritual* conventions, Defoe also (it is interesting to note in passing) confirms the prevailing patriarchal *economic* norms for minor characters: Roxana's daughters are condemned to a downward mobility; only her son enjoys the fruits of her immoral labours and prospers as, of course, a merchant. *Roxana* is Defoe's most careful study of the tension between female individualism circumscribed by a patriarchal social system. It is also, in a formal sense, his best novel because he has allowed the radical individualism to transcend the sin–repentance–forgiveness equation of *Moll Flanders*. Defoe leaves the reader vexed with the paradoxes, moved by Roxana's inability to repent, and finally shows the psychological turmoil in an individual whose vast social ambition has led to the murder of her daughter and the severing of all the important human ties that bind.[22] When Ian Watt remarks that 'Defoe flouts the orderliness of literature to demonstrate his total devotion to the disorderliness of life',[23] it is difficult to know in what, precisely, that 'orderliness ' consisted. His greatest achievement is to break through all social structures – including 'literature' itself – and emerge into a hinterland of guilt and lonely self-confrontation where there are no poets or priests to give meaning, consolation, or precedent.

⌐ ➔consequences for all

A Journal of the Plague Year

Defoe published two novels between *Moll Flanders* (1722) and *Roxana* (1724). *A Journal of the Plague Year* (1722) is not the confessional autobiography of a sinner but the admonitory, indignant record of a corrupt society anatomized during a national disaster. It is, as it were, the fictional autobiography of the city reflected by one of its marginal members. The tenacious pattern of sin–repentance–forgiveness is here even more in evidence, and becomes implicitly a theory of cyclical history. Narrated by a survivor, 'H. F.', the *Journal* re-creates in compelling detail the bubonic plague year of 1665, which wiped out 70,000 people, in order to warn contemporary England of a possible reoccurrence in the year 1722. An imaginative reconstruction of history is thus used as a tract for the times.[24] The *Journal* contains structural and moral patterns common to all of Defoe's novels: a first-person narrative, an evolving conviction of a divine purpose working through human disaster, and a fundamentally Puritan sense of individual moral election or damnation. As in Bunyan's *Pilgrim's Progress* the individual who is saved must first run the gauntlet of social ostracism. Bunyan's Christian must reject the world, but Defoe's Dissenter starts with an advantage, being already discriminated against. Whereas Moll reckons up her material wealth after each sexual transaction, here the statistical accumulation includes the number of burials within the Bills of Mortality (an important element in the verification of this 'authentic' history), the compilation of lists (for example, the number of clergymen who died of the plague, 237), the careful account of dates, months, seasons, and weather conditions, and the cartographical and demographic focus. In a passage such as the following, the steady accretion of 'realistic' detail has the cumulative effect of a surrealistic nightmare:

> I liv'd without *Aldgate* about mid-way between *Aldgate* Church and *White-Chapel-Bars*, on the left Hand or North-side of the Street; and as the Distemper had not reach'd to that Side of the City, our Neighbourhood continued very easy: But at the other End of the Town, their Consternation was very great; and the richer sort of People, especially the Nobility and Gentry, from the West part of the City throng'd out of Town, with their Families and Servants in an unusual Manner; and this was more particularly seen in *White-Chapel*; that is to say, the Broad-street where I liv'd: Indeed nothing was to be seen but Waggons and Carts, with Goods, Women, Servants, Children &c. Coaches fill'd with People of the better Sort, and Horsemen attending them, and all hurrying away; the empty Waggons, and Carts appear'd and Spare-horses with Servants, who it was apparent were returning or sent from the Country to fetch more People: Besides innumerable Numbers of Men on Horseback, some alone,

> others with Servants, and generally speaking, all loaded
> with Baggage and fitted out for travelling, as any one
> might perceive by their Appearance. (7)

This is the first literary examination of refugee psychology, and
again Defoe's eye is on the details which reveal a process. Social
distinctions of wealth and property are carefully observed at the very
moment when their social function has become redundant. Driven by
fear and the instinct for self-preservation, society is levelled by a
common enemy. Defoe's 'H. F.', a Dissenter and therefore normally
a marginal man, occupies a central position as narrator and is therefore
quick to appreciate the irony of exclusive social conventions, and
particularly religious sectarianism, temporarily abolished under the
impact of a subsuming fear of mortality. Medical quackery and superstition thrive in the face of an unintelligible disaster; prophets of doom
are themselves visited by the dead cart (234); Anglican clergy desert
their sheep, while dissenting clergymen remain, sometimes at the cost
of their lives (235).

The apocalyptic vision and the peculiar horror of a dead city
returning to life are finally understood in terms of an awesome Providence.[25] The random nature of the deaths, like H. F.'s (and Robinson
Crusoe's) random opening of the Bible in search of solace, *can* be
explained as a 'terrible Judgment upon the whole Nation' from 'the
hand of God' in a 'Season of Divine Vengeance', but again the
documentary realism, what Ian Watt has called Defoe's 'circumstantial
realism', provides the essential texture of the *Journal*. In addition to the
Providential theme, Defoe also provides a host of biblical parallels (the
deliverance of the Israelites, for example) and a social confirmation of
the individual's tendency to regard repentance as a single, temporary
act, extracted by the exigencies of a moment's crisis but having no
necessarily longer-term effect on conduct.

Colonel Jacque

The narrator of the *Journal* enjoys the uncomfortable privilege of
witnessing the moral artifice of his society. The plague reveals more
than a biological nastiness; its visitation rends the veil of class and
established power; it reveals gaping sectarianism; and above all exposes
the fraudulent, if comfortable, doctrine that man alone controls his
fate. Defoe's sense of society as a system of evasions or disguises is

exemplified in *Colonel Jacque*, published in the same year as *Moll Flanders* and *A Journal* (1722). Once again, Defoe chooses (perhaps this is too deliberative for what seems an instinct) a first-person, retrospective autobiography as the method of narration, and as in *Moll* and *Roxana* the urge towards upward social mobility is the dominant energy again. Like these rogues also, Colonel Jacque invokes 'Necessity' both to account for his crimes and also to excuse them. But unlike any other of Defoe's novels the repentance is utterly unconvincing, the retrospective patterning of a life by Providence is a tired recourse to a convenient commonplace, and in its origin absurd: it is stimulated by 'a violent Fit of the Gout, which . . . clears the Head, restores the Memory, and Qualifies us to make the most, and just, and useful Remarks upon our own Actions'.[26] But this novel also explores the idea of gentility at greater length than anywhere else outside the pages of Defoe's treatise *The Compleat English Gentleman*. In addition, Defoe's Preface at least recognizes the distinction between fiction and literal truth, and, for once, declines to adopt his usual technique of stressing the transparency of the narrative process: '*neither is it of the least Moment to enquire whether the Colonel hath told his own Story true or not; If he has made it a* History *or a* Parable, *it will be equally useful, and capable of doing Good*' (2).

Led into a criminal life as a child, Colonel Jacque survives in an amoral state and becomes an expert thief, his pocket being the centre of a soulless world, his moral sense only 'a strange kind of uninstructed conscience' prompted by a 'strange original notion . . . of my being a gentleman'. An equally strange kind of chastity, both in word and deed, signals a romantic theme of the lost child and the probability that the novel will end with the restitution of its hero to wealth and social position. The question put to Jacque by an old man, 'Is this like a gentleman?' becomes a totem throughout the novel. He learns to read and write, earns a salary for a time, joins the army, deserts, and instead of arriving in London finds he has been hijacked to Virginia, where he prospers as overseer on a tobacco plantation. Horrified at his duties (which include horsewhipping the Negro slaves), Jacque implements a system of pardons, a disciplinarian policy which curiously reflects that of contemporary England, where the criminal law 'made it possible to govern eighteenth-century England without a police force and without a large army . . . [making] enough examples to inculcate fear, but not so many as to harden or repel a populace that had to assent, in some measure at least, to the rule of property'.[27] The irony of representing this kind of policy through Jacque, a transported thief with no moral sense but high social ambitions, seems not to be Defoe's intention. But the social and spiritual efficacy of pardon colours the conclusion of each of Defoe's major novels except *Roxana*. In Jacque it reveals an untutored humanitarianism directed by less than altruistic aims: 'it appeared that *Negroes* were to be reason'd into things as well as other People, and it was by thus managing their Reason that most of the Work was done' (149).

As in the case of *Moll Flanders* we are to admire Jacque's New-World regeneration as a plantation owner, 'in a method exactly honest, with a reputation that nothing past will have any effect upon', and again like Moll, prosperity brings with it a retroactive guilt at past crimes, 'that without Honesty, Human Nature was Sunk and Degenerated . . . that it was Honesty, and Virtue alone that made Men Rich and Great' (157). Jacque's gentlemanly ambitions are advanced by learning Latin from a scholarly mentor, also a transportee, who tells him that '*Newgate* . . . was a place that seldom made Penitents, but often made Villains worse, till they learn'd to defie God and Devil' (164). But with his help, Jacque's reformation begins and he makes a return to England, where he lies low among the French community in London and marries a woman whose natural vivacity threatens Jacque's monogamous views, his bank balance, and his need for sober privacy. Without physical courage, Jacque refuses to fight a duel over his ex-wife's debts, but subsequently regains his self-respect as a soldier in France, whereupon he is promoted to the rank of lieutenant-colonel. But beneath the gentleman's uniform lurks the merchant's apron and the looter's instinct: 'I gain'd the Reputation of a good Officer, but I happen'd to be in some particular Posts too, by which I got somewhat that I lik'd better, and that was a good deal of Money' (209). As a prisoner of war he is paroled in Italy. In marrying instead of seducing his host's daughter Jacque makes the reader an accomplice to an act of unaccustomed and unintentional honesty, presumably failing yet again to enact the part of a gentlemanly seducer. She subsequently adds to his social discomfiture by cuckolding him, and an uneasy vein of social comedy runs increasingly against Jacque himself as a deluded husband. He believes that he has killed his wife's lover in a duel and returns to England once more.

Like Crusoe before him, however, a retired and private life is insufferable: 'I had got a wandring kind of Taste' (233), he remarks, and thus poses as a Frenchman to the English and an Englishman among the French. This relationship does not prevent Jacque from marrying a third time, privately, and he enjoys perfect happiness for six years until his wife degenerates through drink and commits suicide. Once more the less-than-innocent Jacque provides a sermon on others' misfortunes, and his pose as the naive injured party is almost certainly to be seen as ironical. His next action, for example, is to pose as a Roman Catholic in order to marry Moggy, with the help of a Catholic priest masquerading as a doctor. The persistent atmosphere of misogyny in all but the last of Jacque's relationships implicates Defoe also, not as a woman-hater but as an artist who too frequently falls back on commonplace writing and tired platitudes. *Colonel Jacque* recycles clichés, including Defoe's own. Jacque's return to Virginia brings a marital reunion with his divorced wife, now a penitent convict. With a nice symmetry, however, Jacque receives a royal pardon for his small part in the Jacobite rebellion (although he actually deserted at Preston) and offers praise to King George's political acumen and clemency, just as Jacque himself had been the instrument of clemency towards disobedient slaves. He ends the book, of course, as an extremely wealthy merchant, with leisure to write down his repentance and enforce on the reader his clumsy perceptions of a Providential pattern in his own life.

At no specific point in *Colonel Jacque* can we disentangle Jacque's dual role as naive hero (who is sometimes a fool, often a rogue) and his emblematic role as mercantile hero. The line between Jacque as a social predator and Jacque as *the* moral reference point for all others' deficiencies is confused. If we are to admire his material success, as 'a great man, a magistrate, a governor or master of three great plantations' (300), how are we to reconcile this with the fact that he is also a bigamist, a religious and political defector, an accomplished dissimulator, a man on the run from his past, and a man driven by greed? Towards the end of the novel he remarks: 'Now was my time to have sat still contented with what I had got; if it was in the power of Man to know when his good Fortune was at the highest . . . but . . . I Dream'd of nothing but Millions and Hundreds of Thousands' (296–97). Restless dynamism in pursuit of even greater wealth is the hallmark of Defoe's characters, but in *Colonel Jacque* Defoe fails to flesh out the too-convenient and commonplace processes of the wheel of Fortune and the hand of Providence with convincing psychological probability.

There are no formal divisions such as chapters or books in Defoe's novels. They are far from completely lacking in meaningful patterns,[28] but the central organizing principle is the life of an individual presented in retrospect and in the first person. Typically, a powerful ego is driven by the need to make moral restitution by a pseudo-public confession whose purpose is to provide moral example for others through the private act of writing. The act of writing thus provides an equation: the subject confronts the self over time in order to justify his or her public existence. But self-analysis is imposed on narrators who are singularly unsuited to its demand for honesty, not simply because they are all (except Crusoe) reliving a criminal past, nor even because their devices for self-scrutiny always involve apportioning blame and credit to an external agency – either the Devil or a providential God. Their

moral evasions stem from a conflict between Defoe's own public role
as an editor and censor external to the text and his artistic interest in
the (potential) realization of character from within the text. The effect
of this is to provide the reader with an opaque text, in which neither
narrator nor author seem aware of the full significance of what is said.
The conclusions of the novels often seem perfunctory and summary,
but more worryingly they are also discontinuous with their character's
dynamism. Artistic exhaustion and the process of ageing induce a
conclusion *and* leisure for repentance, if not grief. Providence is not
only omnipotent and omnipresent: it is often the *only* structural
principle.

But we can, as literary critics, become as pious in our own way as
Defoe's characters in theirs. Defoe warns his readers often enough
against adopting an attitude of moral condescension towards the
victims of Necessity, with a 'There but for the grace of God go thou'
admonition, and it would be absurd to demand infallible heroes as our
moral exemplars (as Fielding is to imply in Squire Allworthy). Defoe
insists (*pace* the Preface to *Colonel Jacque*) that his literary fiction is
literal truth, a self-effacing, transparent medium. He seems to subject
art to an overriding didactic function, but he also provides novels
whose artistic energies stem from an extraordinary fictional imagination, both Defoe's own imagination and his readers'. Reading Defoe
involves direct and actual confrontation with the methods we all use
to comprehend reality by shaping it, selecting from it, and on
occasions lying about it. Defoe's most important single realization is
that there existed in the early years of the eighteenth century a market
for fiction *per se*. All of his characters wrestle awkwardly with the
problem of casting their individual lives inside the framework of a
public morality. But there seems to be, in Colonel Jacque's words,
another market principle at work created by the gradual secularization
of the imagination. The intrinsic pleasure of fiction crept upon Defoe's
conscious mind in 1722, his most prolific year:

> Perhaps, when I wrote these things down, I did not
> foresee that the Writings of our own Stories would be so
> much the Fashion in *England*, or so agreeable to others to
> read, as I find Custom, and the Humour of the Times has
> caus'd it to be . . . 'tis evident by the long Series of
> Changes, and Turns, which have appear'd in the narrow
> Compass of one private mean Person's Life, that the
> History of Men's Lives may be many ways made Useful,
> and Instructing to those who read them, if moral and
> religious Improvement, and Reflections are made by those
> that write them. (307)

Notes

1. Peter Earle, *The World of Defoe* (London,1976), p. viii.

2. *The Life and Strange Surprizing Adventures of Robinson Crusoe of York, Mariner,* edited by J. Donald Crowley (Oxford, 1981), p. 194.

3. See J. R. Moore, *A Checklist of the Writings of Daniel Defoe* (1960; second edition, Hamden, Connecticut, 1971).

4. Mark Schorer, for example, states that *Moll Flanders* should be read as 'the allegory of an impoverished soul' – Defoe's: see 'A Study in Defoe, Moral Vision and Structural Form', *Thought*, 25 (1950), 275–87.

5. Ian Watt, *The Rise of the Novel: Studies in Defoe, Richardson and Fielding* (London, 1957), p. 106.

6. *Captain Singleton,* edited by Shiv K. Kumar (London, 1969), p. 277.

7. [Charles Gildon] *The Life and Strange Surprizing Adventures of Mr. D———DeF———, of London* (1719). Pat Rogers sees this as 'something between a critique and a parody': see *Robinson Crusoe,* Unwin Critical Library (London, 1979), p. 129. This book is a mine of information and the best single introduction to the themes, sources, structure, style, and critical history of *Crusoe.*

8. Watt, *Rise of the Novel* p. 63. For two contrary responses to Watt's influential chapter, '*Robinson Crusoe*: Individualism and the Novel', see Diana Spearman, *The Novel and Society* (London, 1966), and Pat Rogers, 'Crusoe's Home', *Essays in Criticism,* 24 (1974), 375–90. Spearman remarks that 'No one in his senses would choose the story of a man cast alone on an uninhabited island to illustrate a theory which only applies to the exchange of goods and services . . . Fundamentally, it is a story of man against nature' (pp. 166, 168). Pat Rogers concludes that *Crusoe* is 'the story of a Caribbean nabob who makes a little England in remote surroundings. Crusoe is *homo domesticus*; his narrative, the epic of home-making and housekeeping' (p. 390). For a detailed study, see M. E. Novak, *Economics and the Fiction of Daniel Defoe* (1962; reprinted New York, 1976).

9. Defoe's criticism of the slave trade is restricted to its harsh methods, not its ethical basis. For the *economic* benefits stemming from humanitarian approaches, see *The History and Remarkable Life of . . . Colonel Jacque,* edited by Samuel Holt Monk (London, 1965), pp. 127–47.

10. Rogers, *Robinson Crusoe,* p. 39, remarks that 'Defoe was a prophet of empire before Britain had fully acquired an empire'.

11. In his Preface to *Colonel Jacque* Defoe writes as Editor on the possible double focus for interpretation without prejudging the reader's preference for either: 'If he has made it a history or a parable, it will be equally useful and capable of doing good, and in that it recommends itself without any other introduction.' For detailed discussion, see J. Paul Hunter, *The Reluctant Pilgrim: Defoe's Emblematic Method and Quest for Form in Robinson Crusoe* (Baltimore, 1966).

12. It was never the bestseller that *Gulliver's Travels* became after 1726, but between its first appearance in April 1719 and 1753 it had gone through ten editions.

13. *Further Adventures of Robinson Crusoe* (Oxford, 1927), pp. 79, 80: Volume III of the Shakespeare Head Edition of Defoe's Novels and Selected Writings.

14. For a detailed discussion of this theme, see G. A. Starr, *Defoe and Spiritual Autobiography* (Princeton, 1965).

15. For an immeasurably more powerful treatment of this theme the reader turns to Conrad's *Heart of Darkness*, of course.

16. Compare *Gulliver's Travels*, Part 4. Swift's hero returns to England after his experience in the rational Utopia of the Houyhnhnms alienated from the human species. Both writers are compared in J. F. Ross, *Swift and Defoe: A Study in Relationship* (Berkeley, 1941).

17. In *Debts of Honour* (London, 1980), p. 181, Michael Foot, for example, describes *Moll Flanders* as 'a feminist tract, justifying the ways of woman to God and man'. Compare Dorothy Van Ghent's Jungian interpretation, *The English Novel: Form and Function* (1953; reprinted New York, 1961), p. 43: Defoe 'gave to Moll the immense and seminal reality of an Earth Mother, progenetrix of the waste-land, sower of our harvests of technological skills, bombs, gadgets, and the platitudes and stereotypes and absurdities of a morality suitable to a wasteland world'.

18. *The Fortunes and Misfortunes of the Famous Moll Flanders*, edited by G. A. Starr (Oxford, 1981), pp. 23–24.

19. But compare her remark on p. 268: 'The Moral indeed of all my History is left to be gather'd by the Senses and Judgement of the Reader; I am not qualified to preach to them.'

20. There is a facsimile edition of *A Review*, edited by A. W. Secord, 22 vols (New York, 1938). This extract will also be found in *Daniel Defoe: Selections*, edited by James T. Boulton (1965; reprinted Cambridge, 1975), p. 131. For a discussion of the role of Necessity in Defoe's novels, see Novak, *Economics and the Fiction of Defoe*, pp. 70–71.

21. *Roxana, The Fortunate Mistress*, edited by Jane Jack (Oxford, 1969), p. 8. The novel's full title indicates its high-life setting: *The Fortunate Mistress: or, a History of the Life and Vast Variety of Fortunes of Mademoiselle de Beleu, afterwards called the Countess of Wintelsheim in Germany Being the Person known by the Name of the Lady Roxana in the time of Charles II*. For Defoe's own non-fictional exposition of marriage as a social institution, see *Conjugal Lewdness; or, Matrimonial Whoredom* (1727), and M. E. Novak's introduction to the Scholar's Facsimiles and Reprints text (Gainesville, Florida, 1967).

22. This is not the common view. G. A. Starr, for example, in *Defoe and Spiritual Autobiography*, p. 165, believes that 'Defoe means to consign Roxana to the devil, and . . . the technical difficulty of making an unregenerate malefactor her own critic is the book's undoing'. M. E. Novak, in *Defoe and the Nature of Man* (New York, 1963), pp. 65–68, includes this warning: 'It would be a mistake . . . to confuse Roxana's tortured self-condemnations with a final judgment on her life.' As G. A. Starr points out in *Defoe and Casuistry* (Princeton, 1971), p. v: 'Nearly all of Defoe's fictional works cause us to identify imaginatively with characters whose actions we regard as blameworthy.' Both of these last two points are discussed in Everett Zimmerman's persuasive chapter on *Roxana*, in *Defoe and the Novel* (Berkeley, 1975). My own view is that Defoe, whether through exhaustion or design, has finally presented in Roxana a convincing state of moral turmoil, and a

terror in Roxana herself, far beyond the reach of moral rescue, and that
Defoe himself found the artistic courage *not* to contain her moral horror
within the iconology of repentance rhetoric.

23. Watt, p. 106.

24. *A Journal of the Plague Year*, edited by Louis Landa (Oxford, 1972). A month
   before the *Journal* appeared Defoe also published *Due Preparations for the
   Plague, as well for Soul as Body* (1722), in response to the plague then raging
   in France: see Landa's Introduction, pp. xxiv–xv. In *Daniel Defoe: Citizen of
   the Modern World* (Chicago, 1958), p. 320, J. R. Moore maintains that *Due
   Preparations* and the *Journal* were written in support of Walpole's unpopular
   Quarantine Act. Manuel Schonhorn has pointed out that Defoe concentrates
   description on those parts of the old London still present in 1720: see
   'Defoe's *Journal of the Plague Year*: Topography and Intention', *Review of
   English Studies*, 19 (1968), 387. For similar examples of Defoe's technique of
   historical reconstruction, see Pat Rogers, 'Literary Art in Defoe's *Tour*: The
   Rhetoric of Growth and Decay', *Eighteenth-Century Studies*, 6 (1972–73),
   153–85.

25. It is impossible to underestimate the horror of a dead city to Defoe. As
   London's unofficial prose laureate, the city's depopulation evokes an
   apocalyptic lyricism, just as its growth and prosperity evokes wonder. In his
   Tour (1724–26) he wrote of London: 'nothing in the world does, or ever did,
   equal it, except old Rome in Trajan's time' (Letter v). See further Pat
   Rogers's discussion in 'Literary Art in Defoe's *Tour*'.

26. *Colonel Jacque*, p. 307.

27. Douglas Hay, 'Property, Authority and the Criminal Law', in *Albion's Fatal
   Tree: Crime and Society in Eighteenth-Century England*, edited by Douglas Hay
   and others (London, 1975), pp. 56–57. Hay estimates that the number of
   capital statutes grew from 'about 50 to over 200 between the years 1688 and
   1820. Almost all of them concerned offences against property' (p. 18), yet
   half of those condemned to death during this period escaped the death
   penalty and were either transported or imprisoned. In 1722–23 Walpole's
   government established the Black Act, creating fifty new capital offences in
   an effort to curtail offences against property, such as destroying trees,
   poaching deer, and adopting disguises for the purpose of highway robbery.
   See E. P. Thomson, *Whigs and Hunters: The Origin of the Black Act* (London,
   1975).

28. The 'pattern' of a fictional biography may be no more than a process of
   accretion held together by a single life, but in each of Defoe's novels there is
   a superimposition of a spiritual equation. For a discussion of additional
   patterns (numerological and Providential), see Douglas Brooks, *Number and
   Pattern in the Eighteenth-Century Novel. Defoe, Fielding, Smollett and Sterne*
   (1973), pp. 18–64. On the question of the secularization of the tradition of
   spiritual autobiography, see Ronald Paulson's remark, *Satire and the Novel in
   Eighteenth-Century England* (New Haven, 1967), p. 43: 'the reader is never
   very certain whether Moll or Jacque is struggling through the streets of the
   City of Destruction and Vanity Fair or through the various allegorical valleys
   and sloughs of his own character.'

Chapter 3
Private Letters and Public Intentions: Samuel Richardson

One can know too much about a writer's intentions. Samuel Richardson stated that his purpose in writing *Pamela; or, Virtue Rewarded* (1740) was to divert and entertain, to inculcate religion and morality, to set forth parental, filial, and social duties, to make vice odious and virtue lovely, to instruct his female readers how to use Fortune and to subdue Passion in a man, to provide practical examples for the modest virgin, the chaste bride, and the obliging wife, 'and all without raising a single Idea throughout the Whole, that shall shock the exactest Purity even in those tender Instances where the exactest Purity would be most apprehensive'.[1] This statement of a comprehensive didacticism has provoked much critical comment. But another feature of Richardson's fiction, the great length of his books, has undoubtedly prevented many readers from getting even this far. His second epistolary novel, *Clarissa; or, the History of a Young Lady* (eight volumes in seven, 1747–8) contains just under a million words. As Richardson himself observed, quite without dry humour, in a preface later to be deleted:

> Length will naturally be expected, not only from what has been said, but from the following considerations: that the letters on both sides are written while the hearts of the writers must be supposed to be wholly engaged in their subjects: the events at the time generally dubious – so that they abound not only with critical Situations, but with what may be called instantaneous descriptions and reflections, which may be brought home to the breast of the youthful reader: as also, with affecting conversations, many of them written in the dialogue or dramatic way.[2]

Prolixity is indeed inevitable, given Richardson's choice of narrative method. And then there is Samuel Johnson's remark on the ratio of plot to sentiment: 'if you were to read Richardson for the story, your impatience would be so much fretted that you would hang yourself. But you must read him for the sentiment, and consider the story as only giving occasion to the sentiment' (Boswell's *Life of Johnson*, 6 April 1772).[3] Even so, the norm of prolixity can be contradicted to extraordinarily dramatic effect. The most alarming letter in the novel is also the shortest. Lovelace writes three sentences to Mr Belford, 13 June: 'And now, Belford, I can go no farther. The affair is over. Clarissa lives.'

More recent criticism has preferred Richardson as a writer of profound psychological insight, the analyst of personality, the mapper of ambiguous motives and unconscious drives, and the medium through which news of profound social changes is being transmitted. Claims are now made for the significance of his work which Richardson might have found astonishing: thus, 'Pamela, Clarissa and Sir Charles Grandison are not only fictional characters: they are also public mythologies, coordinates of a mighty moral debate, symbolic spaces within which dialogues may be conducted, pacts concluded, and ideological battles waged between the bourgeoisie and the aristocracy . . . pitting the values of thrift, peace and chastity against a violent and profligate nobility'.[4] In his own time, and in his own terminology, a narrower ideology governed the self-conscious artist in Richardson. He saw his fictions as mere vehicles for 'the sentiment', i.e. as devices to convey a moral education. An intelligent reader will not permit his response to the novels to be entirely defined by their author's stated intentions, even if, as in the case of Richardson, they are unusually clear and insistently didactic. His own last word on his fiction, and a sign of his determination to control his readers' interpretation of it, was a publication with this title: *Collection of the Moral and Instructive Sentiments, Maxims, Cautions, and Reflexions, Contained in the Histories [sic] of Pamela, Clarissa, and Sir Charles Grandison. Digested under Proper Heads, With Reference to the Volume, and Page, both in Octavo and Twelves, in the respective Histories* (1755). The novels are here gutted of their imaginative power and reduced to a vade-mecum of practical ethics, such as the Good Man, Female Dignity, Platonic Love, Piety, Retribution, Marriage, and advice to Masters, Mistresses, and Servants. Its only value to us is to remind us of the immense imaginative achievement which Richardson won from such dull compilations as the Puritan conduct-books which inspired his moral artistry. And yet within the novels themselves, quite apart from numberless occasions in his correspondence, prefaces, and postscripts, Richardson returns to this educative purpose. This didactic insistence was fed by his unremitting campaign to change reading habits: he refers scathingly to the 'light novel, or transitory romance' foolishly preferred above narratives which serve as 'a vehicle to Instruction'.[5] Charlotte Grandison remarks that 'the French only are proud of sentiments at this day; the English cannot bear them: Story, story, story, is what they hunt after, whether sense or nonsense, probable or improbable'.[6]

'Story and sentiment' says Richardson: Defoe says 'a history or a parable'. These distinctions are, of course, inessential. In both novelists the act of writing ('histories' or memoirs in Defoe's case, letters in Richardson's) creates and is the only reality which we can confront. All literary characters are created by writing about them, the difference between Defoe and Richardson is simply that in the latter it is more obvious. We can imagine Moll's semi-literate foul papers being edited by Defoe: but if Pamela and Clarissa were deprived of their pens, there would be no novels at all. It is a commonplace to point out the vast difference between Richardson and Fielding, but the difference between Defoe and Richardson is equally profound. Broadly speaking, Richardson's heroines struggle against sexual seduction with the same energy that Defoe's use to escape poverty. For Pamela and Clarissa all actions are considered by a pre-existing conscience, whereas Defoe's characters can only understand moral action long after it has taken place. In Richardson's novels the operation of self-analysis is unremitting and constant; in Defoe's the self-analysis is retrospective and sporadic. Economic necessity drives personality in Defoe, but in Richardson's work we are mostly concerned with reasons for inaction. The former renarrates the past in an effort to understand its (spiritual) pattern, the latter writes 'to the moment', in a continuous present which creates the present and the future in the process of describing it. The first of Moll's many evasions is to conceal her real name, but Pamela's first act of self-determination is to sign herself 'Your dutiful Daughter'. In the one, social and economic pressures are the reality and personality is unknowable; in the other, an immovable and exceptional integrity of the self is on a collision course with fixed social mores. Defoe's women are desexualized in the process of conquering their patriarchal society; Richardson's heroines either force their patriarchal society to recognize and adjust to their claims on it (*Pamela*) or, in the case of *Clarissa*, choose death rather than surrender to its repressiveness. Putting it bluntly, Defoe's battle for wealth and social position becomes in Richardson's novels a battle for the soul of woman at a peculiarly appropriate moment in English social history[7]: as Pamela remarks at one point, 'my *soul* is of equal importance with the soul of a princess'. Roxana actually becomes a princess, but loses her soul. The order of priorities is reversed.

Pamela; or, Virtue Rewarded

Richardson's novelistic roots are in the conduct-book, a recognition first made by Fielding's antagonistic comic parody of *Pamela*, entitled *An Apology for the Life of Mrs Shamela Andrews, In which the many notorious Falshoods and Misrepresentations of a Book called Pamela, Are exposed and refuted; and all the matchless Arts of that young Politician, set in a true and just Light* (1741). Shamela's library includes some of the worst (i.e. most prurient) of contemporary pornography alongside Richard Allestree's *The Whole Duty of Man*. *Pamela* (Volumes I–III, 1740) is Richardson's first novel, but its completion in 1742 (Volumes III–IV, 7 December) involved putting aside a prior project, a collection of sample letters which included a series from 'A Father to a Daughter in Service, on hearing of her Master's attempting her Virtue' (*Familiar Letters on Important Occasions*, 23 January 1741; 164–65). *Pamela* is prefigured here, but its development was stimulated by the popularity of previous epistolary novels and the discovery of an absorbing pattern of social and sexual tensions.

Pamela is a fifteen-year-old servant. Her mistress has died before the novel opens, leaving her temporarily anxious about her future until her mistress's son, known as Mr B, but more commonly as 'my master', appears as her benefactor and new protector.[8] It is Pamela's parents, 'careful, but loving', who first communicate their suspicion of B's motives, signalled by many intimate gifts and, eventually, by a direct approach (Letter XI). Pamela's confusion is partly at the narrowing of the social distance between master and servant, and she resolves to move to the home of Lady Davers, Mr B's sister. Letter XXV narrates, in the past tense, how Mr B conceals himself in her bedroom closet. It is the first of many symptoms of his voyeuristic nature. Mr B talks and behaves beneath Pamela's expectations, she above his. In Letter XXX Mr B expresses his love for Pamela ('thou art a perfect nun', he remarks) and gives her money, the effect of which is to replace Pamela's fear of B's rage by fear of his kindness. But his proposal to marry her to his chaplain, Parson Williams, she greets with horror. She writes a ten stanza poem on her going away (121–23) which is immediately followed by Richardson's own interpolation, an account of Pamela's delivery to Mr B's Lincolnshire estate, where Pamela's letters to her parents are intercepted by 'honest' John, one of B's servants. Among the false information which B feeds to her parents is the charge that Pamela has had an affair with Mr Williams, thinks everybody is in love with her, and reads romances and novels. In Lincolnshire Pamela is now alone, surrounded by B's people, employees and servants who owe him their livelihood and therefore unquestioned loyalty. Mrs Jewkes, B's housekeeper, reappears to Pamela as 'a wicked procuress'. With Parson William's help, Pamela hides her letters, and a marriage between the two seems likely until Williams is arrested and jailed through Mr B's agency as magistrate. Not for the first time Pamela confronts her ambiguous feelings about Mr B:

> Just now we heard, that he had like to have been drowned in crossing a stream, a few days ago, in pursuing his game. What is the matter, that, with all his ill usage of me, I cannot hate him? To be sure, in this, I am not like other people! He has certainly done enough to make me hate him; but yet when I heard his danger, which was very great, I could not in my heart forbear rejoicing for his safety; though his death would have set me free. Ungenerous master! If you knew this, you surely would not be so much my persecutor! But for my late good lady's sake, I must wish him well; and O what an angel would he be in my eyes yet, if he would give over his attempts, and reform! (218)

Pamela's difficulty is also the reader's problem. Though minute psychological interest centres on Pamela's complex motives and shifting loyalties, the portrait of Mr B contains more than it requires, an odd selection of melodramatic male postures rather than a psychological entity. He is not the moustachio-twirling villain of a Victorian melodrama, but neither is he easily or ordinarily intelligible. He adopts a female disguise in order to get into Pamela's bedroom, touches Pamela's breasts while Mrs Jewkes holds her down, but desists when Pamela faints away. Pamela shrewdly puts the image of B's deceased mother between herself and his further desires, and B makes the following unexplained (but significant) confession: 'I cannot endure the thought of marriage' (251). He attempts to strip Pamela's clothes off, but only in search of her concealed letters (271), and the last page of Volume I describes B as the spoiled child of an indulgent parent. If Pamela protests too much, Mr B's predatory nature is continually checked by a contrary impulse, a desire not only for Pamela's body but for the moral rectitude which she represents. Such an ambiguity prefigures Richardson's purpose at the end of the novel, to some extent, but it is Mr B who is the weakest psychological presence in the book even so.

It is not what Pamela says, but what she *writes* that has the greatest effect on reforming Mr B, since he, like Lady Davers and her conver-

sion to Pamela's side later on, must read before he understands. The
process of writing also elicits Pamela's half-conscious motives. Thus,
very early in the second volume (283) the pen once again outpaces her
conscious mind. She writes to her parents:

> to be sure, I must own to you, that I shall never be able
> to think of any body in the world but him! Presumption!
> you will say; and so it is: but love, I imagine, is not a
> voluntary thing – *Love*, did I say! But come, I hope not: at
> least it is not, I hope, gone so far, as to make me *very*
> uneasy: for I know not *how* it came, nor *when* it began;
> but it has crept, crept, like a thief, upon me; and before I
> knew what was the matter, it looked *like* love.[9]

This kind of equivocation is not the irresolute moral muddle of Defoe's
characters but the subtle discovery and recognition of changing, and
not entirely desirable, unconscious desires. Mr B is moved by her
compassion for his near-drowning, expresses his love for her, and
Pamela (responding to his 'condescension' but now also motivated by
love) rushes back to his sick-bed. It is Lady Davers who stalls the
predictable union by warning her brother not to marry beneath him.
Mr B also warns Pamela of the enormous social gulf which separates
them, but it is at this point that Pamela overtly assumes the role of
moral exemplar both for Mr B and for Richardson's larger social
purposes: Mr B exclaims 'I shall find some of my own bad actions
atoned for by your exemplary goodness, and God will bless *me* for *your*
sake . . . I will now defy the saucy, busy censures of the world' (301).
His role model will now be Pamela, and his aggression is redirected
against the constraints of his sister. Pamela's presentation to the Darn-
fords is a triumph (Lady Davers excepted), a moment in which the
possibility of a social accommodation is realized. In an age when peers
married actresses, the possibility of upward mobility for an impoverished female servant by marriage with the landed gentry may seem the
merest fantasy of a scheming vixen who trades her virginity for a
settlement. Pamela's forthcoming marriage does seem like an apotheosis to her father, who dreams of Jacob's ladder 'and angels descending
to bless me, and my beloved daughter' (334). But, as Richardson
clearly demonstrates, the real battle is to be fought neither in spiritual
nor in materialistic terms. Lady Davers, unaware of Pamela's private
marriage to Mr B, makes a catastrophic mistake in treating Pamela
with contempt, physical abuse, and imprisonment. She replaces Mr B
as Pamela's tormentor, but this time Pamela's vulnerability to social
ostracism is minimal: she now shares the social status of her husband
and it is Davers who must be instructed by her reformed brother.

Moral ennoblement of the husband is to be the only role for a woman who crosses the social boundaries:

> a man ennobles the woman he takes, be she *who* she will; and adopts her into his own rank, be it *what* it will: but a woman, though ever so nobly born, debases herself by a mean marriage, and descends from her *own* rank, to that of him she stoops to marry . . . when a duke lifts a private person into his own rank, he is still her *head*, by virtue of being her husband: but, when a lady descends to marry a groom, is not that groom her *head*? Does not that difference strike you? (441, 442)

Lady Davers, perhaps understandably, accuses Pamela of converting a rake into a husband and a husband into a Puritan preacher. But B's reputation as a rake is, finally, explained away. He fought a duel, certainly, but only in defence of a friend. He enjoyed the sexual favours of Sally Godfrey, certainly, but had been trapped into the affair with his landlady's daughter at university. Mr B, it seems, always had the potential for moral rectitude but, as he informs Pamela (463), was a victim of enfeebling educational and marital practices among the upper classes. Pamela deduces forty-eight rules for the marriage state and the novel begins its steep decline into the vapid and nerveless moralizing which characterizes the next two volumes. Pamela is reconciled to all those who betrayed her – Jervis, Longman, John Arnold; there is a great deal about money matters (her parents are to get a farm from Mr B), and Pamela asks her parents for a list of 'honest, industrious poor, as may be true objects of charity' (490) on whom to spend her quarterly allowance. An account of these charitable transactions will be compiled under the title 'Humble RETURNS for DIVINE MERCIES'. Pamela as moral exemplum becomes Pamela as moral proselyte, sending Farmer Jones three guineas' worth of good books, i.e. a family Bible, *The Book of Common Prayer*, and *The Whole Duty of Man*. Pamela's last words to her husband take the form of a poem on humility.

It is not difficult to discern the weaknesses of Richardson's first novel. Pamela's doubts, moments of paradoxical motivation, and increasing self-awareness are brilliantly and minutely mapped in her letters; but Mr B's function as the representative of a rigid patriarchy, his stereotypical role as seducer and reformed rake, and his ambiguous psychological status (voyeur, sadist, clothes fetishist, protector, patron, employer) creates a part-adolescent and part-paternal split in his personality which disables him. Mr B is not reformed because he never has been a rake. At the end of the novel he is exculpated as a victim of social circumstance. Whatever power he possesses in the novel is therefore to be understood as socially conditioned role-playing: when the disguise is removed he is as pious as Pamela herself.

Fielding was only the first of many to see, and mercilessly ridicule in *Shamela*, that the novel could also be interpreted as the cheapest form of romantic wish-fulfilment, the bartering of virginity for status and property on the altar of moral expediency.[10] Contemporary reaction to the novel was violently partisan, and to some extent continues to be so. Richardson's undeniable contribution to the novel lay not in his moral earnestness, nor in the social didacticism based on conventional gender roles with which the novel ends, but in the literary process of creating personality through the writing of letters and the articulation of thought processes. The outstanding weakness of the complete four-volume *Pamela* is that the incipient (and, in the two-volume sequel, the terminal) collapse into the conduct-book type of moral didacticism is accelerated.[11] Richardson turns from radical questioning of the male–female stereotypes, gender roles constructed by social conventions, to a reinforcement of bourgeois values in a rigidly stratified society. Nothing less than artistic genius reversed this process of social accommodation in his second novel, *Clarissa*.

Clarissa; or, The History of a Young Lady

Three years before the first volumes appeared, Richardson had a complete plan of *Clarissa*, even though the composition of the novel was incomplete.[12] He had determined from the outset that Clarissa's ending should be 'triumphant', that is, it should end with the deaths of Clarissa and Lovelace, and in the case of Clarissa this intention was sustained against popular pressure. He refused to repeat *Pamela*. In a letter (7 November 1748) he said: 'I intend more than a Novel or Romance by this Piece . . . it is of the Tragic Kind.'[13] It is in fact the first great tragic novel in English.

Richardson's formal control over this vast, and in effect serially published novel, extends beyond its broad narrative symmetry, its double set of correspondents ('two young ladies of virtue and honour' and 'two gentlemen of free lives') to imagery, episode, viewpoint, and theme. As in *Pamela*, personality is written, created by the pen, existing only in letters, self-projections, and confrontations with the self, only 'real' if able to be read about and therefore interpreted. One way to comprehend the novel and illustrate Richardson's now firm control is to look at its larger lineaments. *Clarissa* begins and ends with a duel. In January, Lovelace has wounded Clarissa's imperious and rash brother for his family's insulting behaviour, and the novel is to end in December of the same year with Lovelace's death at the hands of Clarissa's cousin, Colonel Morden, who exacts from Lovelace the ultimate penalty for the rape of Clarissa. Clarissa leaves her family home, Harlowe Place, in the spring; the rape takes place in June (Midsummer Night), and she dies in December. This seasonal cycle is paralleled by the emblem of eternity on Clarissa's coffin (a serpent with its tail in its mouth). There are three broad episodes in the novel: the first two volumes, in Richardson's words, are 'chiefly taken up with the altercations between Clarissa and the several persons of her family . . . the Foundation of the whole' (1498–99). At the end of the second volume Clarissa is tricked into running away from her family with Lovelace. In the middle of the novel (i.e. from the end of Volume III to Volume VI) Clarissa is a prisoner of Lovelace, and most of this time is spent at Mrs Sinclair's 'vile house'. Clarissa escapes at the beginning of Volume VI and the last two volumes describe the deaths of Clarissa (VII) and Lovelace (VIII). The dominant point of view in the first third of the novel is Clarissa's; in the middle it is Lovelace's; in the last third Clarissa and Lovelace are seen through the letters of Belford, who is a friend to both, a character whose moral function is inseparable from his structural role, 'a midway point between the good of the one and the evil of the other . . . He moves like an awkward ambassador between the courts of virtue and vice'.[14]

Each of the volumes ends on a note of anticipatory anxiety. Volume I ends with the Harlowe dilemma, 'So they are to lose a son, or to conquer a daughter' (206); Volume II with Anna Howe's breathless letter to Clarissa, 'Good God of heaven and earth! – but what shall I say? – I shall be all impatience for particulars' (371); Volume III concludes with Clarissa's acute anguish, 'in a wilderness of doubt and error; and never, never, shall find my way out of it' (566); Volume IV shows Lovelace at the peak of expectation – 'I am on tiptoe, Jack, to enter upon this project' and swearing that 'I will have Miss Howe, if I cannot have her more exalted friend!' (753); Volume V with Lovelace telling Belford (945) that the move to Hampstead will be Clarissa's final 'trial' (she is in fact taken to Mrs Sinclair's brothel); Volume VI with Belford's admonishing letter (IV, 8) to Lovelace (an essay on man as predator and a statement of her own sister Arabella's cruelty, and with a restatement of Clarissa's own prescient ironic signal (1020): 'Let me repeat that I am quite sick of life; and of an earth in which *innocent* and *benevolent* spirits are sure to be considered as *aliens*, and be made sufferers by the *genuine sons* and *daughters of that earth*'; Volume VII ends with Belford's description of Clarissa's coffin (which she uses as a writing desk) and his anxiety about Clarissa's state of mind (1316–17); the final volume describes Lovelace's death, and also the marriage of Belford to Charlotte Montague (1493–94).

The principle of the procrastinated rape is thus complemented by anticipatory fictional climaxes at the end of all but the final volume. The novel's publication in instalments delayed both Lovelace's gratification and the reader's: Richardson's reading public had to wait five months (until 28 April 1748) for the second and third volumes. Seven months elapsed between the fourth volume of the first edition, ending with Clarissa's escape, and the final three volumes (6 December 1748). As Lovelace says of marriage, 'the joys of *expectation*, the highest of all our joys, would salubriate and keep all alive' (873) – a remark just as true for the libertine as it is for the inquisitive reader. As F. W. Hilles has remarked, the 'symmetry of the plot suggests a highly stylized dance in which two chief performers change places: Clarissa's element is the country, Lovelace's the city; in the early part of the novel Clarissa is "nettled and alarmed" by her family's remorseless pressures and Lovelace's plotting; at the end of the book she is facing death'.[15] At the beginning, Lovelace is initially confident and swaggering; at the end he is 'THE MOST MISERABLE OF BEINGS' (1490). Certain patterns throughout the novel metamorphose sexual conflict into elemental, almost cosmic metaphors of strife. These metaphors translate the attraction of Lovelace to Clarissa and their eventual habitation in opposed worlds into terms which can only suggest the intense and dialectical imaginative energy of Richardson's involvement. To Lovelace Clarissa is an angel, and he is a devil. He compares himself with Milton's Satan (772), perhaps subconsciously responding to Clarissa's earlier remark, after her betrayal in the garden, 'Your *rattle* warns me of the *snake*' (439).[16] After the rape (not described) Lovelace says of both: 'As soon as she found her wings, the angel flew from me. I, the reptile kneeler, the despicable slave, no more the proud victor, arose' (930). Lovelace swears by pagan gods, Clarissa invokes and eventually chooses the Christian hereafter for justice and peace. Lovelace torments her with an entirely secular world-view, and one in which all power over her is apparently concentrated in his hands: 'O Madam, I have read the Bible as a fine piece of ancient history' (II, 88 in Everyman edition; omitted in Ross edition). And yet, in his final dream Lovelace, like Faustus, sees himself falling to the blackest Hell.[17] The play of polar opposites in conflict leads to tragic ironies of entrapment and blight: 24 July is Clarissa's birthday, for example, but the moment is paradoxical – 'Blooming, yet declining in her blossom!' – as Belford remarks (1124).

In its broad structural sweep, and in its local detail, *Clarissa* is a sustained emotional crisis, so much so that the rape itself is almost incidental. Much more than the defloration of a virgin was at stake here, and, of course, Richardson was to reject completely any notion of repeating Pamela's social accommodation after the rape of Clarissa. Lovelace's crime is a crime against nature, for which there can be no reparation in social terms. Even though the greed of the Harlowe family for self-aggrandizement through property and social position drives Clarissa into the arms of Lovelace, the solution to Clarissa's victimization is never seen in terms of a bourgeois settlement. Clarissa exclaims to Lovelace's profession of love: 'I will never marry any other man. I have seen enough of your sex; at least of *you*. A single life shall ever be *my* choice – while I will leave you at liberty to pursue *your own*' (593).

On the other hand, it might be said that Richardson simply avoids the social consequences of Clarissa's refusal to take part in a property marriage by the apotheosis of Clarissa herself. Certainly the lengthy, elaborate, and almost stifling ritual preparations for her death are oppressively and even at times grotesquely paraded. Even here, perhaps, Richardson might be thought to be falling back on a clumsy kind of moral and didactic exhibitionism. And yet the power of this novel resides in the inescapable nature of its conclusion. It *arises* from a context of power. Lovelace is a justice of the peace: he sees himself as entitled by his class to scorn the secular law and to exercise his droit de seigneur with impunity. Richardson has transcribed the polarized sexual politics of his day: socially conditioned gender roles dictate that Lovelace is the lord of his temporal world and Clarissa's role is to be spiritually passive, and therefore marginal. These powerful social determinants are questioned, toppled, and eventually abandoned by Clarissa's transcendent death. As Margaret Doody says, 'Richardson is the first major English novelist to present sexuality as a constant vital principle of human life, both conscious and unconscious. At the same time he is also one of the first (and few) novelists to treat spiritual life seriously.'[18]

Clarissa's family demands her passive acceptance of a property marriage with the odious Mr Solmes. Clarissa's grandfather has bequeathed the family estate not through the male line but, out of love, to Clarissa. She is trapped between an alienated family whose bourgeois demands for ennoblement she cannot fulfil and a sexual liaison with Lovelace which threatens to divide her integrity. Lovelace, after the rape, justifies his action by *reducing* Clarissa to a sexual stereotype. He says to Belford, 'when all's done, Miss Clarissa Harlowe has but run the fate of a thousand others of her sex – only that they did not set such a romantic value upon what they call their *honour*; that's all' (885). Clarissa's tragic ending is inevitable once she determines that there can be no separation of her sexuality from her identity as an *individual* (that is, after all, what the word means). Richardson is totally unambiguous on this point. While other characters rehearse possible alternative 'social' endings (Dr Lewes suggests legal proceedings against Lovelace, and Arabella Harlowe suggests that Clarissa should spend a few years in Pennsylvania until the scandal subsides), Clarissa herself adopts a deliberate ambivalence designed to free herself from all possible endings but one. There are several examples of this ambivalence, but the most significant is her visit to an undertaker in order to purchase a coffin, which Clarissa terms her 'house' (1273). The secular world's demands appear to be met when she announces her resolve to return to 'her father's house'; but it is the spiritual home to which Clarissa intends to go. Clarissa's language, i.e. her 'pardonable artifice', indicates that she already exists on another experiential plane: alternative denouements seem grotesquely ironic, just as the continuing squabbles of the Harlowe family about their worldly goods seem, finally, obscene.

In death Clarissa is transformed into an icon of injured innocence. It is Colonel Morden who remarks that 'Her beatification commenced yesterday afternoon, exactly at forty minutes after six' (1369). Her letters continue to arrive, post-mortem, defying mortality and finally free of the pressure to accommodate, even if only in words, to social expectations.[19]

The reasons for Richardson's emblematic intention and his ritualized treatment of Clarissa's death-bed scene are even clearer once we realize that Clarissa's exemplification of a serene holy dying is point for point in strategic contrast with the horrific death-bed scenes of the sinners Belton and Mrs Sinclair. Belton has 'all the classic symptoms of the dying sinner, as represented in devout literature' of the time – mental torment, a self-mortifying anxiety, fear, and guilt – and Mrs Sinclair's end is 'likewise a picture of death in despair . . . a picture of hell'.[20] Lovelace similarly dies in a mist, enigmatic, unplumbed, lost, an appropriate end for a soul driven by passions he can neither understand nor control. Whereas Clarissa's death dominates the last quarter of the novel, Lovelace's death is described perfunctorily, by a servant. Unable to enact the conduct-book's specified social, secular, and bourgeois roles of dutiful daughter married off by her father's will to become a dutiful wife, Clarissa turns a secular tragedy into a spiritual victory for the individual self. Moreover, and however unpalatable to modern sensibilities, Clarissa does finally enact that radical paradox at the centre of the Christian world-view (Puritan and Catholic alike), which gives the lie to Harlowe materialism. Clarissa is like Christiana (no less than Christian) in Bunyan's *Pilgrim's Progress*, who must reject the world in order to gain it. At Vanity Fair the act of renunciation includes 'Houses, Lands, Trades, Places, Honors, Preferments, Titles,

Countries, Kingdoms, Lusts, Pleasures and Delights of all sorts, as Whores, Bawds, Wives, Husbands, Children, Masters, Servants, Lives, Blood, Bodies, Souls, Silver, Gold, Pearls, Precious Stones, and what not'.

Clarissa's death is not only inevitable, given her holistic view of body and soul; it is also an affirmation of a traditional Christian topos familiar both to herself, from her own reading in secular as well as devotional literature, and to her readers from the same sources. Lovelace's quotations (and misquotations) from secular literature are selectively designed to bolster his cynical view of women's claims to equality and spirituality (as in his citations from Restoration comedy, Bernard Mandeville's *The Fable of the Bees, or, Private Vices Public Benefits*, 1714 and 1723, or the ironic banter intended in the line from Pope's Epistle, *Of the Characters of Women*, 1735, 'But every woman is at heart a Rake', for example). Clarissa quotes from the heroic tragedies of Otway and Dryden. Lovelace is an arch misreader, a sceptical disbeliever in the candidacy of women for spiritual consideration. At one point he picks up Clarissa's copy of Jeremy Taylor's two books, *Holy Living* (1650) and *Holy Dying* (1651), and sneers to her:

> A smart book, this, my dear! – This old divine affects, I
> see, a mighty flowery style upon a very solemn subject.
> But it puts me in mind of an ordinary country funeral,
> where the young women, in honour of a defunct
> companion, especially if she were a virgin, or *passed for
> such*, make a flower-bed of her coffin. (1002)

But the literary emblems of Clarissa's dying are charged with peculiarly powerful energies which are allowed to obliterate such cynicism. Having been abandoned by her family, Clarissa finds herself without either wardrobe or money. Yet she has some books, forwarded to her, she suspects, by her spiteful brother, and these include *Drexelius on Eternity* (1710) and Bayly's *Practice of Piety* (1613; fifty-ninth edition by 1735), texts which enforce the doctrine of damnation, salvation, and the proximity of death. These are ideas with which she increasingly identifies herself. In another book by Jeremiah Drexel we may find (as perhaps Richardson himself found) prototypes of Clarissa's own dying. In Chapter 29 of *The Considerations of Drexelius Upon Death*, entitled 'A Coffin is the last Throne of our Pride', we are told of the sombre funerary rituals of Abraham, the Austrian Emperor Maximilian, Charles V, and the following:

> Ida, a Woman of approv'd Chastity, order'd a Coffin to
> be made her long before her Death; which she twice a day

fill'd with Bread and other Victuals, and as often emptied
it to the Poor. The study of Virtue is the best Preparatory
to Death. No death stains Virtue. He easily contemns all
things, who always thinks he is dying.[21]

If such examples lie behind Clarissa's own emblematic death, then
they are signs of Richardson's intention to textualize Clarissa as a
Christian emblem.[22] Their most important effect is to render Clarissa
unintelligible to the predatory Lovelace, although he does occasionally
perceive her innocence: 'Miss Clarissa Harlowe is above all artifice. She
must have some meaning I cannot fathom' (1290). Neither his reading
nor his social conditioning equip him to comprehend what Clarissa
represents. Moreover, his busy repertoire of gender-crossing disguises
and his charivari of stage-managed plots finally reveal only the
separateness of Clarissa. Like a second-rate playwright trapped inside
the conventions of old drama, Lovelace discovers that his control of
both plot and chief character has been an illusion from the beginning.
As Lovelace's personae proliferate, Clarissa's individuality intensifies;
she fits none of his scripts, and eventually they do not speak even the
same language.

In *Pamela* Richardson believed that erotic love warped by a masculine lust for domination could be tamed by a woman's resistant virtue
and accommodated within conventional marriage. The result is
achieved essentially by a subsequent recasting of the rapist as a misunderstood adolescent and a victim of patriarchal class attitudes. In *Clarissa* the evil is unregenerate and virtue, specifically the integrity of body
and soul, is proof against all pressures for social compromise. Like the
letter itself, whose form is principally defined from within, *Clarissa*'s
concern is to realize the inner self and her individual consciousness in
the act of writing. It is more than an accident that the novel form, itself
marginal and without a respectable social or literary lineage at the time,
takes as its subject the social and spiritual marginality of women. Richardson enacts the paradox of conventional devotional theories (as found
in Allestree's *The Ladies Calling*, 1673, for example, where woman is
man's spiritual equal but his social subject), by *opposing* its materialistic
social theory and a spiritual equality of the sexes. The novel as a whole
thus examines several concepts of power. The erotic passions of Mr
B and Lovelace (in the latter to an almost psychotic extent) are roused
by distress and pain. Power is channelled into lust, and lust is described
as power. Lovelace's 'freedoms' are licences to oppress. Imprisoned at
Mrs Sinclair's 'vile house', the future object of Lovelace's mawkish
fantasies of maternity, breast-feeding, wifely adoration, and of his own
marital condescension, Clarissa arouses in Lovelace a grotesquely
literary as well as a libidinal reaction:

redoubling her struggles to get from me, in broken
accents, and exclamations the most vehement, she
protested that she would not survive what she called a
treatment so disgraceful and villainous; and, looking all
wildly round her as if for some instrument of mischief,
she espied a pair of sharp-pointed scissors on a chair by
the bedside, and endeavoured to catch them up, with
design to make her words good on the spot.

Seeing her desperation, I begged her to be pacified; that
she would hear me speak but one word, declaring that I
intended no dishonour to her: and having seized the
scissors, I threw them into the chimney; and she still
insisting vehemently upon my distance, I permitted her to
take the chair.

But, oh the sweet discomposure! – Her bared shoulders
and arms, so inimitably fair and lovely: her spread hands
crossed over her charming neck; yet not half concealing its
glossy beauties: the scanty coat, as she rose from me,
giving the whole of her admirable shape and fine-turned
limbs: her eyes running over, yet seeming to threaten
future vengeance: and at last her lips uttering what every
indignant look and glowing feature portended; exclaiming
as if I had done the worst I could do, and vowing never
to forgive me; wilt thou wonder that I could avoid
resuming the incensed, the already too-much-provoked fair
one? (724–25)

Lovelace is to describe such scenes as 'a frolic only, a romping-bout,
and laughed off by nine parts in ten of the sex accordingly' (728). But
its significance for Clarissa herself is precisely the opposite. It is a
verbal prelude to physical rape, an obliteration of Clarissa's individual
identity and selfhood by the superimposition upon her of a sexual stereotype. Clarissa is to be the means of Lovelace's self-gratification; *his*
self-realization can only be achieved by destroying that which *she*
values most. As Anna Howe remarks to Clarissa, 'Your merit is your
crime' (237). Clarissa's individual *difference* is not compatible with his
notion of her gender or sexual roles. One of the injunctions in her will
states that her body 'shall not be touched but by those of my own sex'
(1413). *Noli me tangere.*

Such moral vigour was an important element in Richardson's determination that *Clarissa* should end unhappily. In what he termed the
'general depravity' of his own time

when even the pulpit has lost great part of its weight . . .
the author thought he should be able to answer it to his

own heart, be the success what it would, if he threw in
his mite towards introducing a reformation so much
wanted; and he imagined, that . . . in an age given up to
diversion and entertainment, he could *steal in*, as may be
said, and investigate the great doctrines of Christianity
under the fashionable guise of an amusement (Postscript to
Clarissa).

In other words, Richardson intended that the relationship between his
novel and the society which was to receive it should be oppositional,
a reminder that the materialistic hedonism of its erotic, social, and
theological affections (not to mention its taste in reading matter) was
radically at odds with Christian duties. This oppositional relationship
is intensified in Richardson's last novel, a book which has never been
accused of understating its didactic purpose.

The History of Sir Charles Grandison

Fielding's *Tom Jones* had appeared in 1749, a year after *Clarissa*. Its
delineation of a profligate benevolence in the character of its hero gave
pain to Richardson's sensibilities. More significantly, it may have
prompted the composition and the theme of Richardson's *Sir Charles
Grandison* (seven volumes, 1753–54). Which of these two novelists
found the other's work more subversive is a matter of debate. *Pamela*
(1741) provoked Fielding's *Shamela* (1741: discussed in Ch. 4); *Clarissa*
(1747–48) finds its counterpart in Fielding's *Amelia* (1752); but *Tom
Jones* (1749), one feels, was the prime *literary* target of *Sir Charles Grandison* (1753). In a 'Concluding Note' to *Grandison* Richardson takes up
some of his readers' criticisms (chiefly those of Mrs Chapone, who is
'answered' by using the arguments of his ally, Lady Bradshaigh), and
the apologia contains this comment on contemporary novels:

It has been said in behalf of many modern fictitious
pieces, in which authors have given success (and *happiness*,
as it is called) to their heroes of vicious, if not of
profligate, characters, that they have exhibited Human
Nature as it *is*. Its corruptions may, indeed, be exhibited
in the faulty character; but need pictures of this be held
out in books? Is not vice crowned with success,
triumphant, and rewarded, and perhaps set off with wit
and spirit, a dangerous representation? And is it not made

even *more* dangerous by the hasty reformation, introduced,
in contradiction to all probability, for the sake of patching
up what is called a happy ending? (III, 466)

Richardson always found in Fielding's novels too much evidence of the
artist's abrogation of proper social and moral responsibility, as did
Johnson. The popularity of *Tom Jones* saddened and possibly induced
envy in Richardson, and in a letter to Astrea and Minerva Hill (4
August 1749) he spoke of the novel directly:

> perhaps I think worse of the Piece because I know the
> Writer, and dislike his Principles both Public and Private,
> tho' I wish well to the *Man*, and Love Four worthy Sisters
> of his with whom I am well acquainted. And indeed
> should admire him, did he make the Use of his Talents
> which I wish him to make; for the Vein of Humour, and
> Ridicule, which he is Master of, might, if properly turned,
> do great Service to ye Cause of Virtue.

In the event, *Sir Charles Grandison*, 'The History of my Good Man',
as Richardson called it, stands in stark contrast to Fielding's notion of
the good man, and also represents in Richardson's *oeuvre* an attempt
to counterbalance the feminization of fiction achieved in *Pamela* and
Clarissa.

Sir Charles Grandison, as his name implies, is a particular kind of
exemplary hero. He is generous, empathic, magnanimous, wealthy,
flawless in his social manners and in all his intents and purposes a
paragon of moral virtue. He is also Richardson's image of the Christian
hero, a rationalist in virtue, and a virtuous rationalist, an emblem of
Richardson's conviction that 'characters may be good, without being
unnatural' (Concluding Note). His Christian rationalism, and the
reason for refusing to duel with Pollexfen, is reducible to a syllogism:

> Courage is a virtue;
> Passion is a vice;
> Passion, therefore, cannot be Courage

(I, 265)

Although Richardson based his hero on historical sources, *Grandison*
is chronologically his most contemporaneous novel, as if to indicate
the urgent need in his society for such morally uplifting characters.[23]
Whereas the tragic Clarissa had been 'a truly Christian heroine', Grandison was to be 'a Man of TRUE HONOUR', and although a great
deal of *Grandison* reinforces this exemplary theme, the tone and much

of the writing in the earlier volumes belong to the world of social comedy. Harriet Byron is bright, intelligent, beautiful, with a mischievous ironic wit, and is unconsciously looking for a husband, the motive which allows Richardson to mark out the fashionable but empty fopperies of his contemporary world. Sir Hargrave Pollexfen and Mr Greville emerge as suitors for Harriet in a section of the novel which is incipiently theatrical and on occasions actually replaces the epistolary narrative mode with stage dialogue. The witty Charlotte Grandison bears some similarity to the level-headed frivolity of the independent-minded Millamant in Congreve's *The Way of the World*, both resenting the prospect of domination and ownership by their respective husbands. Her presence in the novel is more than an entertaining light relief from the serious discussion of right moral conduct and the nature of love, the central theme enacted by Sir Charles, Clementina (his first love) and Harriet (the woman he will marry). Harriet explains the difficulty which faces Charlotte in her relationship with Lord G, an inequality which she herself clearly fears, but one which she will escape from with Grandison:

> What can a woman do, who is addressed by a man of talents inferior to her own? Must she throw away her talents? Must she hide her light under a bushel, purely to do credit to the man? She cannot pick and choose, as man can. She has only her negative; and, if she is desirous to oblige her friends, not always *that*. Yet it is said, Women must not encourage Fops and Fools. They must encourage Men of Sense only. And it is *well* said. But what will they do, if their lot be cast only among Foplings? If the Men of Sense do not offer themselves? And pray, may I not ask, If the taste of the age, among the Men, is not Dress, Equipage, and Foppery? Is the cultivation of the mind any part of their study? The men, in short, are sunk, my dear; and the women but barely swim. (I, 230)

As Emma's similarly speculative opinions and behaviour, based on an inequality of intellectual if not social peers, are finally restrained by Mr Knightley in Jane Austen's novel, so Harriet's pre-marital anxiety about the inequality between the sexes is authoritatively soothed by Grandison, both in words and because he is a model husband. Beneath the superficial and polite raillery, male patriarchy asserts itself through Grandison (see III, 248–49); it is accepted not only because Grandison is its model representative, but also because behind Grandison there is an unimpeachable moral authority: 'When Sex ceases', he says to Charlotte, 'inequality of Souls will cease; and women will certainly be on a foot with men, as to intellectuals, in Heaven' (III, 250). This is an ancient and a mixed consolation; but although the doctrinal shadow of the conduct-book hangs over this novel (one of the characters is actually called Allestree), in this particular scene Richardson sparks off brilliant high comedy. In Charlotte he catches the authentic tone of an intellectually proud woman glimpsing in her brother's reply the kind of equal partnership between the sexes which her own marriage denies her. The light raillery in this scene is completely integrated with Richardson's serious concerns, so that what is said, and the manner of its saying, deepen theme and character in several directions at once.

Similarly, the central and dominant tension in the novel is shared between its three main characters, each of whom adjusts to the presence of the other two. Harriet (in a private letter, I, 309) declares her love for Grandison before he declares his for her; she is then stunned to discover that Grandison's past contains a passionate relationship with the Italian (and Catholic) Clementina. What looks like the makings of a conventional romantic rivalry and a dilemma for Grandison is eventually transcended. Clementina returns to England, having run away from parental and filial pressure to marry Count Belvedere. She arrives in a state of acute mental distress, hysteria not madness, and appeals to Grandison. He is, of course, solicitous, but his emotional response is that of a brother or an uncle, not that of a possible sexual partner. He expands his moral sympathy in order to accommodate Clementina (and Harriet) in a new and richer relationship, converting what might have been a moral embarrassment into a further strength. Grandison welcomes her, but with an indication of the only relationship possible in the new situation: 'Generous, noble Clementina! – Your happiness is indeed essential to that of us *both*. My Harriet is another Clementina! You are another Harriet! Sister-excellencies I have called you to her, to all her relations' (III, 343). Within a very few pages it is Harriet's turn to expand her emotional repertoire. It is not only her 'frankness of heart' (III, 355) but also her emotional confidence in Grandison's example which enables her to empathize with and, to some extent, relive Clementina's distress without Clementina's consequences. They weep in unison, a scene utterly remote from the tearful mawkishness of later novels of sensibility.

Grandison is psychologically static. His poise has been attained before the novel begins and his prehistory is narrated to Harriet by his sisters, Charlotte and Caroline, in a lengthy interpolated narrative (I, 310–86). The son of a rakish, poetical, spendthrift, and duelling absentee father whose insouciance killed his principled, benevolent, and sensitive wife, Grandison's moral elegance is presented as an already achieved compromise between the sins of his father (heedless self-indulgence) and the passive and reflective piety of his exploited mother.

Grandison neither duels nor 'frights gay company with grave maxims' (II, 379). He is wealthy, intellectually accomplished (a classically educated man, as Richardson himself was not), a model landowner, son, brother, guardian, lover, a perceptive judge of both men and women. He is the moral reference point for everyone in the novel. Richardson was soon made aware of the dangers of his almost faultless hero. In spite of his 'tendencies to pride and passion' (III, 464) Grandison's presence in the book clearly indicates that it was Richardson's purpose to exhibit an already good man, not the process whereby a good man is made. His very presence elicits reform and benevolence in all who come into contact with him. Harriet's uncle observes (III, 184): 'He can court without speech: He can take one's heart, and say never a word.' Grandison wins his battles by the force of moral example. A brilliant swordsman, he refrains from violence: 'My sword is a sword of defence, not of offence' (I, 208). The impetuous Sir Hargrave Pollexfen, from whose clutches Grandison had rescued Harriet, is converted from his brutal and antiquated vices of wenching and duelling by the new and 'truly heroic' moral resistance of a Christian hero. Harriet's last words in the novel describe no mere husband but a moral machine; typographically, almost, a god:

> But could HE be otherwise than the best of HUSBANDS,
> who was the most dutiful of SONS; who is the most
> affectionate of BROTHERS; the most faithful of
> FRIENDS: Who is good upon principle, in every relation
> of life?
>   What, my dear grandmamma, is the boasted character
> of most of those who are called HEROES, to the un-
> ostentatious merit of a TRULY GOOD MAN? (III, 462)

The moral energy of Richardson's elevated prose here is something not ordinarily met with outside descriptions of religious revelation. This is not accidental. Richardson's imagination is fired by the prospect of realizing a social and moral revolution. In converting the old notion of the heroic from one in which relationships are defined by power and domination into a new heroism in which there is a communal (if here only matrimonial) celebration of a passive and selfless altruism, Richardson displaces actuality with a social vision. If Grandison seems too good to be true, then social truths are to be questioned. Richardson's endings (the death of Clarissa, the bliss of Harriet) are vindications, in fictional terms, not of social realism but of social possibility. The extension of Grandison's individual moral code into a social principle is, I think, the subject of Richardson's knowing irony. When James Bagenhall says to Solomon Merceda, 'See what a Christian can do,

Merceda. After this, will you remain a Jew?', Merceda replies, 'Let me see such *another* Christian, and I will give you an answer' (I, 254). Grandison is, of course, exceptional.

The essential difference between Richardson and Fielding is that Richardson's pose as editor of others' texts is an enabling device; it frees the author to step aside from autonomous characters and allows them to develop as moral beings beyond the world of social actuality. It is not simply a coincidence that the newly emerging novel, itself a marginal and socially dubious form at this time, takes as its subject a social minority. In all of Richardson's novels power resides in male hands, through the laws of justice, property, inheritance, and family. In *Pamela* Sir Simon Darnford is not impressed by the prospect of Pamela's rape: if Mr B wishes to have her, 'He hurts no family in this' (I, 172). In two of his novels Richardson's fictional plot arises from the possibility of a corrupt masculine world reformed by the moral leadership of an individual woman. In *Grandison* Richardson's own stereotype is reversed, but only by depicting a man who holds the patriarchal powers in reserve. Grandison is a brilliant swordsman and also controls his family by absolute power. But he chooses to exercise neither potentiality. The sword is there, but it is never drawn; he has chosen 'to give, and not take a life' (I, 262) and adds, 'I love to communicate pleasure, but not pain' (I, 394). Richardson is able to suspend the stereotyped gender roles by invoking Christian imperatives. Without the overt Christianity, Richardson's thematic preoccupation surfaces again in the novels of D. H. Lawrence and Patrick White.[24] In all three writers there is a conviction that sexuality is much more than a social construct. In Richardson's conscious imagination, and embedded in the implications of his fiction, there is a concept of human personality two centuries ahead of its time. As Anna Howe puts it in her memorial of Clarissa (1468): 'Let our sex therefore (she used to say) seek to make themselves mistresses of all that is excellent and not incongruous to their sex in the *other*; but without losing anything commendable in their *own*.'

Notes

1. *Pamela; or, Virtue Rewarded*, edited by Peter Sabor (London, 1980), p. 31 (Preface by the Editor). All references to *Pamela I* are to this edition and are given in the text. This comprises only the first and second volumes of the four-volume *Pamela*. For *Pamela II*, i.e. Volumes III and IV, see note 11 below.

2. Quoted in A. D. McKillop, *Samuel Richardson: Printer and Novelist* (1936; reprinted Chapel Hill, 1960), pp. 124–25. Compare Richardson's comment on his own prolixity: 'Nineteen or Twenty Vols. Closely printed! A Man of Business too! – Monstrous! – Reflecting upon my *now* habitual unconquerable Reluctance to the Pen, I wonder myself at my enormous Luxuriance. All I have to say for myself is, *first*, that the new Manner of writing – to the Moment – betray'd me into it; flattering myself, that hardly any-one, who would attempt the same Manner, would be able to avoid the same Excess; and *next*, to convince the Public that I know when to stop; and that I make not its Patience the Measure of my Impositions; and that Avarice was not the Motive that governed my Pen' (*Selected Letters of Samuel Richardson*, edited by John Carroll (Oxford, 1964), p. 329: to Lady Bradshaigh, 9 October 1756).

3. For a discussion of Johnson's preference for Richardson's novels over those of Fielding, see Bernard Harrison, *Henry Fielding's Tom Jones: The Novelist as Moral Philosopher* (London, 1975), pp. 11–27.

4. Terry Eagleton, *The Rape of Clarissa: Writing, Sexuality and Class Struggle in Samuel Richardson* (Oxford, 1982), pp. 5–6.

5. *Clarissa; or, The History of a Young Lady*, edited by Angus Ross (Harmondsworth, 1985), p. 35. All references are to this edition and are given in the text.

6. *The History of Sir Charles Grandison*, edited by Jocelyn Harris, 3 vols (Oxford, 1972), iii, 228. All subsequent references are to this edition and are given in the text.

7. Two years before *Pamela* appeared, in 1739, a pamphlet possibly written by Lady Mary Wortley Montagu (1689–1762) was published under the title *Woman Not Inferior to Man*, a caustic criticism of patriarchal society which pushed the feminist cause further in the direction indicated by Mary Astell (1668–1731), the 'Ingenious Lady' to whom Defoe alludes in his *Essay on Projects* ('An Academy for Women'), and the author of *A Serious Proposal to the Ladies for the Advancement of their True and Great Interest* (1694). Both Astell and Montagu define gender as a social construct. For further discussion, see Katherine M. Rogers, *Feminism in Eighteenth-Century England* (Carbondale, 1982) and, for a more popular account, Dale Spender, *Women of Ideas . . . from Aphra Behn to Adrienne Rich* (London, 1982), pp. 73–85. A brief poem by Aphra Behn shows a distinctly more subtle and ironic awareness of the cosmic and social double standards ranged against women:

> How prone we are to Sin, how sweet were made
> The pleasures, our resistless hearts invade!
> Of all my Crimes, the breach of all thy Laws,
> Love, soft bewitching Love! has been the cause;
> Of all the Paths that Vanity has trod,
> That sure will soonest be forgiven of God;
> If things on Earth may be to Heaven resembled,
> It must be love, pure, constant, undissembled:
> But if to Sin by chance the Charmer press,
> Forgive, O Lord, forgive our Trespasses.

8. Mr B's name is almost certainly Brandon: see *Pamela*, i, 179.

9. Some of Richardson's editorial tinkering was designed to tone down the sexual fantasies of Pamela by providing psychological explanations: see, for example, pp. 187–88 and note 137, dealing with Pamela's escape attempt and her mistaken identification of the cow for a bull.

10. Compare Arnold Kettle's remark in *An Introduction to the English Novel*, 2 vols (London, 1951), I, 68–69: 'The hard-headed scheming of the girl and her parents for a decent social position is presented in terms of a high-falutin religiosity.'

11. It is symptomatic of Richardson's imaginative failure that in the two-volume sequel to the 1740 *Pamela* Mr B's moral re-education (or his moral self-discovery) includes sub-editing Pamela's own conduct-book. See *Pamela*, Volume II, Everyman's Library edition (London, 1976), p. 472.

12. *Clarissa* first appeared in eight volumes, but use of smaller type for the last two meant that it was published in seven.

13. In his Postscript to *Clarissa*, pp. 1495–99, Richardson cites Aristotle for his tragic authority. For further discussion, see Ira Konigsberg, *Samuel Richardson and the Dramatic Novel* (Lexington, 1968), pp. 74–94, and Richardson's letter to Lady Bradshaigh, 15 December 1748, *Selected Letters*, p. 108.

14. Margaret Anne Doody, *A Natural Passion: A Study of the Novels of Samuel Richardson* (Oxford, 1974), p. 182.

15. F. W. Hilles, 'The Plan of *Clarissa*', *Philological Quarterly*, 45 (1966), 236–48.

16. Lovelace's quotation from *Paradise Lost* includes phallic imagery. At the inn on Hampstead Heath he is grimly amused that one of the maids looks at his foot, expecting to find it cloven (772–73). Other recurrent antitheses are devil/angel; hunter/wounded deer; spider/fly; serpent (i.e. Satan)/serpent (Clarissa's funerary symbol of eternity); black/white; miner or pioneer/citadel; chicken/tiger (935); wolf/lamb(?); fire/water or ice; etc. Lovelace also sees himself as a rake *naturally* conditioned to prey upon women's (hypocritical) pretence to chastity.

17. Clarissa's comment to Miss Rawlins is reported in dialogue form by Lovelace to Mr Belford: 'He can put on the appearance of an angel of light; but has a black, a very black heart!' (790).

18. Doody, p. 106.

19. Compare Eagleton, p. 75: [Clarissa's] 'elaborate dying is a ritual of deliberate disengagement from patriarchal and class society . . . she refuses incorporation into social discourse and transforms herself instead into a pure self-referential sign.' Presumably, God is her intended reader. For a reading of *Clarissa* based on Jungian myths, see Dorothy Van Ghent, *The English Novel: Form and Function* (1953; reprinted New York, 1961), pp. 45–63, 307–22, and for the novel's sexual symbolism, pp. 315–16.

20. See Doody, pp. 151–87, for a discussion of the death-bed scene in contemporary devotional literature.

21. In N. Bailey's translation of 1699, published in London, p. 65. Part II, Chapter 9 (pp. 237–38) also illustrates Clarissa's evasive use of the grave as her 'house', again a commonplace. Jeremiah Drexel (1581–1638) was a Jesuit writer. An English translation of his *Considerations on Eternity* (1620) was published in 1710. Both books include emblematic engravings, and were reprinted several times during the eighteenth century.

22. Richardson's printing firm published Defoe's *A New Family Instructor* (1727) and *Religious Courtship* (1722: which Pat Rogers describes as 'the most imaginative treatment of domestic life under the Puritan ethos which had yet

appeared': *The Augustan Vision*, London, 1974, p. 269). Katherine Hornbeak examines the influence of domestic conduct books in 'Richardson's *Familiar Letters* and the Domestic Conduct Books', *Smith College Studies in Modern Languages*, 19 (1938), 1–29, as does Rita Goldberg in the more recent *Sex and Enlightenment: Women in Richardson and Diderot* (Cambridge, 1984), pp. 24–65. In her edition of *Grandison* cited above, Jocelyn Harris points out (I, xviii) that 'Stylistically, the pattern in *Grandison* of maxim, illustrative scene, and commentary is traceable to the conduct books, probably by way of Defoe's *Family Instructor* (1715), *Religious Courtship* (1722), and *A New Family Instructor* (1727)'.

23. William Villiers, Viscount Grandison, a Royalist in the Civil War, is described in Clarendon's *History* as 'a young Man of so virtuous a habit of mind, that no temptation or provocation could corrupt him . . . and of that rare Piety and Devotion, that the Court, or Camp, could not show a more faultless Person' (quoted Doody, p. 249). In his pamphlet 'A Letter to a Lady' (1754), printed to increase the novel's circulation, Richardson states that the action of *Pamela* is set thirty years before, that of *Clarissa* twenty years previously, and that of *Grandison* 'pretty near to the present time' (*Grandison*, III, 467). There seems no doubt as to where Richardson believed the most urgent sexual reform should begin.

24. Patrick White, *The Twyborn Affair* (London, 1979), p. 360: 'True friendship . . . if there is anything wholly true – certainly in friendship – comes, I'd say, from the woman in a man and the man in a woman.'

Chapter 4

Forms for Public Art: Henry Fielding

Pamela, Fanny Hill, and Shamela

The fact that Henry Fielding's career as a novelist began with a pseudonymous parody of Richardson's *Pamela* is both undeniable and prob-
lematical. *Shamela* is certainly not the last word on its model, nor is
it an adequate prefiguring of Fielding's subsequent artistic character.
Shamela reveals more about Fielding than it does about Richardson,
and it marks not a bridge but a frontier between the two novelists. Like
all parody, *Shamela* is a reading and a rewriting of its model, an
interpretation of it, a version which selects and distorts (or misreads)
in order to redirect its unacceptable claims. *Shamela* simplifies and
polarizes its model according to a totally different moral system.
Fielding ridicules Pamela's lack of education; he reinterprets her naivety
as low cunning, her fear of sexual advances as a lewd and hypocritical
'knowingness', her friendship with Parson Williams and her literary
taste as evidence of her equally promiscuous moral and literary preferences. Pamela's chastity of mind and body is recycled into an exclusively sexual obsession, a screen for the lowest form of fortune-hunting.
Thus Shamela writes of her wedding night with Squire Booby:

> In my last I left off at our sitting down to Supper on
> our Wedding Night, where I behaved with as much
> bashfulness as the purest Virgin in the World could have
> done. The most difficult Task for me was to blush;
> however, by holding my Breath, and squeezing my
> Cheeks with my Handkerchief, I did pretty well. My
> Husband was extreamly eager and impatient to have
> Supper removed, after which he gave me leave to retire
> into my Closet for a Quarter of an Hour, which was very
> agreeable to me; for I employed that time in writing to
> Mr. *Williams*, who, as I informed you in my last, is
> released, and presented to the Living, upon the Death of

the last Parson. Well, at last I went to Bed, and my
Husband soon leapt in after me, where I shall only assure
you, I acted my Part in such a manner, that no
Bridegroom was ever better satisfied with his Bride's
Virginity. And to confess the Truth, I might have been
well enough satisfied too, if I had never been acquainted
with Parson *Williams*.[1]

Shamela is a superbly barbed and specific form of close textual transformation. But it is, of course, a travesty of Richardson's novel. It
appeared on 4 April 1741, and less than a year later it was followed
by Fielding's first novel, *Joseph Andrews*. Joseph is the imputed brother
'to the illustrious *Pamela*, whose Virtue is at present so famous'; thus
Fielding shaped and timed his novel with Richardson in mind. Fielding
saw in Richardson's novel a vulgarized and exclusively sexual concept
of chastity – 'Vartue' not 'Virtue'. In place of Pamela's defence of *her*
chastity against a predatory Mr B, Fielding puts Joseph's defence of
his chastity against a predatory Lady Booby. Joseph's elevation from
human scarecrow to his Lady's personal manservant is the limit of his
upward social mobility within the Booby household, as sly a reference
to Pamela's social success as the final resolve of Joseph never to be
'prevailed on by any Booksellers, or their Authors, to make his
Appearance in *High-Life*'.[2] The anti-*Pamela* satire is only a part of
Fielding's artistic purpose in *Joseph Andrews*. Specific cross-references
between the two novels decline steeply after I, xi, where Joseph turns
away from his parental home and his sister's estate and proceeds
towards the Booby country seat in search of his childhood sweetheart,
Fanny Goodwill (whose illiteracy is determined by parodic intentions
but also by an increasingly obvious sense of Fielding's unwillingness
to consider the social implications of Pamela's marital alliance before
the idea of chastity and charity have been redefined). *Pamela* provides
Fielding with a starting-point for a plot, and an oppositional frame of
social and moral reference. Of all the possible reasons for Fielding
turning away from another *Shamela* in *Joseph Andrews* the most likely
is that narrow intertextual parody was simply too cramping for
Fielding's purposes. *Joseph Andrews* does not start with anti-*Pamela*
material but with a careful and deliberate critical essay on what, to
Fielding, a novel actually should be.

Certainly, Fielding found *Pamela* morally pretentious and its cult-
following a ludicrous overestimate of a crude experiment. Among
Fielding's ultimate purposes in *Tom Jones* was a definition of virtue
which had little to do with a narrowly sexual chastity. His admiration
for Richardson's *Clarissa*, consequently, was immediate, sustained, and
genuine, though a remark he makes in *Tom Jones* (IX, 1) seems unde-

niably a stylistic hit equally applicable to *Pamela* and the later *Clarissa*: 'To the Composition of Novels and Romances, nothing is necessary but Paper, Pens and Ink, with the manual Capacity of using them.' One notorious underground literary classic dared to examine *overtly* the crucial difference between Richardson and Fielding's literary treatment of the nature of female sexuality, and without either Richardson's moralizing strait-jacket or Fielding's recourse to sly innuendo in *Shamela*. John Cleland's *Memoirs of a Woman of Pleasure* (1748–49) has been seen as a mid-point between Pamela's sexual nervousness and Shamela's brazen knowingness. In the first unabridged edition since its original publication, Peter Sabor claims that 'Fanny's physical resemblance to Pamela is not gratuitous; she is a Richardsonian creation, modified by the wit and good humour of Fielding. Drawing on the strengths and parodying the weaknesses of the two great mid-eighteenth-century novelists, Cleland's *Memoirs of a Woman of Pleasure* deserves a permanent place not only in libertine literature but in the canon of the English novel'.[3] The last point is undeniable, but it would be difficult to see Fanny Hill either as one of Pamela's daughters or as one of Shamela's acquaintances. This novel's virtuoso sexual explicitness is both joyous and guiltlessly exuberant; it is a celebration of sensuality without equal in its time, a sufficient reason alone for its suppression. The *Memoirs* is neither a bad book, nor is it badly written. Its connection with Richardson's novel is partly formal (the two volumes are in the form of two letters, and there are occasional allusions to Richardson's device of 'writing to the moment') and partly thematic (Fanny's early companion Esther reflects a mercantilist attitude towards her 'VARTUE' (3) which is not shared by Fanny herself). But in all other respects these novels are worlds apart. The framework of Fanny's initiation into the joys of heterosexual pleasure is her love relationship with Charles, whom she eventually marries after an extremely athletic sexual reunion (182–86). Between her initial innocence and her arrival 'in the bosom of virtue' (187) she is the witness to a series of sexual acts (heterosexual and homosexual) and the increasingly expert participant in many heterosexual partnerships (some private, others public). Fanny herself isolates the horror of mere lust as a joyless and loveless animal coupling as vividly as D. H. Lawrence was to do. But in sexual relationships between consenting adults the narrative style becomes linguistically euphoric: there are more than fifty metaphors for the phallus alone. Cleland's critical aversion to boring the reader is as keen as his desire to avoid charges of hypocrisy. At the beginning of the second volume, in a discourse itself saturated with sexual allusion, Fanny wrestles not with her lovers but with language itself (91):

MADAM,

If I have delay'd the sequel of my history, it has been purely to afford myself a little breathing time, not without some hopes that, instead of pressing me to a continuation, you would have acquitted me of the task of pursuing a confession, in the course of which, my self-esteem has so many wounds to sustain.

I imagined indeed, that you would have been cloy'd and tired with the uniformity of adventures and expressions, inseparable from a subject of this sort, whose bottom or ground-work being, in the nature of things, eternally one and the same, whatever variety of forms and modes, the situations are susceptible of, there is no escaping a repetition of near the same images, the same figures, the same expressions, with this further inconvenience added to the disgust it creates, that the words *joys, ardours, transports, extasies,* and the rest of those pathetic terms so congenial to, so received in the *practice of pleasure,* flatten, and lose much of their due spirit and energy, by the frequency they indispensibly recur with, in a narrative of which that *practise* professedly composes the whole basis: I must therefore trust to the candour of your judgment for your allowing for the disadvantage I am necessarily under, in that respect, and to your imagination and sensibility the pleasing task of repairing it, by their supplements, where my descriptions flag or fail: the one will readily place the pictures I present before your eyes, the other give life to the colours where they are dull, or worn with too frequent handling.

What you say besides, by way of encouragement concerning the extreme difficulty of continuing so long in one strain, in a mean temper'd with taste, between the revoltingness of gross, rank, and vulgar expressions, and the ridicule of mincing metaphors and affected circumlocutions, is so sensible, as well as good-natur'd, that you greatly justify me to myself for my compliance with a curiosity that is to be satisfied so extremely at my expence.

Fanny's subject and language are inextricably connected. She avoids romantic cliché and the hackneyed language of literary eroticism just as she avoids smuttiness, titillation, and apologetic guilt. The confessional mode of her memoirs is neither exhibitionist nor (as in Moll

Flanders's curiously asexual memoirs) self-censoring. In the following passage, from the concluding pages of the novel, Fanny describes an area of sexual experience far beyond Pamela's sexual timidity and equally distant from Shamela's reductive voyeurism, and in language rarely seen since the poetry of Donne (184):

> As we were giving then a few moments of pause to the delectation of the senses, in dwelling with the highest relish on this intimatest point of re-union, and chewing the cud of enjoyment, the impatience natural to the pleasure soon drove us into action. Then began the driving tumult on his side, and the responsive heaves on mine, which kept me up to him: whilst as our joys grew too mighty for utterance, the organs of our voice, voluptuously intermixing, became organs of the touch: And, now! now! I felt! to the heart of me, I felt the prodigious keen edge, with which love, presiding over this act, points the pleasure: Love! that may be stiled the attic salt of enjoyment: and indeed, without it, the joy, great as it is, is still a vulgar one, whether in a king or a beggar: for it is undoubtedly love alone, that refines, ennobles, and exalts it.
>
> Thus happy then, by the heart, happy by the senses, it was beyond all power, even of thought, to form the conception of a greater delight, than what I was now consummating the fruition of.
>
> *Charles*, whose whole frame all convulsed with the agitation of his rapture, whilst the tenderest fires trembled in his eyes, all assured me of a perfect concord of joy, penetrated me so profoundly, touch'd me so vitally, took me so much out of my own possession, whilst he seem'd himself so much in mine, that in a delicious enthusiasm I imagin'd such a transfusion of heart and spirit, as that coaliting, and making one body and soul with him, I was him, and he, me.

Cleland's final appeal is that the reader should not see Fanny's respectable marriage to Charles as a social and literary cover-up for a gratuitously erotic subject, 'the paultry finesse of one who seeks to mask a devotee to Vice under a rag of a veil, impudently smuggled from the shrine of Virtue' (187). This disclaimer failed to prevent the authorities from deconstructing Cleland's erotic masterpiece into a subversive intrusion into both literary and social no-go areas. Not the least achievement of this novel is its finale; the stylized operatic climax of its closing pages elaborates both the heights of sexual bliss and the sensual enjoyment of literature itself. In Roland Barthes's terms, this is a novel of 'Pleasure', not of 'Desire'. It does not *disappoint* the reader.[4]

Cleland's recognition of exuberant female sexuality has nothing in common with either Richardson or Fielding, and there is, in turn, a class difference between Richardson and Fielding both as men and novelists. Richardson was a self-educated and eventually wealthy writer whose origins were artisan; Fielding was a member of the public school and university-educated professional classes from a distinguished aristocratic and military family, dogged by poverty. There is a species difference between their respective self-images, as between their novels. The class antagonism between them is indicated by Johnson's reported remarks of Richardson's inference from reading Fielding's work: 'Richardson used to say, that had he not known who Fielding was, he should have believed he was an ostler' (Boswell's *Life of Johnson*, 6 April 1772). As a *writer*, the patrician Fielding, it seems, could strike the socially ambitious artisan as the merest proletarian. Lady Mary Wortley Montague commented in a letter to her daughter the Countess of Bute (20 October 1755), that Richardson's novels revealed ignorance of the ways of social high life, and one of Fielding's closest friends turned his intended compliment to Richardson around a similarly fixed view of social categories: 'The sordid views of trade have not (as usual) been so far able to engross you, as to withdraw you from the contemplation of more rational, more ingenuous, and (what perhaps may sound strange to many of your neighbours) more interesting subjects.'[5] A more recent commentator puts a similar assumption more bluntly:

> What really bothered Fielding about *Pamela* was that it was subversive. It overthrew classical literary decorum in making a low, ungrammatical female its heroine; it overthrew social barriers in presenting a misalliance as not only possible but in given circumstances desirable. It even questioned the multiple standards of sexual morals. *Shamela* shows what a revolutionary book *Pamela* could seem. Richardson's novel affronted the old Etonian in Fielding, and he registered the reaction of the Establishment.[6]

In their technical approach to writing novels each takes a quantum leap in opposite directions. Richardson's technique of 'writing to the moment' (the phrase is used by Lovelace as well as his creator) is essentially an exploratory mode in which personality, reality, and truth are interdependent and provisional – 'All the letters are written while the hearts of the writers must be supposed to be wholly engaged in their subjects (the events of the time generally dubious)', as Richardson points out. In Fielding's novels everything has been 'written' already, either in the 'Book of Nature', or in other books. Fielding's purpose is to persuade the reader that what is commonly agreed is also commonly true. Whereas in Richardson letters are continuously subject to change – by interception, interpretation, suppression, loss, forgery – the central and reliable truths are generally already possessed by Fielding himself as author. The process of enlightening the reader is a gradual, sometimes teasing sequence of authorial revelation and suppression utterly alien to Richardson's narrative absenteeism, where autonomous texts jostle for privilege. Although neither Richardson's nor Fielding's names appear on the title-pages of their novels, Fielding leaves his authorial signature everywhere throughout the novels, carefully establishing a collusion between the reader and himself in relation to a third entity, the text itself. Fielding's acute sense of the novel's literary form enables him to index the reader's attention and redirect his interpretation by direct exhortations. In contrast, Richardson disappears as author (as does 'the reader') and becomes merely a literary factotum, a servant of the text, a means whereby the text is produced and rendered meaningful, but not the instrument of its invention. 'Richardson's' letters are primary utterances by other people. Fielding's narrative art is just that, an open and public gathering to watch the author shape a literary fiction. Very few of these characteristics could be served by another *Shamela*; all are present in *Joseph Andrews*.

The author's Preface to *Joseph Andrews* establishes the *difference* between his prose fiction and that of his predecessors (both in form and subject) and the *similarities* or generic links with a heretofore unrecognized family history of the novel. Fielding's 'comic Epic-Poem in Prose' has distant classical antecedents in Homer's lost comic epic, more proximate European roots in Cervantes's *Don Quixote*, and precedent for its emblematic and parabolic procedures in the universal narrative of the Bible. Thus the 'new' form springs from an old stock and the 'foundling' novel of Defoe and Richardson is returned to its rightful high social place. Fielding's restitution of the novel to a dignified place in literary history seems to provide an aristocratic origin, but in fact Fielding's purpose is to democratize the epic in order to include 'high' and 'low' life possibilities within an extremely broad framework of literary traditions. For the first time in the history of the English novel a space is created between the mode of writing and the subject-matter, a space which is filled with authorial irony, a public manipulation of surfaces, appearances, styles, expectations. Fielding's novels do not *depend* for their success on literary props (a detailed knowledge of the classics, of Cervantes, of Shakespeare, Dryden, Swift, or even of the Bible itself), but Fielding's imagination, by contrast with Richardson, does work on a much denser and more various *literary* context of patterns and allusions than any previous novelist to date. His acute sense of literary form may owe much to his years of experience as a dramatist, but his novels also relate moral meaning to aesthetic shape in new ways. *Tom Jones* (1749) is the obvious example, but such formal and thematic patterns also shaped his first novel. Like all of Fielding's novels the structural division of *Joseph Andrews* into books and chapters, its balancing or contrasting episodes, interpolated narrative episodes which parallel, contrast with, or anticipate the novel's larger thematic concerns, all underline and assume the necessity for an artistic form which itself carries meaning. Fielding is the first of the major English novelists *not* to pretend that his prose fiction is anything else but an artefact. This is not, of course, the same as saying that his novels are inauthentic. In Richardson, only that which is written is real: in Fielding, that which is said often turns out to be the opposite of what is done, and an ironic and situational comedy is the result. The 'real thing' in Fielding's work as a novelist is the play of an intellectual imagination on the moral history of 'HUMAN NATURE', in which 'the Excellence of the mental Entertainment consists less in the Subject, than in the Author's Skill in well dressing it up' (*Tom Jones*, I, 1). Fielding is also the first novelist in English to incorporate into the novel itself instructions to the reader on how to 'read' the novel; he creates his preferred readers' response by synchronizing moral preference with the determinations of plot.

The History of the Adventures of Joseph Andrews

Although Fielding's Preface (3) records his disapproval of 'those voluminous Works commonly called *Romances*, namely Clelia, Cleopatra, Astraea, Cassandra, the *Grand Cyrus*',[7] *Joseph Andrews* nevertheless utilizes some romance commonplaces, and its Preface advances a theory of the novel which is also 'strikingly similar' to that expounded by the French writers of heroic romance.[8] Joseph's birth is obscure; he is only '*esteemed* to be the only Son of Gaffar and Gammar *Andrews*', and the existence of his real father, the reformed rake Mr Wilson, is accompanied by the discovery of a strawberry birthmark. The initial description of Joseph (38) includes 'an Air, which to those who have not seen many Noblemen, would give an Idea of Nobility', and subsequent mention of his fair skin (61, 66, 298) signals the probability of gentle birth – a motif which Smollett was also to use in *Humphry Clinker*, and for the same purpose.[9] Whatever trials and discomfiture Joseph suffers, he will nevertheless find his appropriate place in the social hierarchy. Unlike Defoe, Richardson, and Sterne, Fielding has no interest in loneliness. As in the case of Tom Jones, the exile's wandering is only a temporary state. The question is not whether both heroes will find their social accommodation, but when. Both heroes seem to have obscure origins, but Fielding is not at all concerned with the psychology of the 'outsider' figure, nor in the economics or morality of a Defoe-like self-determination.

Obscure birth is more than a device of plotting, however. Temporary separation from rightful social register serves several purposes. In both *Joseph Andrews* and *Tom Jones* the hero is ejected from an apparently stable social context (Booby Hall, Paradise Hall, respectively) by external forces (Lady Booby's frustrated sexual designs on Joseph, Mr Allworthy's displeasure at Tom's apparent dishonesty) which, in retrospect, are to be seen as necessary agents of Joseph and Tom's eventual social, romantic, and moral success. Fielding uses Fortune as a metaphor for this process. Secondly, the ejection precipitates a wandering quest, a journey through life (Joseph with a mentor, Parson Adams, Tom with the pedagogue Partridge) which enables both to be reunited with their 'fathers' (a real father in Joseph's case; Tom's father has died, but Allworthy welcomes Tom back as a surrogate father and a real nephew). Thirdly, the temporary social deracination of each provides Fielding with the means of exposing the hypocrisy and snobbery of a society which bases its behavioural expectations, both within and between all social levels, on rank. The social politics of rank and interest fascinates Fielding: Chapter 13 of Book II discusses the 'Ladder of Dependence' as it relates to '*High* People' and '*Low* People'. It is Lady Booby who exemplifies the imprisonment of the individual by a social class-consciousness to the exclusion of all other considerations. She resents the crossing of social boundaries by Pamela (whom Fielding characterizes as a snob) and affects to complain of the tyranny of Fashion, to Slipslop, when her lust for Joseph is at its most urgent (265):

> Is he not more worthy of Affection than a dirty Country
> Clown, tho' born of a Family as old as the Flood, or an

idle worthless Rake, or little puisny Beau of Quality? And
yet these we must condemn ourselves to, in order to avoid
the Censure of the World; to shun the Contempt of
others, we must ally ourselves to those we despise; we
must prefer Birth, Title and Fortune to real Merit. It is a
Tyranny of Custom, a Tyranny we must comply with:
For we People of Fashion are the Slaves of Custom.

In Fielding's view, social rank ought to have a necessary correlation
with moral standing, but in practice it does not. High people differ
from low people not only in the extent of their abuse of power over
their social inferiors, but in their abrogation of certain social responsibilities. The worst offenders are those like Slipslop, Miss Grave-airs,
Pamela, and Lady Booby, who either affect to be what they are not
or try to have it both ways. In both cases the prime motive is self-
interest and beneath the comedy of manners Fielding exposes the ugly
social manoeuvres. Slipslop's malapropisms are themselves signs of
social ambition conflicting with social place. At the inn (II, 5) she
scornfully rejects Miss Grave-airs's condescension towards mere
servants. But a mutual realignment takes place when social connections
threaten to change the operation of patronage: 'That prudent Gentlewoman, who despised the Anger of Miss *Grave-airs*, whilst she
conceived her the Daughter of a Gentleman of Small Fortune, now she
heard her Alliance with the upper Servants of a great Family in her
Neighbourhood, began to fear her Interest with the Mistress'(110).
Fielding questions the operation of social privilege, but does not
argue for its abolition. Through Parson Adams he offers the example
of a good man whose revolutionary, levelling Christian example is
qualified, even ridiculed, by his unworldly eccentricity. The implied
social criticism is achieved by an ironic juxtapositioning of styles. Lady
Booby's attempts to prevent the marriage of Joseph and Fanny include
threatening Adams with unemployment. But he replies: 'I know not
what your Ladyship means by the Terms *Master* and *Service*. I am in
the Service of a Master who will never discard me for doing my Duty.'
Behind all of Lady Booby's chatter about her reputation there is an
echo of the old conflict in many Restoration comedies, the dilemma
of fashionable women attempting to satisfy their sexual needs without
at the same time disturbing the social myth of female chastity. This
'double standard' is a subject for *Tom Jones*, but its presence in *Joseph
Andrews* is a foreshadowing of the later novel.
The formal elegance of *Joseph Andrews* may be described diagram-
matically.[10] The novel is composed of three parts, each with distinct
thematic and topographical features, as shown below.

Part One	Part Two	Part Three
Bk i, 1 – i, 10	Bk i, 11 – iii, 13	Bk iv
City	Road	Country/home
(the Booby town house)		(the Booby country house)
7 days	11 days	9 days
Chastity	Charity i, 11 – iii, 13; City and country in Wilson's narrative iii, 3–4	Marriage

The novel is framed by situations and characters drawn from Richardson's *Pamela* (Books I and IV), but from the outset Fielding interpolates critical essays which fill the canvas within the Richardsonian frame with his own material. The Preface offers a critical definition of the subsequent novel: Book I opens with remarks on the art of biography; Book II with a discussion of 'the Art of Division', i.e. the formal division of the novel into (4) books and chapters, with analogies drawn from Homer's *Odyssey* (24 books), Virgil's *Aeneid* (12 books), and Milton's *Paradise Lost* (10 in the first edition, 12 in the second); Book III returns to a theory of biography and adds a theory of characterization ('I describe not Men, but Manners; not an Individual, but a Species'), and a definition of the function of satire; Book IV has no critical preface. In other words, Fielding's interest in the art of fiction moves from external structures into a new area in which form and content have become inseparable. Of the three interpolated narratives (Leonora's story, II, 4; the 'History of two Friends', IV, 10; Mr Wilson's story, III, 3) the latter is the most important. It is at the physical mid-point of the novel; it enacts (without comedy) the structural poles of the novel's opposition between city and country and their associated values; and it provides Joseph (at the time unaware that he is listening to his father) with a means of moral education at one remove from direct involvement. Fielding signposts this narrative for the reader's careful attention by anticipatory thematic parallels and by some overt critical theory. Thus Mr Wilson addresses Adams (who is described by Joseph in III, 5 as 'the best Teacher of a School in all our Country'): 'To this early Introduction into Life, *without a Guide* [my italics], I impute all my future Misfortunes.' The father's deficiency is, of course, supplied to the son not only by Adams's exemplary presence, but also by Joseph's own ability to learn from bad examples to do otherwise. Moreover, Fielding has already instructed his readers how to react to this parallelism. In an effort to establish each other's bona fides Adams and Wilson discuss Homer. Adams repeats some of Fielding's own ideas in the Preface, particularly his regret for the loss

of Homer's comic epic, and the single characteristic of Homer's epic
which meets with Adams's greatest approval is its relation of episode
to structure and meaning in a harmonious whole, the 'Harmotton, that
Agreement of his Action to his Subject . . . from which every Incident
arises, and to which every Episode immediately relates' (176). Mr
Wilson's subsequent autobiographical narrative is to be understood in
exactly the same way in relation to Joseph's own experience in the
context of the novel as a whole.

Additional contexts evoked by the novel, too obvious to need sign-
posting for Fielding's contemporary audience, include the parallels
between Abraham Adams and the biblical patriarch Abraham, a type
of Christian devotion.[11] Whereas Abraham is ready to sacrifice his own
son Isaac in obedience to God's wishes, Adams is desolated at the
supposed loss of his favourite son by drowning, and forgets his recent
lecture on Christian stoicism to the grief-stricken Joseph, who believes
he has lost Fanny. Adams's pre-lapsarian innocence is not simply a
matter of his bookish naivety. As Martin Battestin has shown, Fielding
represents in him the pattern of true moral goodness by which he
wishes to be known as a writer.[12] Fielding's typology of character
through the use of significant names (Mr Allworthy, Messrs Square
and Thwackum, in Tom Jones, for obvious examples) underpins the
men/manners and individual/species distinctions drawn in Joseph
Andrews III, 1. Fielding's moral purpose is 'not to expose one pitiful
Wretch, to the small and contemptible Circle of his Acquaintance; but
to hold the Glass to thousands in their Closets, that they may contemplate their Deformity, and endeavour to reduce it, and thus by
suffering private Mortification may avoid public Shame' (168–69).
Once more, the potential of the novel form is being realigned: its
purposes are to coincide with those of the dominant contemporary
satirical writings of Pope and Swift, but without the latter's fiercely
negative and unforgiving satirical strategies.

A self-conscious form exemplifies more than a gratuitous aesthetic
shape. For much of the novel Fielding's ironic narrative style determines a plurality of possible interpretations and outcomes. The
narrator's attitude towards Adams, at least initially, is ostensibly
ambiguous. Adams's character sketch in I, 3 presages possible triumph
and possible disaster simultaneously; he is seen as an overbalanced
character whose learning and good nature are both out of step with
the real world. His innocence of the world's ways is, though admirable, also dangerously naive:

> Mr. Abraham Adams was an excellent scholar. He was
> a perfect master of the Greek and Latin languages; to
> which he added a great share of knowledge in the Oriental

tongues, and could read and translate French, Italian and Spanish. He had applied many years to the most severe study, and had treasured up a fund of learning rarely to be met with in a university. He was besides a man of good sense, good parts, and good nature; but was at the same time as entirely ignorant of the ways of this world as an infant just entered into it could possibly be. As he had never any intention to deceive, so he never suspected such a design in others. He was generous, friendly, and brave to an excess; but simplicity was his characteristic: he did, no more than Mr. Colley Cibber, apprehend any such passions as malice and envy to exist in mankind. (I, 3: 19)

If the world's institutions and moral behaviour are ignorant and corrupt, then Adams provides an example which it cannot tolerate. Fielding's flickering irony (introduced by the word 'but' in both cases) seems to share the world's judgement. But the purposes of the novel are to tip the balance in Adams's favour, to indicate that a cloistered virtue not only can be praised but become an active principle in determining the lives of others for the better. Although it seems that the fickle and pagan goddess Fortune is in charge of *Joseph Andrews*, coincidence and chance meetings (such as the charitable pedlar's with Adams in II, 15) are eventually redefined as instruments and agents of a benevolent principle which loves order, symmetry, reunification, and reconciliation. Fielding is to his artefacts as a benevolent God is to the Art of Nature. Martin Battestin has argued in relation to *Tom Jones*, 'As the general frame and architecture of *Tom Jones* is the emblem of Design in the macrocosm, so the narrative itself is the demonstration of Providence, the cause and agent of that Design . . . his novels may be seen as artful and highly schematic paradigms of the human condition'.[13] Although this analogy may seem less overt in Fielding's first novel, its presence is unmistakable. In IV, 15, neatly balancing his first appearance in II, 15, the pedlar establishes Joseph's identity by enquiring about the strawberry birthmark. The pedlar then volunteers to find Joseph's parents, but Fielding has so arranged the plot that when human agents resolve to act in accordance with certain benevolent moral principles, Fortune aids in their realization. Fielding remarks:

> But Fortune, which seldom doth good or ill, or makes men happy or miserable, by halves, resolved to spare him this labour. The reader may please to recollect that Mr. *Wilson* had intended a Journey to the West, in which he was to pass through Mr. *Adams's* Parish, and had

promised to call on him. He was now arrived at the Lady
Booby's gates for that purpose. (306)

The reader's role is therefore a co-operative witnessing of the workings
of a benevolent Providence. If the reader remembers the pedlar's first
appearance in II, 15, he will recall a spontaneous act of Christian charity
rather like that of the postilion in I, 12, who provides the naked Joseph
with his own coat (but who is later transported for robbing a hen-
roost). The pedlar, once a gentleman, is the instrument of both
Joseph's reinstatement and of his own: his own reward from Mr
Booby is to become an exemplary exciseman (a collector, in Johnson's
definition, of that 'hateful tax levied upon commodities' and adjudged
by 'wretches'), admired for his justice. The individual reforms the
institution by his example.

Fielding's narrative skills are therefore not employed for the sake
of 'formal realism' as Ian Watt defines it, but for a fundamentally
emblematic purpose. Both characters and plot convey, in their interaction, a representation of an abstract moral pattern in human affairs
which is itself characterized by a Providential justice. The romantic
interest which centres upon Joseph and Fanny is fulfilled in their
marriage; the morally rich Adams acquires some rather more worldly
wealth; Lady Booby's dissipated and fragmentary character is recon-
nected to a social world in which distraction is the essence; her appetites are satisfied by casual and random affairs in London and a
perpetual round of card parties (the *fashionable* game of Fortune, a
parody of Providential patterns).

This distribution of just rewards provides the reader with an
aesthetic sense of an ending, and a schematic image of idealized social
processes. It is futile to complain, as many critics have done, that the
denouement of this novel is 'an artificial expedient'.[14] If Fielding is not
concerned with formal realism then his novel is not subject to the
demands of a truth-to-life literalness. At the most, Fielding's concern
is with morally desirable social conduct qualified by a disillusioned
sense of an imperfect humanity. Against Richardson's preferred mode
of stimulating moral reform by altruistic examples, Fielding substitutes
social actualities for social potentialities. *Joseph Andrews* is therefore a
self-conscious artefact which only *seems* to portray reality. Even the
much-praised 'social realism' of the inns and houses visited by Joseph
and Adams on their journey is to be seen in other terms, i.e. as Quixotic castles inhabited by avaricious tyrants (Mrs Tow-wouse, Parson
Trulliber) or as malicious parodies of feudal hospitality (the squire in
II, 16). Having accepted so much emblematic artifice and authorial
manipulation the reader can hardly object to the resolution of a tangled
plot (already based on mysterious births and gipsy kidnapping) by the

devices of accidental meetings and the fortuitous reappearance of minor characters. As he points out in III, 1, Fielding is concerned neither with 'Individuals' nor with 'Universals' but with generic types who are in continuous existence and unlocated in time, place, and social position:

> Are not the Characters then taken from Life? To which I answer in the Affirmative; nay, I believe I might aver, that I have writ little more than I have seen. The Lawyer is not only alive, but hath been so these 4000 Years, and I hope G – will indulge his Life as many yet to come. He hath not indeed confined himself to one Profession, one Religion, or one Country; but when the first mean selfish Creature appeared on the human Stage, who made Self the Centre of the whole Creation; would give himself no Pain, view no Danger, advance no Money to assist, or preserve his Fellow-Creatures; then was our Lawyer born; and whilst such a Person as I have described, exists on Earth, so long shall he remain upon it. (168)

Fielding thus provides a literary pattern broad enough to provide for the reader's own experience to play an active confirmatory role – even, perhaps, a self-recognizing part. He reminds us of what we should already know rather than instructing us in what we do not know. In exchange for a role in his novels Fielding offers us the compliment of knowledge superior to all of his characters. Abraham Adams and Joseph Andrews are not permitted to ponder their own moral significance, nor do other characters see them as signifying moral paradigms. Their limited autonomy as characters is designed to emphasize, not conceal, Fielding's real concern with the moral education of the reader.

Tom Jones

One of the differences between an abstract philosophical argument and a work of imaginative literature is that the act of interpretation is an essential part of the latter's meaning. Bernard Harrison has perceptively remarked:

> Fielding does not . . . present the reader with an abstractly formulated thesis illustrated by bare and schematic

'examples'. He draws him, as spectator and judge, into a
complex imagined world in which he must actually
exercise moral judgement in circumstances which force
him to reflect upon what he is doing in making such
judgements.[15]

In reading Fielding's novels we are certainly witnesses and
accomplices to acts of choice and judgement, and the choices often lie
between reflecting and non-reflecting judgements. Nothing provokes
Fielding's irony more readily than figures like Adams, Allworthy,
Square, and Thwackum, whose cock-eyed views of the world are
based on a priori theories which exempt either themselves or the rest
of the world from full participation. In all these characters judgement
either precedes full knowledge of the facts (Adams, Allworthy), or
suppresses the awkward complexity of things in order to prove an
elegant and simplistic thesis (Square and Thwackum). The former can
change their judgements as their view of reality is modified by experience, and thus adjust to the world they inhabit; the latter's inadequacy
is exposed as hypocrisy masquerading as authority. Both sets of
characters learn that human nature includes themselves and that it is
a quality subject to change and a very untheoretical weakness which
prohibits such self-exempting. Fielding does, however, provide in *Tom
Jones* an 'abstractly formulated thesis' in relation to the novel's structural disposition. At the mid-point of the novel (the 104th chapter in
a total of 208) Tom stands on Mazard Hill, like Hercules facing the
choice between a virtuous good and a self-indulgent vice. He thinks
of Sophia Western and his past life at Paradise Hall, but then begins
a descent which will soon end in Mrs Waters's bed. Hilltops are
dangerous places in the novel. As Partridge points out (VIII, 10), 'if the
Top of the Hill be properest to produce melancholy Thoughts, I
suppose the Bottom is the likeliest to produce merry ones, and these
I take to be much the better of the two'.[16] Mr Allworthy, the paragon
of moral benevolence, lives at Paradise Hall and on a peak of moral
complacency too abstracted from ground level and ordinary mortals.
The Man of the Hill inhabits the foot of a hill which is at the other
extreme. He is a misanthrope – 'human nature is everywhere the same,
everywhere the object of detestation and scorn' (VIII, 15). A cloistered
virtue and a misanthropy are equally the products of myopic partial
views. Tom's role is to avoid both, by experiencing the conditions of
each. For him, Fortune's wheel will stop neither at the bottom nor at
the top.
     The symmetry of Fielding's novel has been frequently praised, care-
fully dissected, and often misunderstood. Its architectural shape has
prompted one commentator to present a ground plan of the novel

based on John Wood's original design for Ralph Allen's Palladian mansion, Prior Park, the home of Fielding's patron and a possible model for Fielding's description of Allworthy's Paradise Hall.[17] Originally published in six volumes containing three books each, the eighteen books are divided into three parts, as shown below.

Part One	Part Two	Part Three
I, 2 – VI, 11	VI, 12 – XII, 14	XIII, 2 – XVIII, 13
21 years	10 days	1 month
Country	Road	City
Paradise Hall	Upton episode	Lady Bellaston's
Tom and Molly	(IX–X)	house
Seagrim	Tom and Mrs	Tom and Lady
(IV–VI)	Waters	Bellaston
	(IX–X)	(XIII–XV)
Tom separated from		
Sophia (VI)		Tom rejoins Sophia
		(XIII)

Many schematic parallels may be drawn in addition to the one above: for example, the number of chapter totals in each of the books (I has 13, 9, 10, VI has 10, 9, 13); parallel episodes which reflect the same theme or situation from a different point of view (Tom's pursuit of Sophia Western and Tom's pursuit by Molly, Mrs Waters, and Lady Bellaston); and the pairing of contrasted characters. Tom and Blifil (who share identical environments and tutors but who inhabit opposite moral worlds); the Hanoverian, stable, benevolent Allworthy and the Jacobite, inconstant, irascible Western; the abstract moral rationalism of Square and the gloomy doctrinal contentiousness of Thwackum (who agree on one thing only: never to mention the word *goodness*). These are only a few of the many apparently dichotomous contrasts in the novel, whose overall effect is that of discordant detail framed by a total harmonic pattern. In a chapter entitled 'Of the serious in Writing, and for what purpose it is introduced' (V, 1) Fielding's 'Art of division' is elevated to a principle of contrast which runs through the whole physical, aesthetic, and literary worlds:

> And here we shall of Necessity be led to open a new Vein of Knowledge, which, if it hath been discovered, hath not, to our Remembrance, been wrought on by any antient or modern Writer. This Vein is no other than that of Contrast, which runs through all the Works of the Creation, and may probably have a large Share in

> constituting in us the Idea of all Beauty, as well natural as
> superficial: for what demonstrates the Beauty and
> Excellence of any thing but its Reverse?[18]

This certainly looks like an authorial signpost to the 'proper'
interpretation of the novel's structural disposition of contraries. But we
should not infer from it that in all matters of moral choice the 'proper'
conclusion lies at either extreme or, least of all, in the middle. The
middle position between the contrasting teachings of Square and
Thwackum is actually a vacuum ('goodness'), each operating at a
theoretical remove from practical moral concerns. Tom's nature only
seems to lie between the optimistic benevolence of Allworthy (who
rejects Tom), and the weak, impulsive self-gratification described in
the pessimistic misanthropy of the Man of the Hill. These are contrary
positions which Tom does not choose between, but transcends. There
are no fixed and absolute terms to describe human nature except relative ones. Tom idealizes the beauty of the absent Sophia, but the
fleshly Molly Seagrim has the advantage of availability. In v, 10, a
marvellous example of Fielding's stylistic comedy, Tom generates an
erotic image of the absent Sophia in his mind's eye which the grubby
carnality of Molly Seagrim happily accommodates. Their sexual liaison
is not described, but Fielding then remarks:

> Some of my Readers may be inclined to think this
> Event unnatural. However, the Fact is true; and, perhaps,
> may be sufficiently accounted for, by suggesting that *Jones*
> probably thought one Woman better than none, and *Molly*
> as probably imagined two Men to be better than one.
> Besides, the before-mentioned Motive assigned to the
> present Behaviour of *Jones*, the Reader will be likewise
> pleased to recollect in his Favour, that he was not at this
> Time perfect master of that wonderful Power of Reason,
> which so well enables grave and wise Men to subdue their
> unruly Passions, and to decline any of these prohibited
> Amusements. Wine now had totally subdued this Power in
> *Jones*. (I, 257)

The choice here lies between condoning Tom's sexual pragmatism or
retiring from the problem into the rarefied world of self-denial. But
Fielding advocates neither. He turns immediately to dissect the
grounds on which judgement itself is possible. Tom's romantic image
of Sophia is just as 'intemperate' as his behaviour with Molly, and the
narrative style distances both by comic allusion (Molly and Tom are
compared with Dido and Aeneas, retiring into a cave to consummate

their love: *Aeneid*, IV, 165–66). Fielding further forestalls and anticipates the reader's judgemental response by the unexpected arrival of
two self-appointed censors of public morality, i.e. Blifil and
Thwackum, who declaim against vice and wickedness, subject Tom
to a moral inquisition, and then a beating. The reader will, of course,
remember that Blifil is a cold-blooded hypocrite (his 'compassionate'
release of Sophia's caged bird is in fact spiteful revenge on Tom
executed without a single thought for Sophia's possible distress), and
that Thwackum's fate has been obliquely foreshadowed by the sexual
exposure of his philosophical colleague in Molly Seagrim's bedroom
('among other female utensils', v, 5). The reader's categorical moral
judgement on Tom is thus deflected and kept provisional. The reason
for this becomes very clear in the opening chapter of Book v, where
the serious re-education of moral censors is undertaken under the
chapter heading 'Of Love'. Higher than mere sexual gratification ('the
Desire of satisfying a voracious Appetite with a certain Quantity of
delicate white human Flesh'), Love is 'a kind and benevolent Disposition, which is gratified by contributing to the Happiness of others',
which can but need not be expressed in sexual terms. Just as beauty
may exist in the eye of the beholder, so vice may be a projection of
an unhealthy mind. A benevolent mind would not deny the existence
of evil, but an avaricious or ambitious mind will reduce others' esti-
mable and selfless motives to mere self-seeking: Why? Fielding suggests
that the root of the problem lies in our moral natures – 'there is scarce
any Man, how much soever he may despise the Character of a Flat-
terer, but will condescend in the meanest Manner to flatter himself'.
This injunction to 'Know thyself' before externalizing moral judgement of others is unequivocally placed at the centre of Fielding's
relationship with his characters. But it is also the single principle on
which Fielding is prepared either to continue or part company with
his readers:

> Examine your Heart, my good Reader, and resolve
> whether you do believe these Matters with me. If you do,
> you may now proceed to their Exemplification in the
> following Pages; if you do not, you have, I assure you,
> already read more than you have understood; and it would
> be wiser to pursue your Business, or your Pleasures (such
> as they are) than to throw away any more of your Time
> in reading what you can neither taste nor comprehend. To
> treat of the Effects of Love to you, must be as absurd as
> to discourse on Colours to a Man born blind. (I, 271)

The gap between the fiction and the reading public has been bridged.
When we consider Tom Jones we are asked to consider our own pre-

sumptive rights to impose moral judgements on others, to cast the first
stone. The extraordinary structural symmetry of this novel's form
provides a whole series of ostensible contrasts, and questions the
conditions of our critical judgement. A similar process is at work in
the central episode of the novel, Tom's meeting with the Man of the
Hill (viii, 10–viii, 15). In this much-discussed episode Tom and
Partridge break their journey from Gloucester at the Man of the Hill's
house and talk through the night. Fielding prepares the reader for the
subsequent arguments about man's depravity by the setting: it is dark,
Partridge's superstitious fear of witchcraft is stressed, and their first
action is to rescue the Man of the Hill from robbers. The Man of the
Hill is dressed, like a provincial Robinson Crusoe, in animal skins, and
is feared in the neighbourhood. He has lived out of the public world
for thirty years, having been betrayed by his first mistress, corrupted
by a fellow collegian, ruined by gambling, reclaimed by a chance
meeting with his good-natured father, and fortified in his misanthropy
by reading Aristotle, Plato, and the Bible. The paradox of his misanthropy is that in order to preserve intact an ideal of human nature he
must avoid all contact with it. Since 'Human Nature is every where
the same, every where the Object of Detestation and Scorn', the Man
of the Hill lifts his eyes away from human corruption to a contemplation of God's 'Power . . . Wisdom . . . and . . . Goodness'. Fielding
presents, as it were, a dramatic dialogue between two opposing points
of view (misanthropy based on a severe and abstract idealism versus
Tom's unreflecting compassionate benevolence), without immediate
authorial comment. To the Man of the Hill the supreme question is
how a benevolent God could 'form so imperfect, and so vile an
Animal' as Man. Tom, like his creator, shifts the grounds of the
discussion from abstract moral philosophy to individual psychology.
Although the Man of the Hill's first error lies in what might be called
his philosophic method (generalizing the character of mankind from
'the worst and basest among them', instead of extrapolating from 'the
best and most perfect Individuals of that Species'), the real cause of his
error lies within his own moral being. As Tom delicately puts it, the
Man of the Hill has been

> unfortunate, I will venture to say incautious in the placing
> your Affections. If there was indeed much more
> Wickedness in the World than there is, it would not prove
> much general Assertions against human Nature, since
> much of this arrives by mere Accident, and many a Man
> who commits Evil, is not totally bad and corrupt in his
> Heart. In Truth, none seem to have any Title to assert
> Human Nature to be necessarily and universally evil, but

those whose Minds afford them one Instance of this
natural Depravity; which is not, I am convinced, your
Case. (I, 485–86)

But this debate between Youth and Age is unresolved. As dawn
breaks (IX, 1) Fielding interpolates a prefatory chapter on prefatory
chapters. The ostensible purpose of this is to indicate the authentic
trademark of his artistic intelligence and to stress the authenticity of
his source material, 'the vast authentic Doomsday-Book of Nature'.
He defines the prerequisites of the historian (or novelist) as Genius, or
Invention and Judgement; Learning; Conversation (a knowledge of the
characters of men drawn not only from books but from knowledge
of the world, the only source of 'the true practical System' of ethics);
and, finally, 'a good Heart . . . capable of feeling'. It is here, in a
critical essay, that Fielding obliquely answers the Man of the Hill in
the same way as Tom had attempted more directly. Misanthropy is
the projection of an unsociable mind conditioned by bad company.
The reclusive Man of the Hill had disqualified himself from serious
consideration by his retreat from the real world. Tom's compassionate
benevolence and the Man of the Hill's stubborn misanthropy are irreducible and irreconcilable opposites: they each inhabit different moral
worlds, and Tom's is the one which encapsulates his creator's positive
energies. The first chapter of Book IX, therefore, reasserts Fielding's
narrative presence, his formal control over the narrative, and his own
moral authority. Again, the reader's judgement of the debate between
Tom and the Man of the Hill awaits Fielding's own delayed response.
    As an interpolated narrative, the Man of the Hill episode functions
as a parable of the novel's larger moral issues. Like Mr Wilson's
narrative in *Joseph Andrews* it outlines a path which the eponymous
hero will not follow: in both cases the younger man has innate moral
resources which the elder lacked, or is simply more fortunate in his
choice of friends. Though their structural positioning is identical in
each novel, their thematic and artistic function is different. Wilson's
narrative shows a path not taken by Joseph – the sins of the father will
not be visited upon the son. The Man of the Hill is *not* Tom's father:
indeed, he is the antitype of Allworthy, Tom's adopted father,
comparable only as benevolence is related to misanthropy as two
species of idealism. The Man of the Hill's story has an integral moral
place in Fielding's discussion of human nature quite independent of
Tom's biography, and its central position in the novel should warn us
that it is neither a mere digression nor a mere device of plot, but a
pivot on which conflicting views of the nature of man turn. Tom's
predisposition, like that of Squire Allworthy to benevolent optimism,
is innate, just as his brother Blifil's predisposition to a miserably

cunning egotism is innate. The former's 'philosophy' is not a theory drawn from experience (like the Man of the Hill's) but a state of mind, an emotional Epicureanism which confronts but cannot impress the misanthrope. As he says to the lawyer Dowling (XII, 10):

> I had rather enjoy my own Mind than the Fortune of another Man. What is the poor Pride arising from a magnificent House, a numerous Equipage, a splendid Table . . . compared to the warm, solid Content, the swelling Satisfaction, the thrilling Transports, and the exulting Triumphs, which a good Mind enjoys, in the Contemplation of a generous, virtuous, noble, benevolent Action?

Unfortunately, Tom's natural good-breeding and his natural goodness are vulnerable commodities among the artifices of society. His relationship with Lady Bellaston is bleakly contractual: he becomes a male prostitute, trading sex for money from a misplaced sense of gratitude. The best of motives may yet produce moral error, and Tom is similarly reprimanded for his too easy forgiveness of Black George's fraud and ingratitude (XVIII, 11). But just as Tom must learn prudence, the subject of Allworthy's sermon to Tom in XVIII, 10, so Allworthy must learn the same lesson. Having completely misread Tom's character and been duped by the appearance of virtue in Blifil, Allworthy must learn from Tom that Justice is not only blind but also harsh – even the villainous Blifil is entitled to an opportunity for repentance. Fielding has reserved for Blifil a worse fate than destitution or banishment: he turns Methodist in order to marry a rich widow, thus revealing at a stroke his unprincipled addiction to materialism without good works.

The ironic distance which Fielding preserves between the internal components of the novel and his external relationship both to it and to the reader through commentaries serves a number of purposes. Firstly, there is always the possibility of a judgemental perspective; secondly, authorial distance sustains a comic atmosphere; and thirdly, Fielding thereby preserves a confidential relationship with his reader. At moments of violence or potential tragedy (Molly's assault by the village mob in IV, 8, the prospect of Tom's hanging in XVII, 1, for example) Fielding's obtrusively comic–epic diction or his teasing pretence of not being in control of subsequent events raises a comic anxiety instead of a tragic or even an empathic involvement in the reader.[19] As Ian Watt has pointed out, the prospect of a village mob violently assaulting the pregnant Molly Seagrim is intrinsically very unfunny. But Fielding's mock-epic presentation of the violence evaporates anxieties. If the narrator does not convey anxieties, why should the reader be alarmed? As for the prospect of Tom's being hanged, this is so much of a comic outrage that Fielding can pause in order to elaborate it. The *possible* denouements outlined in xvii, 1 include a couple of murders, Sophia's marriage to Blifil, Tom's suicide, and the consequent need for the reader to take a front-row seat at Tyburn gallows. But, as Fielding points out, he is tied to psychological probability, not to the fantastic and improbable; Tom will escape the hangman's noose and Blifil will be exposed for the same reason – the career of evil is entirely dependent on the temporary blindness of those with the power to eradicate it. In a Providential world everything except benevolence is provisional: in Fielding's *Tom Jones* everything, including the narrator and the reader, is subject to ironic controls.

Jonathan Wild and *Amelia*

In spite of the publisher's best efforts, Fielding's last novel was a commercial and critical failure. To put it another way, contemporary readers expected *Amelia* to be another *Tom Jones* and were disdainful when their expectations were not fulfilled. But then most modern readers have similarly expressed their dissatisfaction with what Fielding called his 'favourite Child'. Gone is that dazzlingly alert narrative irony, to be replaced by an earnest didacticism; intellectual playfulness gives way to a sombre social exposure of the corruption of innocence; a vicious society subverts powerless individuals in *Amelia* with an almost documentary vividness and veracity. *Amelia* is the closest Fielding gets in his three major novels to social realism. It is a magistrate's view of social disease, not a comic artist's transformation of it, and the consequence of this is that the whole restorative basis of comic fiction is thrown into question.

Amelia's themes and methods are, respectively, foreshadowed by and vividly contrasted with Fielding's earlier novel *The History of the Late Mr. Jonathan Wild the Great*, which formed the third and last volume of Fielding's *Miscellanies* (1743).[20] Although the moral indignation in *Jonathan Wild* is buoyed up by a sustained and inventive irony, the social horrors in *Amelia* have no palliative and elevating stylistic comedy. *Amelia* is the *least* romantic novel in the whole of eighteenth-century fiction. *Wild* seeks to educate its readers morally by assuming their agreement and taste for irony; *Amelia*, as some contemporary readers found out to their dismay, confronts the reader with an unremitting exposure of endemic, institutionalized corruption. In the former, Fielding's rhetorical irony is the medium of moral expression: in *Amelia* the narrative mode is dramatic, objects stand for nothing but themselves, and the narrator refuses to provide a comic filter. Fielding's *Jonathan Wild* is an extensively ironic work, a black comedy, using a range of satirical devices such as Swiftian political allegory (the scene in Newgate, III, 3, is an image of the political state of England, divided by two parties differing only as two wolves in a sheepfold). The structural irony, as in Gay's *Beggar's Opera*, draws a parallel between criminality and politics. Wild is a type of all 'Great Men', and of Walpole in particular. It is also a parabolic mirror for corrupt magistrates, a sometimes caustic and sometimes sentimental exposure of vulnerable innocence in the Heartfree family.

As a whole, *Jonathan Wild* affects to subvert the positive moral programme recommended in all of Fielding's other novels. It blames constancy, prudence, friendship, tolerance, and benevolence as foolish weakness of mind; and it praises treachery, self-seeking, carnal lust, bigotry, and the ruin of innocence by cynical opportunism, as the world's wisdom. Wild's 'greatness' is defined in negative terms; he lacks 'humanity, modesty and fear', whereas Heartfree's weaknesses are that he is 'good natured, friendly, and generous to an excess'. Wild's criminal career is nourished not only by Heartfree's naive and trusting ingenuousness but also by a society which rewards corrupt and successful sophistication if it is based on an appearance of high rank, which prefers the 'outside' to the 'inside', and which operates a legal system mostly divorced from principles of moral justice. Wild's career begins to crumble before the law catches up with him. He is manipulated by Laetitia and cuckolded by Fireblood; he gradually becomes the victim rather than the hero, and Fielding asks dryly for the reader's sympathy. Heartfree, like Adams in *Joseph Andrews*, possesses not only an exemplary innocence but a religious tolerance which is Fielding's own (he asserts that an honest believer, whether Turk, Presbyterian, Anabaptist, or Quaker will be saved, whereas 'a dishonest and deceitful Christian' will not), and his eventual survival becomes a social icon. As Wild is the paradigm of all the villains and hypocrites in Fielding's fiction, so the Heartfrees are called by their neighbours 'the family of love'.[21] The specific agents of Wild's downfall are a change in the machinery of the law (which makes it a capital offence to procure others to steal) and, as in *Amelia*, a just magistrate:

> The justice, having thus luckily and timely discovered
> this scene of villainy, *alias* greatness, lost not a moment in
> using his utmost endeavours to get the case of the
> unhappy convict [Heartfree] represented to the sovereign,
> who immediately granted him that gracious reprieve which

caused such happiness to the persons concerned; and which
we hope we have now accounted for to the satisfaction of
the reader. (141)

Fielding's narrative switches then to Mrs Heartfree's adventures at
sea, her marooning on the African coast, her rescue by a French
vegetarian Robinson Crusoe figure, a virtuous hermit who nevertheless
threatens her chastity. The only thematic relevance of this lengthy and
structurally awkward episode, apart from the trial of her innocence,
is to provide Fielding with another mirror for magistrates.[22] Mrs
Heartfree tells of a magistrate who is 'the only slave of all the natives
in this country', a concept of judicial responsibility of which Fielding
himself was the real-life exemplar. In *A Voyage to Lisbon*, that moving
account of Fielding's last doomed attempt to recover from appalling
physical illness and chronic overwork, he sees himself as like 'those
heroes who, of old times, became voluntary sacrifices to the good of
the public' (193). But the whole of this episode is an odd miscellany
of echoes of *Gulliver's Travels, Robinson Crusoe*, and political allegory,
never quite articulating its purpose, and concluding with the bald
assertion, 'THAT PROVIDENCE WILL SOONER OR LATER
PROCURE THE FELICITY OF THE VIRTUOUS AND INNO-
CENT' (161). Fielding's particular gift for fusing moral seriousness
with comic form is not best represented by this novel; but for all its
imperfection it is perhaps the clearest statement of Fielding's systematic
and sustained moral convictions, whose very strength permits the
subversive confidence exemplified in the fifteenth maxim of the
Machiavellian Wild's credo of greatness: 'That the heart was the proper
seat of hatred, and the countenance of affection and friendship' (174).
In *Jonathan Wild* 'greatness consists in bringing all manner of
mischief on mankind, and goodness in removing it from them'. In his
last novel, *Amelia* (1751), the trial of innocence and naivety proceeds
without the presence of a protective and reassuring narrative irony.
Fielding tells us exactly what this novel is to be about in the opening
sentence, and his expressive rhythms are sombre: 'The various Acci-
dents which befell a very worthy Couple, after their uniting in the
State of Matrimony, will be the Subject of the following History.' As
for its purpose, the dedicatory epistle to Ralph Allen is similarly transparent and a curious combination of diffidence and aggression:

> The following Book is sincerely designed to promote
> the Cause of Virtue, and to expose some of the most
> glaring Evils, as well public as private, which at present
> infest the Country; tho' there is scarce, as I remember, a
> single Stroke of Satire aimed at any one Person

throughout the whole . . . The good-natured Reader, if his
Heart should be here affected, will be inclined to pardon
many Faults for the Pleasure he will receive from a tender
Sensation; and for Readers of a different Stamp, the more
Faults they can discover, the more, I am convinced, they
will be pleased. (3–4)

Booth, like Heartfree, Adams, Tom Jones, Allworthy, and Dr
Harrison, is a naive hero and a man of 'good nature'. All of Fielding's
good men share a benevolent and social instinct which prompts
empathic concern for the distresses of others and a charitable
response.[23] As such, they are immediately in conflict with the operative
social modes, which generally favour a primarily self-regarding social
ethic. Like Joseph and Tom before him, but unlike Heartfree, Booth
has a protector in the shape of Dr Harrison, a moral guardian and a
benefactor, a constraint on self-destructive instincts. Booth's problem
is that he is suffering from a form of moral illiteracy. He believes that
since men are driven by their passions none can be held responsible
for the moral consequences of their actions – a doctrine which Fielding
associated with the Methodists, and one which James Hogg much later
articulated in his astonishing novel, *The Private Memoirs and Confessions
of a Justified Sinner* (1824). Booth's moral passivity leads him to impute
to Fortune what properly lies at his own front door. As Fielding signals
to the reader: 'Life may as properly be called an Art as any other; and
the great Incidents in it are no more to be considered as mere Acci-
dents, than the several Members of a fine Statue, or a noble Poem' (17).
    Demonstrating this relationship between fatalism and moral self-
responsibility in aesthetic terms, the central episode in the novel is Mrs
Bennet's account of the merits of Christian fortitude (VII, 1–10) which,
like the Man of the Hill and Mr Wilson's stories, serves as a negative
warning, an emblem for the whole. But the remarkable difference
between *Amelia* and all the other novels is that the actual and titular
hero is a woman. Amelia is never subject to the kind of undercutting
irony from which Sophia Western suffers in *Tom Jones*: she is neither
sensualized nor distanced by mock-heroics. She is depicted as an
exemplar of marital devotion and fortitude, a Job in petticoats, a
personification in the female sex of Fielding's moral philosophy. As
we might expect, *Amelia* also contains a significant symmetry, the
formal sign of Fielding's conviction that the hand of Providence guides
human action. Mrs Bennet's past history is seen by Amelia as a portent
of her own possible fate. In VII, 7, *Amelia* says: 'I look upon you, and
always shall look upon you, as my Preserver from the Brink of a
Precipice; from which I was falling into the same Ruin, which you
have so generously, so kindly, and so nobly disclosed for my Sake.'

Amelia's strenuous defence of her marriage contrasts with the adultery of Booth with Miss Matthews, an echo of Sophia's pre-marital chastity and Tom's profligacy; the comic grotesqueries of some marriages in the earlier novels give way here to the sombre errors of Mrs James, Molly Bennet, and that of the Trents. In short, the symmetries and thematic preoccupations of the earlier novels remind us of what Fielding had done in *Tom Jones*, but shift the comic tone from reconciliation to stark and minatory warning. In a shrewd discussion, Claude Rawson has spoken of *Amelia*'s 'irresistible factualities which cannot be mastered by displays of authorial understanding', and of its uneasy combination of a stylish and urbane gentlemanliness now accompanied by a 'strange desperate tang' which implies that 'gentlemanliness (and its best properties of confidence and civilized righteousness) are no longer any help'. Certainly, the later writings as a whole (including the *Voyage to Lisbon*, the *Late Increase of Robbers*, the *Effectual Provision for the Poor*, as well as *Amelia*) all reveal a painful struggle in Fielding's writing between his faith in benevolence and 'an increasing, at times obsessional, sense of the depravity of man'.[24] *Amelia*'s happy ending is no more contrived than the similar endings of *Joseph Andrews* and *Tom Jones*, but in Fielding's last novel the structural needs are no longer supported by a conviction that fictional artifice mirrors achievable public realities. *Amelia* is a domestic epic and a mirror for magistrates, but it also leaves us with Fielding's unresolved conviction that the institutionalized corruption of society is endemic and ineradicable, so much so that innocence and benevolence on an individual level can only survive within Art. When Fielding dropped the first-person prefatory chapters after Book I of *Amelia* he removed the comforting comic filters of the comic–epic narrator and allowed himself to confront the moral nastiness of his society. Paradoxically, *Amelia* is both Fielding's gloomiest book and one in which his heroic battle against the forces of corruption is most honestly confronted. As an example of Fielding's Art of Fiction, *Amelia* may be a failure, but it is the clearest proof of Fielding's abiding moral seriousness.

Notes

1. *Joseph Andrews and Shamela*, edited by Douglas Brooks (Oxford, 1980), p. 347. The text of this edition is that prepared by Martin C. Battestin for the Clarendon Press edition (Oxford, 1967).

2. Fielding's words recall not only the subtitle of the two-volume *Pamela* of 1741, but also the spurious continuations, e.g. John Kelly's *Pamela's Conduct in High Life* (1741). For a note on this, see *Joseph Andrews*, edited by Martin C. Battestin (Oxford, 1967), pp. xv–xvi.

3. *Memoirs of a Woman of Pleasure*, edited by Peter Sabor (Oxford, 1985), pp. xxv–xxvi. *Memoirs of Fanny Hill* was the title of Cleland's own abridgement (1750). The novel was completed while Cleland was imprisoned for debt in the Fleet prison. Publication of the *Memoirs* led to his arrest on a charge of obscenity. Cleland hinted at the possibility of a third volume, but it never appeared. The novel was legally available in America only since 1975, and in England since 1970.

4. Roland Barthes, *The Pleasure of the Text*, translated by Richard Miller (London, 1975), p. 58: 'so called "erotic" books . . . of recent vintage . . . represent not so much the erotic scene as the expectation of it, the preparation for it, its ascent; that is what makes them "exciting", and when the scene occurs, naturally there is disappointment, deflation. In other words, these are books of Desire, not of Pleasure. Or, more mischievously, they represent Pleasure *as seen by psychoanalysis*. A like meaning says, in both instances, that *the whole thing is very disappointing*.'

5. James Harris to Samuel Richardson, 9 January 1752: see *The Correspondence of Samuel Richardson*, edited by Anna Laetitia Barbauld, 6 vols (London, 1804), I, 162–63. Richardson and Harris exchanged presentation copies of each other's books, and in 1744 Fielding called Harris 'the Man whom I esteem most of any Person in this World'.

6. Margaret Anne Doody, *A Natural Passion: A Study of the Novels of Samuel Richardson* (Oxford, 1974), p. 74. For contemporary reactions, see *Henry Fielding: The Critical Heritage*, edited by Ronald Paulson and Thomas Lockwood (London and New York, 1969).

7. The first and last are by Madeleine de Scudéry (10 vols, 1654–60; 10 vols, 1649–53 respectively); *Cléopâtre* (12 vols, 1647–58) and *Cassandre* (10 vols, 1642–43) are by de la Calprenède; *L'Astrée* (five parts, 1607–27) was by Honoré d'Urfé. For further remarks by Fielding on their improbability, see *Joseph Andrews*, III, i: 'Romances, or the modern Novel and *Atlantis* writers . . . without any Assistance from Nature or History, record Persons who never were, or will be, and Facts which never did nor possibly can happen.' For a recent discussion of Fielding's 'reading' of *Don Quixote*, see Stephen Gilman, 'On Henry Fielding's Reception of *Don Quijote*', in *Medieval and Renaissance Studies in Honour of Brian Tate*, edited by Ian Michael and R. A. Cardwell (Oxford, 1986), 2738.

8. Irène Simon, 'Early Theories of Prose Fiction', in *Imagined Worlds: Essays on some English Novels and Novelists in Honour of John Butt*, edited by Maynard Mack and Ian Gregor (London, 1968), p. 24.

9. Compare Aaron Hill's letter to Richardson (29 December 1740): 'Like the snow, that last week, upon the earth and all her products [Pamela] covers every other visage with her unbounded whiteness.' Cited in *Tom Jones*, edited by Martin Battestin, 2 vols (Oxford, 1967), I, xv.

10. See F. Homes Dudden, *Henry Fielding: His Life, Works, and Times*, 2 vols (Oxford, 1952), I, 344–50, for a detailed discussion of the novel's time-scheme and a summary of events. For an analysis of its formal patterns, see

Brooks, *Number and Pattern in the Eighteenth-Century Novel*, pp. 65–91. Brooks analyses the novel's 'chiastic ABBA form' (p. 85) and suggests that it is, 'structurally speaking, a virtuoso *jeu d'esprit*' (p. 67).

11. Dudden, I, 344, points out that 'Joseph Andrews', 'Abraham Adams', and several names in *Tom Jones*, are to be found in one of Fielding's favourite books, i.e. Gilbert Burnet's *History of my Own Time* (1724–34). This does not, of course, minimize their emblematic function in the novels, but rather nicely illustrates Fielding's theory of characterization as a representative mode of individualism.

12. Martin Battestin, *The Moral Basis of Fielding's Art: A Study of Joseph Andrews* (Middletown, Connecticut, 1959).

13. Martin Battestin, *The Providence of Wit: Aspects of Form in Augustan Literature and the Arts* (Oxford, 1974), p. 151. Chapter 5, 'The Argument of Design', and 6, 'The Definition of Wisdom', discuss Fielding's artistic theology, i.e. the theme of Providence and the doctrine of Prudence.

14. Dudden, I, 352. But compare Arnold Kettle's remark in *An Introduction to the English Novel*, 2 vols (London, 1951), I, 83, about 'the carefully contrived but entirely non-symbolic plot' of *Tom Jones*.

15. Bernard Harrison, *Henry Fielding's Tom Jones: The Novelist as Moral Philosopher* (London, 1975), p. 56.

16. *The History of Tom Jones: A Foundling*, edited by Martin Battestin and Fredson Bowers, 2 vols (Oxford, 1974), I, 443. All subsequent quotations are from this edition and are given in the text.

17. My discussion draws upon the following: F. W. Hilles, 'Art and Artifice in *Tom Jones*', in *Imagined Worlds*, pp. 91–110; Brooks, pp. 92–111. In the latter, Brooks points out (p. 101), 'two main structural themes operating in *Tom Jones* – a large scale chiasmus, in which each of the books in the first half of the novel is answered in reverse order by the books of the second half (ABCDDCBA), and also a bipartite scheme, in which the second half is a direct echo of the first (ABCD: ABCD)'.

18. See Martin Battestin's note in his edition of *Tom Jones*, I, 212, for a comment on Fielding's 'old and familiar aesthetic principle'.

19. See R. S. Crane's seminal article, 'The Plot of *Tom Jones*' (1950), reprinted in *Essays on the Eighteenth-Century Novel*, edited by R. D. Spector (Bloomington and London, 1965). Crane writes (p. 121): 'We look forward to the probable consequences of [Tom's] indiscretions . . . with a certain anticipatory reluctance and apprehension – a kind of faint alarm which is the comic analogue of fear.'

20. In pointing to the 'darker and more monitory' tone of *Amelia*, Martin Battestin calls the novel 'the first novel of social protest and reform in English – a kind of book scarcely attempted again on such a scale before Dickens': see *Amelia*, edited by Martin C. Battestin (Oxford, 1983), p. xv. All subsequent quotations are from this edition. In his Introduction, Battestin discusses in detail the autobiographical dimension of *Amelia* as the 'disguised and sentimentalized' image of Fielding's own life with his first wife, Charlotte.

21. The phrase is used by Fanny Hill (II, 93), and by Win Jenkins about the Bramble family towards the end of Smollett's *Humphry Clinker* (1771).

22. Compare this with the gipsy episode in *Tom Jones*, xii, 12, another parable of power, directed at exposing the Jacobite ideal of civil happiness under an absolute monarch.

23. For Fielding's definition of 'good nature', see *An Essay on the Knowledge and Characters of Men* (1743), in *Miscellanies by Henry Fielding, Esq: Volume One*, edited by Henry Knight Miller (Oxford, 1972), pp. 153–78.

24. C. J. Rawson, *Henry Fielding and the Augustan Ideal Under Stress* (London, 1972), pp. 86, 96. For a discussion of *Amelia* as an artistic failure, see Andrew Wright, *Henry Fielding: Mask and Feast* (London, 1968), pp. 105–21.

Chapter 5

Satire and Romance: Tobias Smollett

Smollett's translation of Cervantes's *Don Quixote* appeared in 1755, a sign of that great Spanish novel's pervasive influence on this least admired and least read of the major eighteenth-century novelists.[1] Although, in general terms, the English novel had developed in opposition to romance, Smollett's five novels indicate a particular relationship with romance which testifies to his careful understanding of that work. *Don Quixote* began as a parody of romance: it is initially a book about literature before it becomes a book about life, and literature remains part of the book's texture. It is also a hybrid: a parody, a pastoral, a romance, a picaresque novel.[2] In Smollett's novels, most notably in *Humphry Clinker* (1771), that hybrid quality, or generic instability, is sustained. *The Adventures of Launcelot Greaves* (1760–61), his penultimate novel, is an English *Don Quixote*, written consciously against the fashion of the time and thus another reminder that general statements about the novel's neat developmental typology in this period are extremely precarious. In the second chapter of *Launcelot Greaves*, Ferret says to its titular hero:

> What! . . . you set up for a modern Don Quixote? The scheme is rather too stale and extravagant. What was a humorous romance and well-timed satire in Spain, near two hundred years ago, will make but a sorry jest, and appear equally insipid and absurd, when really acted from affectation, at this time a-day, in a country like England.[3]

In reply, Smollett's Yorkshire knight acknowledges the lunacy of Don Quixote for what it was, but nevertheless clearly separates the knight of La Mancha's delusions from the urgent contemporary need to continue the war upon 'the foes of virtue and decorum . . . the natural enemies of mankind'. Greaves is a friend of the downtrodden and an antagonist of the bourgeois tyrants who wield arbitrary power over the poor and defenceless. Perhaps because this novel was written for serial publication in *The British Magazine* (January 1760 to December

1761) it is, next to *Humphry Clinker*, Smollett's least disorganized and certainly his most amusing novel, full of mock-epic battles, parodies (Captain Crowe is the equivalent to Sancho Panza), apparently coincidental meetings, sudden imprisonments, equally Providential escapes, and epic commonplaces (Greaves's London experiences are, as if in the underworld of classical epic, located in 'the Mansions of the Damned'). But unlike *Don Quixote*, where Quixote's beloved Dulcinea remains a fiction of the mind and never in fact appears in the novel, *Launcelot Greaves* ends with comic reconciliations and marriage. Don Quixote dies a figure of pathos, but sane; Greaves has never been mad, marries his Dulcinea, Aurelia Darnel, and lives happily ever after.

Throughout the novel Smollett sustains both romance, parody of romance, and a barbed moral and social satire. Greaves is no more irrational than the world around him, but the important difference is that he is a good deal more humane. Insanity in any case is not a literary joke for Smollett. Sir Launcelot is kidnapped while searching for Aurelia/Dulcinea and immured in a madhouse. He is only too well aware that here 'every violent transport would be interpreted into an undeniable symptom of insanity'. This madhouse is in England, a place where doctors are permitted to talk nonsense by the hour and are deemed oracles; where, *unlike* the Bastille in France and the Inquisition in Portugal, 'the most innocent person upon earth is liable to be immured for life under the pretext of lunacy . . . without question or control'. Smollett's madhouse is the central image for a network of social tyranny which spreads its tentacles over every area of individual freedom. Its servants are corrupt and untrained magistrates, tyrannical squires, venal guardians, brutal parents, exhibiting the uniform (but not the human face) of the army, the navy, the schoolmaster, the university tutor, the fashionable beau monde, and – in some specific ways, given Smollett's Scottish origin – the very institutional structure of English society itself. In the last chapter of *Launcelot Greaves*, the nasty Ferret remarks to the hero:

> I perceive . . . you are preparing to expostulate, and
> upbraid me for having given a false information against
> you to the country justice. I look upon mankind to be in a
> state of nature, a truth which Hobbes has stumbled upon
> by accident. I think every man has a right to avail himself
> of his talents, even at the expense of his fellow-creatures;
> just as we see the fish, and other animals of the creation,
> devouring one another . . . let those answer for my
> conduct, whose cruelty and insolence have driven me to
> the necessity of using such subterfuges – I have been
> oppressed and persecuted by the Government for speaking

> truth – your omnipotent laws have reconciled
> contradictions. That which is acknowledged to be truth in
> fact is construed falshood in law; and great reason we have
> to boast of a constitution founded on the basis of
> absurdity . . . I know how far to depend upon generosity,
> and what is called benevolence; words to amuse the weak-
> minded – I build upon a surer bottom – I will bargain for
> your assistance. (204)

Ferret's view of a Hobbesian world determined by predation and institutionalized hypocrisy is savage enough. But Smollett himself, in a letter to David Garrick, added another characteristic which takes Ferret's view out of all moral frameworks:

> I am old enough to have seen and observed that we are all
> playthings of fortune, and that it depends upon something
> as insignificant and precarious as the tossing up of a
> halfpenny whether a man rises to affluence and honours,
> or continues to his dying day struggling with the
> difficulties and disgraces of life.[4]

Smollett's statement about life is imprinted on his first three novels. With the exception of *Humphry Clinker* (an exceptional novel) and the morally vile Ferdinand Count Fathom in the novel that bears his name, each of Smollett's male protagonists finally gets the upper hand in a society driven by indifference, tyranny, sadistic cruelty, and moral perversion. They triumph not because of any moral superiority, but partly through chance, partly through a cast-iron insensibility to moral horror, and partly because each of them is, at any cost, a survivor. In formal and aesthetic terms, Smollett excavates conclusions to each of his novels from romance. The 'happy ending' becomes a monotonous and predictable formula, literary escapism from the bleak and morally bankrupt world which Smollett reveals, and not, I think, presented to us as an *acknowledged* literary artifice. His characters take their colours and their moral characters from their social context and, having won through to wealth and happiness, they retire both from the novel and the world into a literary convention, part-romantic and part-pastoral.

   Smollett's first novel, *The Adventures of Roderick Random* (1748), was published in the same year as Richardson's *Clarissa*, a fact which in itself testified to the extraordinary contrasts within the novel genre at the time. It was published one year before Fielding's *Tom Jones* (1749), a novel which Smollett enjoyed attacking and from a novelist whose doctrine of benevolent optimism he mocked.[5] His last novel, *The Expedition of Humphry Clinker* (1771) appeared three years after Sterne's last novel, *A Sentimental Journey*, the year of Smollett's death and of

Sir Walter Scott's birth. In the intervening period he wrote *The Adventures of Peregrine Pickle* (1751), *The Adventures of Ferdinand Count Fathom* (1753), and *The Adventures of Launcelot Greaves* (1760–61). He also published translations of Le Sage's *Gil Blas* (1748), Fénelon's *The Adventures of Telemachus* (1776), and Voltaire's *Works* (1761–65). In 1756 he edited *A Compendium of Authentic and Entertaining Voyages* (seven volumes), launched the *Critical Review* in the same year, and in 1766 published *Travels through France and Italy*, an autobiographical and epistolary account of his own travels through some of the countries in which his novels are set. Smollett wrote quickly, and his range of interests was unlimited.

All of Smollett's heroes are male, and all of their female lovers are (with the exception of Clinker's Win Jenkins) versions of Dulcinea, kept aloof from the circumambient corruption, and preserved for a morally uplifting marriage. Roderick Random, Peregrine Pickle, Ferdinand Count Fathom, Launcelot Greaves, and Humphry Clinker are all displaced persons. They are usually rejected from their rightful place in society by parental tyranny or the inhumanity of guardians. They are all moral orphans thrown out into a hostile world. They are all attractive to women (and sometimes to men also), born with an abundance of native wit, and are all quick learners. With the notable exceptions of Launcelot Greaves and Humphry Clinker, they are all predators in a world of dog eat dog. A reductive animal imagery is common in all of his novels, but the metaphor of the sea is ubiquitous. The sea is an image of chance, fortune, unpredictability, threat. But the sea is also subject to regular pattern – it has a sequence of high and low tides irrespective of occasional squalls and inundations, and in every one of his novels except *Ferdinand Count Fathom* Smollett permits the ebb of poverty and misfortune to be followed by a spring tide of social success, marital union, and material justice. One of the questions for the reader is whether Smollett's 'happy endings' are dictated by the demands of an extrinsic literary form (the inherited pattern of anti-romance plus romance), or signs of a recuperative view of individual and social morality, or more simply aspects of private human experience of no relevance at all to Smollett's predominantly satiric purposes.

The Adventures of Roderick Random

Smollett wrote a Preface to *Roderick Random* in which he traced the 'fable in prose' from romance, via Xenophon's *Cyropaedia* to

Cervantes's anti-romance, to Le Sage's *Gil Blas*. This Preface regards the story as merely the vehicle of the satire. It says nothing about the novel form as such. For this we must go to *Ferdinand Count Fathom*, where we find a somewhat evasive analogy drawn with painting, and a concept of structure which gives prominence to a single character to whom everything else is subordinated:

> A Novel is a large diffused picture, comprehending the characters of life, disposed in different groups, and exhibited in various attitudes, for the purposes of an uniform plan, and general occurrence, to which every individual is subservient. But this plan cannot be executed with propriety, probability or success, without a principal personage to attract the attention, unite the incidents, unwind the clue of the labyrinth, and at last close the scene by virtue of his own importance.[6]

Unfortunately, the novel in which this comment appears contradicts Smollett's claim in virtually every respect. *Roderick Random* is a better example, and its first chapter contains the most arresting single image of Smollett's intentions. The pre-natal dream of Roderick's mother is that 'she was delivered of a tennis-ball, which the devil (who, to her great surprise, acted the part of midwife) struck so forcibly with a racket that it disappeared in an instant'. The premonition is a pre-figuring not only of Roderick's subsequent career, but of all Smollet's subsequent novels.

Abandoned by his family, Roderick is nevertheless intensely proud; he becomes a surgeon, sets out for London ('the devil's drawing room'), and meets Miss Williams. Her story – a *récit* – is the first of several interruptions in the chronological biography of Roderick, providing the first major example of innocence corrupted by naivety and ignorance of the world's ways, similar in some respects to the plot of *Moll Flanders*. Roderick, like all of Smollett's heroes, is instinctively drawn to characters who share his own status of social victim in a world increasingly depicted as brutally conscience-less. Roderick is press-ganged, put aboard a man-of-war, and witnesses the obscene violence of war. As a literary descendant of Spanish and French picaresque, Roderick appropriately describes these and other incidents with a detached and almost operatic insouciance: 'The head of the officer of Marines, who stood near me, being shot off, bounced from the deck athwart my face, leaving me well-nigh blinded with brains.'[7] Back in England, he becomes Narcissa's footman, falls in love with her, is entranced by her beauty and by her musical skill, and writes poems to her. But Narcissa also is a victim of (Sir Timothy's) tyranny and she is taken away to France. Roderick reunites by chance with his uncle, Tom Bowling, who has been and will continue to be a recurrent benevolent presence in the novel. He enlists in the French army, fighting against the English, and is most astonished at the grotesque illusion of military patriotism, 'the absurdity of a rational being, who thinks himself highly honoured in being permitted to encounter abject poverty, oppression, famine, disease, mutilation, and evident death, merely to gratify the vicious ambition of a prince, by whom his sufferings were disregarded, and his name utterly unknown' (245).

Roderick learns to take nothing and nobody on trust, meets competition with hatred, constraint with violence, idealism with scorn. After many 'adventures', which convince him that being Providence's stepson is synonymous with being a victim of chance, he is imprisoned for debt. He listens to Mr Melopoyn's Grub Street autobiography (a thinly veiled image of Smollett's own career,[8] Ch. 62 and 63), and is eventually rescued by Tom Bowling. As much as any physical distress, such violent reversals of fortune are a severe test of Roderick's fortitude. They also strain the reader's credence. The novel concludes with reunion with his 'lost' father, the wealthy Don Rodrigo, marriage to Narcissa, and a return to the feudal society of Scotland. Symmetrically, an initial and appalling emotional and social deprivation is finally counterbalanced and apparently erased by an equally extravagant access of social bliss: 'As there is no part of the world in which the peasants are more attached to their lords than in Scotland, we were almost devoured by their affection' (Ch. 69).[9]

The Adventures of Peregrine Pickle

Roderick Random is, for much of his life, a victim of chance. In Smollett's second novel, The Adventures of Peregrine Pickle (1751), society is the victim. Pickle is a precociously cunning infant, a drinker, a dissimulator, a moral blackmailer of the adults around him, quick-witted, a deflator of pretensions, a consummate practical joker, a tyrant over his peer groups. Roderick was severed from his parents by his grandfather's anger at his illegitimate birth; Peregrine Pickle is disowned by his mother and adopted by Commodore Trunnion. He forms an anarchic, terrorist triumvirate with Hatchway and Pipes. School cannot hold him; at Winchester he becomes 'master of the revels' and leads an insurrection there. He elopes from school in order to enjoy Emilia Gauntlet. Oxford University cannot control him, neither can magistrates. He responds only to those whose will is stronger than his, either with defiance (as to Emilia's brother, Godfrey), or with contempt (as to any husband who gets in the way of his sexual ambitions for married women). England cannot contain him, nor France, where he matures into the 'professed enemy to all oppression' (212). Before returning to England, 'sufficiently qualified for eclipsing most of his contemporaries', Pickle is imprisoned in the Bastille, where he plays one of his characteristically sadistic practical jokes. Knowing of the imminent release from imprisonment of both himself and his companion Pallet, he nevertheless informs his testy companion that although free himself, Pallet has been condemned to life imprisonment. He seduces one woman after another (including a reluctant nun in Ch. 63), scours the Low Countries, London, and Bath, and lays siege to Emilia (who discerns his immaturity clearly enough).

The novel becomes a mere list of variations on a theme, except that in Chapter 88 Smollett interpolates a 50,000-word episode of no clear relevance to the novel at all, i.e. 'The Memoirs of a Lady of Quality'.[10] Pickle's skills as a mimic are extended to a 'Pygmalion' device whereby he passes off (successfully, for a time) a 'hedge inamorata' as a fine lady, his own social version of the Trojan horse designed to sabotage the credulity of fashionable society's reliance on surfaces. At this point, Pickle loses virtually all of his money, becomes dependent on the patronage of a government minister, is lectured by a misanthrope (Crabtree), becomes an author, and is imprisoned for debt. During this forced immobility he listens to the story of M——, 'one of the most flagrant instances of neglected virtue which the world can produce' (735) and conceives 'a rancorous resentment against mankind in general' (748). He is brought back from the depths of depression by Emilia's unforced acknowledgement of love for him, by a lecture on the sin of pride ('no better than self-murder', 755), the return of some of his fortune, and inheritance of his father's estate. The novel ends with marriage to Emilia and acclamations from the parishioners, though not from the beau monde.

As in *Roderick Random*, so in *Peregrine Pickle*: there is a final structural necessity for a romance ending, but one which collides everywhere with a view of the universal nastiness of human life bordering on the pathological. An idealized mistress is reserved for a conventional ending, an improbable discontinuity after a series of grotesque acts of betrayal, cruelty, malicious violence, and (it should be added) black comedy. Yet if Peregrine Pickle is bad, Ferdinand Count Fathom makes him look like an apprentice in the trade of moral anarchy. All three heroes acquire the skills of hypocrisy and dissimulation in order to ensure their own survival.

The Adventures of Ferdinand Count Fathom

Fathom's view of human society is that of Ferret in *Sir Launcelot Greaves*. Life is like a human zoo, without the restraint of cages:

> He had formerly imagined, but was now fully persuaded, that the sons of men preyed upon one another, and such was the end and condition of their being. Among the principal figures of life, he observed few or no characters that did not bear a strong analogy to the savage tyrants of the wood. One resembled a tyger in fury and rapaciousness; a second prowled about like an hungry wolf, seeking what he might devour; a third acted the part of a jackall, in beating the bush for game to his voracious employer; and a fourth imitated the wily fox, in practising a thousand crafty ambuscades for the destruction of the ignorant and the unwary. This last was the department of life for which he found himself best qualified by nature and inclination. (56)

Fathom has the moral fibre of an alley cat. More subversive than Iago, more dangerous than Edmund in *King Lear*, he is a social chameleon in the 'vast masquerade' of London life, now a forger of Cremona violins, now a veritable bloodhound when on the scent of others' family secrets. He debauches Celinda and then makes her a drug addict (Ch. 34), betrays Renaldo, his 'guardian, his saviour, his second father' (281), and apparently drives the beautiful orphan mistress Monimia to her grave. Ferdinand is also the instrument of Smollett's sardonic satire of the English. In Chapter 49 Monimia attends a church, 'according to the laudable hospitality of England, which is the only country in Christendom, where a stranger is not made welcome to the house of God' (238). The English are described as xenophobic and racially prejudiced; they judge by appearances, and are therefore easy prey to imposture (Ch. 31); they create the conditions whereby plausible rogues may prosper, and have foolishly been taken in by fashionable philosophers who claim that man has an innate predisposition towards virtue and that benevolence is a central human characteristic. Thus when Ferdinand, now acting the part of a doctor in order to invade the family secrets of others, accidentally cures a merchant's wife (Ch. 53) he becomes famous. Unlike real doctors, who only prosper after malpractice and bad publicity, Ferdinand is given credit for skills which he does not possess by a credulous public. Smollett points out their moral delusion, probably with reference to Shaftesbury and Fielding:

> Success raised upon such a foundation, would, by a
> disciple of Plato, and some modern moralists, be ascribed
> to the innate virtue and generosity of the human heart,
> which naturally espouses the cause that needs protection:
> but I, whose notions of human excellence are not quite so
> sublime, am apt to believe it is owing to that spirit of self-
> conceit and contradiction, which is, at least, as universal, if
> not as natural, as the moral sense so warmly contended for
> by those ideal philosophers. (263)

Ferdinand's career continues its downward moral spiral. He seduces a clergyman's wife, takes a prostitute as his 'wife', is prosecuted for debt after his medical practice fails, and is driven away from pagan fortitude towards Christian resignation in prison. Count Renaldo Melvile's search for Monimia dominates the novel from this point. Having visited Monimia's tomb, he discovers Ferdinand's real character ('a venomous serpent, which it was incumbent on every foot to crush', Ch. 63: 321). Nine years before the appearance of Walpole's *The Castle of Otranto* (1764), Smollett anticipates the Gothic novel, and signals a sentimental conclusion, in this description of Renaldo's visit to Monimia's tomb:

> the soul of Melvile was wound up to the highest pitch of
> enthusiastic sorrow. The uncommon darkness of the night,
> the solemn silence, and lonely situation of the place,
> conspired with the occasion of his coming, and the dismal
> images of his fancy, to produce a real rapture of gloomy
> expectation, which the whole world would not have
> persuaded him to disappoint. The clock struck twelve, the
> owl screeched from the ruined battlement, the door was
> opened by the sexton, who, by the light of a glimmering
> taper, conducted the despairing lover to a dreary isle, and
> stamped upon the ground with his foot, saying, 'Here the
> young lady lies interred'.
>
> (Ch. 62: 317)

In believing Monimia to be dead, Renaldo, Ferdinand, and the reader, have 'mis-read' the world which Smollett has created. She is the heroine of black social satire, remarkable for her exceptional innocence, but she also *belongs* to the literary world of Providential romance. She is in fact alive. Moral corruption is not allowed to determine everything in this novel, for her 'death' was a stratagem designed by Mrs Clement to outwit Ferdinand. Not only this, she is also Serafina, the long-lost daughter of Don Diego, Renaldo's father-in-grief. Ferdinand, unlike every other Smollett hero at this point, is 'insensible, convulsed, and seemingly in the grip of death . . . wore to the bone either by famine or despair . . . the extremity of indigence, squalor and distress, could not be more feelingly represented' (353).

There is no idealized mistress for Ferdinand, only Elinor, whom he had once debauched. There is no sudden inheritance of wealth or land for Ferdinand, hence no social triumph over adversity. He has been and remains a victim of chance. Smollett's literary imagination returns to Count Fathom in his last novel, as we shall see, but for the romantic pair, Renaldo and Monimia, another pattern has worked its way. The reader is asked to see a Providential pattern in their happiness, a pattern which displaces Ferdinand in the last part of the novel. Smollett's self-consciously artful chapter titles, a device possibly copied from Fielding's *Tom Jones*, provide an increasingly obvious pattern within which the reader's response is predetermined and manipulated *above* the consciousness of any individual character.[11]

As a picture of unregenerate evil, *Ferdinand Count Fathom* is Smollett's masterpiece in satirical black comedy. Moreover, for a Smollett novel it is unusually clear in its outline. Its relative simplicity encourages the belief that there is an organic connection between its shape and its content. But Smollett achieves a morally and aesthetically satisfying ending for all participants only by splitting the satire from the romance. Ferdinand (exemplary viciousness), Renaldo (an equally exemplary but opposite 'model of a fine gentleman'), and Monimia ('the paragon of beauty', 454) represent respectively the contrivance of Chance and two examples of the contrivance of Providence. For one commentator, the implications of this coincidence of plot and design are clear:

> *Fathom* possesses an elaborate symmetrical structure, which
> clearly [sic] fulfils a symbolic function by exalting the
> forces of good (Renaldo, Monimia, Farrel, etc.) over
> Fathom, the embodiment of evil . . . Fathom's story, as
> Smollett indicates, is that of a child of Fortune; but
> Monimia's and Renaldo's is just as explicitly Providential.
> The asymmetry of the one is overridden by the precise
> balance of the other to create, for the first time in
> Smollett's fiction, a compelling Providential paradigm.[12]

I think this overstates the case for *Count Fathom* possessing significant form. But equally, other critics have underestimated Smollett's shaping skills. Donald Bruce has remarked that 'the Picaresque novel was more an escape from the severities of form than an imposition of them. . . . So far as Smollett was concerned, the Picaresque novel was no more than a form which took in a wide range of characters from eighteenth-century society and proceeded by the rapid accumulation of moving or entertaining incidents'.[13] The formulaic quality of Smollett's novel is not difficult to discern, and yet a progression within the *minimal* form of the picaresque genre should not be dismissed as an accident. Fathom is Smollett's only real loser, but in case we think his misery is deserved, Smollett indicates the reason for his failure: 'Had he been admitted as a pupil to any political academy, he would have certainly become one of the ablest statesmen in Europe.' In other words, Smollett's satire and the novel's plot depend on the assumption that the world is run by delinquents in high authority, and that the individual who falters in that view, if only for a moment, will suddenly find the world closing in on him. There is a satirical consistency in this, if not a resolution of the vast stresses between the novel's split between the impossibly vile and the impossibly good. Ferdinand Count Fathom is not only a failure, and therefore in Smollett's terms disqualified as a hero; he is also a fool, whereas Roderick Random and Peregrine Pickle qualify as heroes because their victimization by society is turned into their exploitation of society. It is a crude moral equation, but it is generated from the same bleak premiss as that of an incomparably greater satirist, Jonathan Swift: 'Happiness . . . is a perpetual Possession of being well Deceived . . . The Serene Peaceful State of being a Fool among Knaves.'[14] In neither writer can we be absolutely sure that such an irony has a comforting and merely literary function. Both Swift and Smollett demur at preaching a message which the world is too foolish to see for itself, and both prefer to turn conventional pieties upside down, in order to show that human society accommodates and nurtures the knave far more successfully than it rewards the honest citizen.

Smollett's choice of rogue biography as his fictional form demonstrates his satirical purpose perhaps too clearly: the man of wealth and property at the end of *Roderick Random* and *Peregrine Pickle* has beaten society at its own game, and only a weak-minded fool believes that God is on the side of the just. This is more than a satirical strategy designed to shock the reader's complacency. It is more than a reflection of the violence and squalor of eighteenth-century life, filtered out by much of the age's literature. And it is something *less* than we have come to expect from the art of the novelist. Smollett's authorial presence and his clinical realism force the satire beyond any 'literary' tradition into a theatre of cruelty, energized by an Epicurean delight in fantasies of separation and pain. It is not a paranoic's view of the world. The world really does seem to hate the outsider, leaving him only the response of frustrated rage and the instinct to revenge his displacement. But if the boot were on the other foot, and the social victim could become the judge and legislator, the urge to pull down would not necessarily be channelled into moral reform:

> Had the executive power of the legislature been vested
> in him, he would have doubtless devised many strange
> species of punishment for all offenders against humanity
> and decorum; but, restricted as he was, he employed his
> invention in subjecting them to the ridicule and contempt
> of their fellow-subjects. (576)

Smollett's pen followed his foot; his imagination traversed widely but always on the surface, mapping the human topography but never stopping long enough to discriminate and hence to dignify the human individual. It is therefore difficult to know whether Smollett chose the picaresque form or the form determined Smollett's moral and artistic imagination. His strength and weakness as a novelist are two sides of the same coin. As Robert Alter notes, it is a part of the picaresque tradition that 'experience should never substantially alter the given character of the hero'.[15] Roderick Random points this out:

> I had endured hardships, 'tis true; my whole life had
> been a series of such; and when I looked forward, the
> prospect was not much bettered – but then, they were
> become habitual to me, and consequently, I could bear
> them with less difficulty – If one scheme of life should not
> succeed, I could have recourse to another, and so to a
> third, veering about to a thousand different shifts,
> according to the emergencies of my fate, without
> forfeiting the dignity of my character, beyond a power of
> retrieving it, or subjecting myself wholly to the caprice
> and barbarity of the world. (136–37)

The problem here is that with 'character' thus hermetically sealed against the hostile world the possibility of internal psychological change in relation to outside circumstance is minimal. If Roderick were to allow the world to penetrate his personality, he would be no more than an existential tennis ball. Thus, when Roderick Random and Peregrine Pickle fall in love (a state of mind *and* body) Smollett is caught. How can he convey the probability of such an experience? He may appear to do so, but it is significant that for both heroes the symptoms of love seem to be entirely physical in their manifestations. 'Physiology', to cite Alter once more, 'is Smollett's only correlative for inner experience.'[16] On the one hand we have the most extensive gallery of literary grotesques known to the novel – Commodore Trunnion, Hatchway, Pipes, the 'female virtuoso' (Narcissa's aunt), Crabtree the misanthrope, and many more – all permanently and rigidly fixed in the satirist's two-dimensional, simplifying and distorting manner, and on the other we have Romance as the device used to introduce and to account for a change of psychological state in characters whose very resistance to psychological pressure has guaranteed their survival.

The speed with which event follows event militates against involvement and does not always provide a comic detachment. Ferdinand's mother, an 'Amazonian' warrior in her own right during the war between the Turkish Empire and Austro-Hungary (1716–18) here attacks an already wounded Turk:

> perceiving the virago approach with fell intent, he brandished his scymitar, and tried to intimidate his assailant with a most horrible exclamation; but, it was not the dismal yell of a dismounted cavalier, though enforced with a hideous ferocity of countenance, and the menacing gestures with which he waited her approach, that could intimidate such an undaunted she-campaigner; she saw him writhing in the agonies of a situation from which he could not move; and, running towards him with the nimbleness and intrepidity of a Camilla, described a semicircle in the progress of her assault, and attacking him on one side, plunged her well-tried dagger in his throat: the shades of death encompassed him, his life-blood issued at the wound, he fell prone upon the earth, he bit the dust, and having thrice invoked the name of Allah! straight expired.
> (IV, 15)

Fielding's controlled mock-heroic description of a village mob attacking the pregnant Molly Seagrim (*Tom Jones*, IV, 8) maximizes the comedy in an equally improbably comic episode.[17] His mock-Homeric literary artifice distances both the event and the reader from the event. But the precise function of Smollett's exercise in mock-heroic is obscure. The analogies (virago, she-campaigner, Camilla) dissipate rather than concentrate the comic effect, and the solitary specificity of the phrase 'plunged her well-tried dagger in his throat' simply underlines by contrast the flaccid prose which surrounds it. Similarly, in his portraits, Smollett composes by accumulating extraordinary and discrete details, a device common in each of his novels, but particularly clearly shown in Matthew Bramble's description of coffee-house patrons in Bath:

We consisted of thirteen individuals; seven lamed by the
gout, rheumatism, or palsy; three maimed by accident,
and the rest either deaf or blind. One hobbled, another
hopped, a third dragged his legs after him like a wounded
snake [*sic*], a fourth straddled betwixt a pair of long
crutches, like the mummy of a felon hanging in chains; a
fifth was bent into a horizontal position, like a mounted
telescope, shoved in by a couple of chairmen; and a sixth
was the bust of a man, set upright in a wheel machine,
which the waiter moved from place to place.[18]

This is incremental and categorical comedy. One detail is allocated to
each object, and the overall effect is surrealistic, a heterogeneous
mixture of shapes, movement, and properties momentarily fixed in a
bizarre dislocation. At this point in the novel Matthew responds to the
world of Bath with bewilderment, with 'equal surprize and
compassion', and like his creator his eyes pick out details metamorphosed into grotesque travesties of the normal. In Matthew's case he
sees the world as a reflection of his own valetudinarian temperament:
he is hypersensitive to certain objects and his view of the world is
eloquently determined by the language of a sick man. *Humphry Clinker*
is remarkable among Smollett's novels for this coincidence of language
and perception.

Language brings things into existence, but Smollett signals an
emotional crisis only by a physical tremor and the language of
romantic cliché. The 'inner' experience of Roderick in love is encoded
in language twice removed from the authenticity of an individual
experience. Fielding also retreats from intimate psychological analysis
of such moments. Tom Jones speaks to and about Sophia in similar
language, but we neither suspect Tom's sincerity nor the narrator's
competence. Fielding has gained the reader's trust and confidence long
before. But when Smollett needs to write about the inner feelings of
his characters we immediately notice the absence of any narrative
bridge between character and self and between author and reader.
Fielding's characters are presumed to have their own private lives as
much as the reader has his, and to investigate either would, we are
informed, be a breach of decorum. Sterne elevates this principle of
decorum into a co-operative theory of understanding and a joint enter-
prise in the search for meaning:

Writing, when properly managed, (as you may be sure
I think mine is) is but a different name for conversation:
As no one, who knows what he is about in good
company, would venture to talk all; – so no author, who
understands the just boundaries of decorum and good

> breeding, would presume to think all: The truest respect
> which you can pay to the reader's understanding, is to
> halve this matter amicably, and leave him something to
> imagine, in his turn, as well as yourself.[19]

Smollett splits the inner world from the outer, dislocating the
psychology of his characters at precisely the moment when their
fortunes bring them back into the world as prosperous and happy men.
To object that Smollett's description of Roderick Random in love is
stilted, artificial, conventional, and unconvincing is pointless, and risks
assuming that everything else in the novel is naturalistic, 'real',
particular, and authentic. Smollett's heroes are *least* accessible to us
when emotionally involved in a love relationship. Our empathic
involvement with them has never been required.

   Each of Smollett's novels awkwardly combines Romance and a
satirist's Realism, the latter being a concentrated but superficial image
of irreducible ugliness and the artistically irresolvable. Quite obviously,
the relationship between the two is signalled in the novels' titles, where
a name taken from romance (Roderick, Peregrine, Ferdinand, Launcelot, Humphry) is yoked to its 'realistic' antonym (Random, Pickle,
Fathom, Greaves, Clinker), suggesting symbolic meanings (chance,
disaster, moral decline, moral despair, and human detritus respectively), as is the case in Sterne's Tristram Shandy.[20] Unlike Fielding,
Smollett's visceral comedy acknowledges no metaphysical framework
or solution for man's moral dilemma, only a literary one. One of the
effects of Smollett's extraordinary narrative energy is to fill the reader's
mind with such a plethora of comic, violent, grotesque, and extremely
detailed incidents that questions about the meaning, or meaningless-
ness, of his created world are simply crowded out. The surgeon cannot
afford to be concerned with his patient's moral character as he wields
the knife on the mortal disease. In Chapter 66 of *Roderick Random* Don
Rodrigo, Roderick's father, draws a curious moral from his son's
buffettings: '[he] blessed God for the adversity I had undergone,
which, he said, enlarged the understanding, improved the heart, steeled
the constitution, and qualified a young man for all the duties and
enjoyments of life, much better than any education which affluence
could bestow' (415).

   This entirely secular explanation gives the lie to the not infrequent
but always perfunctory insertions of a Providential pattern in Smollett's novels and critical claims to an overall metaphysical purpose. God
does not play tennis, and it is the weak-minded Lydia and the meth-
odistical Humphry who prattle on about Providence in Smollett's last
novel.

The Expedition of Humphry Clinker

Why if thou must write, thou had'st better compose
Some *novels*, or elegant letters in prose.
Take a subject that's grave, with a moral that's good,
Throw in all the temptations that virtue withstood
In epistles like PAMELA'S chaste and devout –
A book *my family's never without.* – [21]

The above quotation comes from Christopher Anstey's *New Bath
Guide* (1766), an amusing and popular satire on the manners and fashions
of those who attended the English spa town for reasons of health,
social display, and for the marriage market it offered. It is one of the
influences on Smollett's last novel, *The Expedition of Humphry Clinker*
(1771). If Smollett took the lady's advice, he added and subtracted
from its recipe. Anstey's book is made up of fifteen letters in verse
from members of the Blunderhead family, each differentiated by metre
and point of view, and including the characters Jenny ('a romantic
young lady'), Sir Simkin (her uncle), Tabby Runt (a maid, who is
impregnated by a Moravian rabbi), and Miss Prudence Blunderhead
(who is elected to Methodism through the supernatural agency of a
dream and by the more fleshly influence of Roger). Sir Simkin, like
Smollett's Matthew Bramble, is a sceptical valetudinarian, plagued not
only by 'vapours and wind', but also by the vagaries of women and
weather. It is from such social comedy that Smollett's novel springs,
and although epitomizing many themes of the earlier novels, *Humphry
Clinker* bears a relationship to Smollett's earlier work similar to that
of Shakespeare's last plays to his earlier tragedies. In this novel Smollett
transcends bleak social pessimism by a recuperative comedy; the
disaffection of age gives way to a new youthfulness, and the novel as
a whole achieves a Sterne-like vivaciousness and liberality of mind.
Formally in the epistolary genre, *Humphry Clinker* stands as a brilliant
example of its kind. Thematically, its peregrination is a part of its
meaning, a search for moral and physical health. In the subject of sickly
humanity travelling from one health spa to another Smollett found a
perfect fusion of his interests in romance and realism, sensibility and
satire, subject and form. In repeating characters and themes from the
earlier novels, Smollett transforms the misanthropy of Crabtree into
the tetchy irritability of Matthew Bramble; the earlier Quixotic Launcelot Greaves is reworked into the prickly pride and scruffy dignity
of Lismahago; and even Ferdinand Count Fathom reappears reformed
and repentant. Each character in *Humphry Clinker* finds a home and a

social place, with the possible exception of Jery Melford, who still searches for happiness amid the world's follies. The novel ends with physical and moral health being reasserted.

Smollett includes much more of himself in this final novel. In Bramble his own self-portrait as a sociable and beneficent patron of writers is discernible. There is a series of amusing testaments to several of Smollett's friends, mentors, relatives, and some notable Scots. In place of the earlier and fairly crude anti-English satire, England and Scotland are set inside a town and country opposition, a version of pastoral myth in which Smollett's own private and public self is reflected in the story of a Welsh family joyfully taking Scotland to its bosom as an example of proud self-dependence, of national pride in its intellectual achievement, and at times an overwhelming generosity towards the outsider. In this final novel Smollett achieves a reconciliation with life as lived.

Most of the eighty-three letters in the novel are written by two correspondents: Jery Melford (to his Oxford tutor Sir Watkin Phillips) and his uncle, Matthew Bramble (to his personal physician, Dr Lewis). It is chiefly through the eyes of uncle and nephew that we see the world of the novel. Matthew begins the novel affecting misanthropy, almost lamed by gout, tortured by constipation, and plagued by his niece, nephew, and sister Tabitha. The whole family has set out to fetch Bramble's niece Lydia away from boarding-school where she has begun an affair with the socially inferior actor, Mr Wilson. By contrast, and at the end of the novel, Matthew Bramble is keenly preparing himself for social life, enjoying 'a considerable stock of health', and has decided 'to renounce all sedentary amusements, particularly that of writing long letters' (351). This social and physical renovation takes place in the context of three marriages: Lydia to Mr Wilson – in reality her social equal Mr Dennison; Tabitha Bramble, after a series of failures to find a man, to Lismahago; and Humphry Clinker to Win Jenkins. Matthew has managed to 'unclog the wheels of life' (339), and Win Jenkins speaks of 'this family of love, where every sole [sic] is so kind and courteous' (338).

With the exception of one letter from Mr Wilson to Lydia (15–16), all of the letters are outgoing and none are received. The interaction *between* characters is created by each correspondent writing in radically different ways about common experiences, and evaluating each other's character and behaviour. For example, Matthew's self-absorbed and apparently misanthropic exterior is accurately penetrated by Jery, whom Matthew regards only as 'a pert jackanapes, full of college petulance and self-conceit' (12). Jery remarks (28) that his uncle 'affects misanthropy, in order to conceal the sensibility of a heart which is tender, even to a degree of weakness', and as the novel progresses

Matthew Bramble is discovered in several acts of secret charity towards
the unfortunate. At Bath and London Matthew Bramble projects his
own misery on the external world. Having said to Dr Lewis 'I have
had an hospital these fourteen years within myself, and studied my
own case with the most painful attention' (23), he sees Bath as 'a
natural hospital . . . none but lunatics are admitted' (34), its elegant
architecture only 'a wreck of streets and squares', and its social life as
an offensive mixing of the social classes ('genteel people' and 'a mob
of impudent plebeians', 37). The same scene suggests to Lydia, who
reads life through the spectacles of literary romance, 'sumptuous
palaces', where 'All is gayety, good-humour, and diversion. The eye
is continually entertained with the splendour of dress and equipage
. . . and the new buildings . . . look like so many enchanted castles,
raised on hanging terraces' (39). Matthew's patriarchal and feudal view
of society is absorbed by Jery's delight in social variety:

> Another entertainment, peculiar to Bath, arises from the
> general mixture of all degrees assembled in our public
> rooms, without distinction of rank or fortune. This is
> what my uncle reprobates, as a monstrous jumble of
> heterogeneous principles; a vile mob of noise and
> impertinence, without decency or subordination. But this
> chaos is to me a source of infinite amusement. (49)

A quarter of the way through the novel Matthew's detached and satirical observations begin to close in on him, although at this stage he
is unaware of the way in which his own youthful past will rejuvenate
his late middle age. As in Sterne's *Tristram Shandy*, the novel's titular
hero, Humphry Clinker, emerges bare-bottomed and late (80). His
present 'significance' is signposted as being more than his current
appearance as a ragged postilion would suggest: he has 'a skin as fair
as alabaster'. He is 'a love-begotten babe, brought up in the work-
house', a Methodist who preaches spiritual equality, the natural son
of Matthew Bramble, and a manifestation of Matthew's suppressed
benevolence (as well as a token of his earlier sexual energy).

The Swiftian indignation of Matthew is not only eroded by the
youthful sensibility of Jery but also by Clinker's human claims on the
former as father and protector. The passion for social satire dies in
Matthew as his health and his family expands.[22] Matthew's beneficence
expands to include the grotesquely disfigured and disputatious Lismahago, whose service to his country in war is an indictment of its
miserly peacetime provision. He is introduced as 'A tall meagre figure,
answering with his horse, the description of Don Quixote mounted
on Rozinante' (188). His quest is for his Scottish family home, but he

ends up in Bramble's household married to Tabitha, who had been 'declining into the most desperate state of celibacy' (29). Tabitha's passion for Methodism declines as her 'passion of love' for Lismahago grows, and as Jery remarks, 'Love, it seems, is resolved to assert his dominion over all the females of our family' (208).

Smollett's native country accelerates Matthew's escape from self-imprisonment. He is intellectually stimulated by Edinburgh, 'a hot-bed of genius' (231), and reacts to Loch Lomond in a way more expected from the romantically inclined Lydia: 'Every thing here is romantic beyond imagination. This country is justly styled the Arcadia of Scotland; and I don't doubt but it may vie with Arcadia in every thing but climate' (248).

Rural Scotland is the antithesis of London's squalor. It is an image of pastoral health, just as the city is the image of physical degradation. The former is a healthy artery which feeds the corrupt heart. But Matthew's stark antitheses become increasingly unsustainable as the novel moves towards its conclusion. Just as Matthew has rescued Clinker from poverty, their roles are reversed when Clinker rescues Bramble from drowning: the 'crab of my own planting in the days of hot blood and unrestrained libertinism' (319) becomes the life-support of Matthew's maturer years. By contrast, Lydia's vacuous romanticism is vindicated, since her persistent lover Mr Wilson metamorphoses into the socially acceptable Mr Dennison. And it is Matthew Bramble himself, as the agent of everybody's expedition, who both repairs the misfortunes of his friend Mr Baynard and who renovates his decayed house into a place of beauty and rural retirement.

The restitution of order and harmony in Humphry Clinker through the comic commonplace of multiple marriages is more than a convenience of plot. Although Jery Melford is still looking for a partner at the end of the novel, the clear implication is that he will find one and end his travels happily. His ironic detachment has yet to find its challenge in romantic love. As the novel ends, Bramble's extended family looks forward to celebrating Christmas in their Welsh home. The events of the novel begin on April Fool's Day (although the first letter is dated 2 April), and it will end in a Christian celebration. As Win Jenkins says in the final letter, 'Providinch hath bin pleased to make halteration in the pasture of our affairs' (352).

This sense of a significant form is not present in Smollett's earlier novels, nor is there such inventive and festive comedy. Win Jenkins's language, for example, is much more than the linguistic comedy of a semi-literate. Her misspellings become metaphors. As one word is turned into another new meanings are generated which reveal the writer's particular obsessions: 'God's grace' becomes 'God's grease'; 'syllable' becomes 'syllabub'; 'hysterics' becomes 'asstericks'; 'Lismahago' becomes 'Kismycago'; 'valet de chambre' becomes 'wally de shamble' and 'valley de shambles'; 'affection' becomes 'infection'; 'eyes' become 'ars', and so on.[23]

The epistolary form of *Humphry Clinker* provides that convincing and individual *self-*consciousness which is absent in each of Smollett's previous fictional works, a sense of individuality conveyed through particular viewpoints, inflexions of language, and habits of mind. As in Richardson's novels, the characters in Smollett's last novel exist only in the words they write. But they also exist in the words of others written about them, so that the reader witnesses and aids in the creation of character above and beyond the level of a single letter. We observe the matrix of letters and a complex network of interconnected experiences. Smollett's characters seem more real in his last novel because they are each given the chance to change in relation to the world and to themselves. None is forced into a predetermined plot; each discovers herself or himself, and what they discover has always been there. Moreover, Smollett's previously overwhelming concern for the squalor and ugliness of eighteenth-century life is now to be seen as more than a satirist's symbolic exposure of moral corruption. In *Humphry Clinker* alternatives are available and solutions are at hand. Smollett's previous heroes, not excluding Ferdinand Count Fathom, all manage to sustain a personal fastidiousness amid the overwhelming corruption and barbarity of their social lives. Again like Swift, Smollett's exposure of decay was prompted by an unwillingness to accept filth and vermin as necessary concomitants of human life. In his last novel some of humanity's diseases are physical and irreparable: but others are psychologically and morally self-inflicted, and can be cured. Matthew's letter to Dr Lewis about the King's Bath (45–48) is simply horrific in its visceral nastiness ('there is, or may be, some regurgitation from the bath into the cistern of the pump . . . we drink the decoction of living bodies at the Pump-room, we swallow the strainings of rotten bones and carcasses at the private bath'), but surrounding the whole town there are 'natural springs of excellent water' as possible alternatives. The antidote to London's vile milk is Welsh and Scottish milk; sociability spells the death of misanthropy; bodily health alleviates moral gloom; marriage alleviates isolation, and, in Jery's words, 'good cheer unites good company; exhilarates the spirits, opens the heart, banishes all restraint from conversation, and promotes the happiest purposes of social life' (60).

It is an irony of history, but not an irony of Smollett's artistic career, that Smollett's last novel, his most positive affirmation of life, appeared only a few months before his death.[24] The paradox is not unlike Fielding's charitable response to the cruel mockery which he suffered at the hands of the English sailors as his diseased and deformed body was winched aboard the ship in his *Voyage to Lisbon* (1755), or Tristram-Sterne's simultaneous flight from death in the last three books of *Tristram Shandy*. All three novels assert the continuity of life against the certainty of death. But this irony of history need have no bearing on a proper understanding of Smollett's last novel. It seems perverse to argue that because Smollett's last novel transcends the bitter satire of the earlier works, Smollett himself had therefore 'gone soft' on his social indignation. Robert Giddings remarks:

> by the 1770s Smollett seems to have tired of telling the world its faults, and was content to compose a novel to amuse his readers. There are some moments of satire in this novel, but the scenes at Bath and Scotland mock only at the superficial, not the essential. *Humphry Clinker* is the classical English bedside book, because it does not make you think.[25]

This comment grossly simplifies the intellectual and moral justification for the satire in the earlier novels and also blithely ignores an important transition between the earlier novels and the last. In the former, a single dominating narrative ego, hell-bent on destruction, subjects the whole experienced world to its own purposes. In *Humphry Clinker* a quintuple set of viewpoints asserts the relativity of all things. *Roderick Random, Peregrine Pickle*, and *Ferdinand Count Fathom* – as novels – are driven at breakneck speed by a satirical energy which leaves little room for psychological depth either in the hero or in others. Hence their factitious romance endings. The world is simply too big, too hostile, and too corrupt for anything other than an aggressive self-defence. In *Humphry Clinker*, however, the ugliness remains unchanged in the outside world (as graphically rendered as in *any* of the other novels), but the individual self reaches an accommodation with it. It is not a book which 'makes you think' as much as a book which shows the individual and multiple processes of thought and opinion reacting to a world impermeable to any *single* act of comprehension. In Smollett's last novel it is as though a final accommodation has been reached with the resistant world: the world's unhoused wretches (Lismahago, Humphry) find both physical shelter and a psychological home; the world is re-created from within the individual and, however bizarre the marriage-matches may seem, the final point is that the rich and comic variety of human life can and does reconcile the misanthrope with a long-lost son and an ageing matron with a grotesquely disfigured half-pay lieutenant. The violent and improbable contrasts of the earlier novels – Ferdinand's black-hearted evil and the snow-white virtue of Monimia and Count Melvile – are, though strategically effective in satire, here given a psychological credibility and a convincing reconciliation.[26] In *Humphry Clinker* Smollett reconciled not only satire and romance: he also returned the novel to that arena of concern for which it is supremely suited – the analysis of conflict between the individual and the world and a sometimes infuriatingly self-contradictory individualism. We can only speculate as to the novels Smollett might have written if *Humphry Clinker* had been his first rather than his last novel, but if the boot had been on the other foot and his social victims had been the judges and legislators, their urge to pull down the social hypocrisies from the outside would still not have produced anything like the settled decorums of Fielding's novels. It is worth repeating the quotation from *Peregrine Pickle*:

> Had the executive power of the legislature been vested in him, he would have doubtless devised *many strange species of punishment* for all offenders against humanity and decorum; but, restricted as he was, he employed his invention in subjecting them to the ridicule and contempt of their fellow-subjects. (576)

One would not, I think, willingly exchange more versions of *Humphry Clinker* for the fierce narrative energy, the raging satirical indignation, and the minutely detailed anatomies of the corrupt body social which rivet our attention in the earlier novels. Smollett's shocking specificity and his sheer splenetic courage are a standing indictment of those who would erect a cordon sanitaire between art and life. As Smollett himself wrote in his first novel, *Roderick Random*: 'Every intelligent reader will, at first sight, perceive I have not deviated from nature, in the facts, which are all true in the main, although the circumstances are altered and disguised, to avoid personal satire' (xxxv). The only substantial difference between Smollett's earlier novels and his last is that a single and tyrannical narrative viewpoint on 'the facts' of social corruption gives way to a multiple set of reactions. The world remains the same, but the solutions to its invasions are now enfolded within a precisely realized concept of human difference.

Notes

1. Smollett's contribution to the development of the novel is twice cursorily mentioned in Arnold Kettle's *An Introduction to the English Novel*, 2 vols

(London, 1951); ignored in Dorothy Van Ghent's *The English Novel: Form and Function* (1953; reprinted New York, 1961); largely ignored in Ian Watt's *The Rise of the Novel: Studies in Defoe, Richardson and Fielding* (London, 1957); and omitted from John Preston's *The Created Self: The Reader's Role in Eighteenth-Century Fiction* (London, 1970). Given this neglect in the major surveys, it is not perhaps surprising to find a tone of strident outrage on Smollett's behalf, in studies such as Donald Bruce, *Radical Dr. Smollett* (London, 1964), and Damian Grant, *Tobias Smollett: A Study in Style* (Manchester, 1977), or in the title at least, of *Smollett: Author of the First Distinction*, edited by Alan Bold (London, 1982). But for more than one viewpoint on Smollett's achievement, see Paul-Gabriel Boucé, *The Novels of Smollett* (London and New York, 1976: translated by Antonia White and the author from *Les Romans de Smollett*, 1971); George M. Kahrl, *Tobias Smollett, Traveler-Novelist* (Chicago, 1945); Lewis M. Knapp, *Tobias Smollett, Doctor of Men and Manners* (Princeton, 1949); and M. A. Goldberg, *Smollett and the Scottish School: Studies in Eighteenth-Century Thought* (Albuquerque, 1959).

2. See Melvina McKendrick, *Cervantes* (Boston and Toronto, 1980), pp. 210–30; Van Ghent, pp. 9–19; Gabriel Josipovici, *The World and the Book: A Study of Modern Fiction* (London, 1971), pp. 149–54 (on some parallel ideas in Swift). For a discussion of Smollett's 'sullen, pessimistic view of the world' and its relationship with Cervantes, see Robert M. Alter, *Rogue's Progress: Studies in the Picaresque Novel* (Cambridge, Mass., 1964), Chapter 4. Sheridan Baker sees Lismahago as 'Smollett's directly Cervantic knight-errant' and, oddly, makes no reference to Smollett's overtly Cervantic *Sir Launcelot Greaves*: see 'Humphry Clinker as Comic Romance', in *Essays on the Eighteenth-Century Novel*, edited by R. D. Spector (Bloomington and London, 1965), p. 158. Boucé, pp. 71–99, discusses the influence of *Don Quixote* and Le Sage's *Gil Blas* on the structure and characters of Smollett's novels, and on *Launcelot Greaves* and *Humphry Clinker* in particular (pp. 179–90).

3. *The Adventures of Launcelot Greaves*, edited by David Evans (Oxford, 1973), p. 12.

4. *The Letters of Tobias Smollett*, edited by Lewis M. Knapp (Oxford, 1970), p. 98.

5. See *The Adventures of Peregrine Pickle*, edited by James L. Clifford (Oxford, 1964: revised by Paul-Gabriel Boucé, 1983), pp. 682–83.

6. *The Adventures of Ferdinand Count Fathom*, edited by Damian Grant (Oxford, 1971), pp. 2–3.

7. *The Adventures of Roderick Random*, edited by Paul-Gabriel Boucé (Oxford, 1981), pp. 167–68.

8. Howard S. Buck, *A Study in Smollett: Chiefly 'Peregrine Pickle'* (New York, 1973), p. 55.

9. Compare Smollett's letter from Chelsea to Alexander Carlyle (1754): 'I do not think I could enjoy Life with greater Relish in any part of the World than in Scotland . . . I am heartily tired of this Land of Indifference and Phlegm where the finest Sensations of the Soul are not felt . . . Where Genius is lost, Learning undervalued, and Taste altogether extinguished, and Ignorance prevails' (*Letters of Smollett*, p. 33). Goldberg, p. 6, cites this letter in support of his argument that Smollett's central concern is with the theme of Primitivism versus Progress. It seems to me that the letter is tetchy rather than philosophical.

10. Buck, p. 20, describes this vast interpolation as 'the controversial storm-centre of the novel', but he does not imply by this that the memoirs of Lady Vane add anything to the novel except bulk. For a discussion of its contemporary significance, see pp. 20–52.

11. See the chapter titles to 55, 61, 64, and 65 for examples.

12. Douglas Brooks, *Number and Pattern in the Eighteenth-Century Novel: Defoe, Smollett, Fielding and Sterne* (London, 1973), pp. 140–41. It is difficult to deny such conclusions: one always hopes for significant symmetries in Smollett's novels, but the reading experience of *Count Fathom* (although patterned in a broad general way, as Brooks suggests) does not, I think, support claims that Smollett's 'balance' is 'precise' or that his 'paradigm' is 'compelling'.

13. Bruce, p. 167, describes his study of Smollett as 'opinionated and contentious', but it is also an entertaining rescue operation.

14. Jonathan Swift, *A Tale of a Tub, etc.* (1704), edited by A. C. Guthkelch and D. Nichol Smith, second edition (Oxford, 1958), pp. 171, 174.

15. Robert Alter, *Rogue's Progress: Studies in the Picaresque Novel*, Cambridge, Massachusetts, 1965, p. 69. Alter goes on to observe that although 'humanity is completely dehumanized by Smollett's quick pen . . . the striking characteristic of Smollett's dehumanization of people is the exhilarating play of unrestrained imagination' (p. 70).

16. Alter, p. 77.

17. Compare Mrs Partridge's assault on her husband in *The History of Tom Jones: A Foundling*, edited by Martin Battestin, and Fredson Bowers, 2 vols (Oxford, 1974), III, 4.

18. *The Expedition of Humphry Clinker*, edited by Lewis M. Knapp (London, 1966), pp. 54–55.

19. *The Life and Opinions of Tristram Shandy, Gentleman*, edited by Ian Campbell Ross (Oxford, 1983), II, 9, p. 87.

20. See Baker, p. 191: among other meanings, 'clinker' is eighteenth-century scatological slang.

21. 'The Ladies Receipt for a Novel', in Christopher Anstey's *The New Bath Guide* (London, 1766; seventh edition, 1770), p. 138. For a discussion of the relationship between Anstey's book and Smollett's novel, see Kahrl, p. 131, and Knapp, p. 322. The architect of Bath, John Wood, published *An Essay towards a Description of Bath* in 1765. Some of its implications for the spa town, particularly its interpretation of buildings as symbols of religious and social harmony and the notion of God as the Divine Architect, are discussed in R. S. Neale's excellent article 'Bath: Ideology and Utopia, 1700–1760', in *Studies in the Eighteenth Century*, edited by R. F. Brissenden and J. C. Eade (Canberra, 1976), III, pp. 37–54.

22. For further discussion, see Clive T. Probyn, 'Gulliver and the Relativity of Things: A Commentary on Method and Mode, with a Note on Smollett', *Renaissance and Modern Studies*, 18 (1974), 63–76.

23. See *Humphry Clinker*, pp. 219, 306–07, 338. John Valdimir Price points out the striking absence in Tabitha Bramble's letters of 'marks of literacy and social grace . . . a curious point when we consider her social status'. See *Tobias Smollett: The Expedition of Humphry Clinker*, Studies in English

Literature, 51 (London, 1973), p. 9. But is not Smollett simply acknowledging the educational disadvantage of women in this period? Lydia's formal education finishes with the boarding-school, but both Matthew and Jery are educated at Oxford.

24. For the circumstances surrounding Smollett's composition of the novel, see Knapp, pp. 286–96. *Humphry Clinker* appeared in June 1771, and Smollett died in the following September. His wife wrote: 'It galls me to the Soul when I think how much that poor Dear Man Suffered while he wrote this novel.' The book was probably completed at Smollett's Italian villa near Leghorn, 'a most romantic and salutary Situation', in Smollett's words.

25. Robert Giddings, *The Tradition of Smollett* (London, 1967). p. 140. Giddings clearly shows the dangers of taking a single perspective on the mixed modes of this novel when he comments that Matthew Bramble's travels 'are in no way a criticism of society and the criticism found along the way is incidental and not organic to the nature and structure of the book . . . the moral framework of *Humphry Clinker* is emphatically not picaresque'.

26. Compare Damian Grant's comment (pp. 205, 207): 'Everywhere in Smollett, and in every way, the genius for comparison serves his turn. It can function equally, though differently, both at the circumference and at the centre . . . only that criticism which is founded in criticism of style will ever be able to perceive the real value of Smollett as a writer.'

Chapter 6
A Form for Self-Realization: Laurence Sterne

Tristram Shandy

'Self', said David Hume, is only 'a bundle or collection of different perceptions, which succeed each other with an inconceivable rapidity and are seen in a perpetual flux and movement'.[1] Sterne's *Tristram Shandy* (1760–67) is the first novel in English overtly about writing and about personality. Its subject is the writing of an autobiography, a textbook on how to reduce the indeterminate mysteries of a single life to the known structures of literary discourse. Writing *Tristram Shandy* is the purpose of Tristram's being, and his being is enacted through his writing. Not even Richardson's Pamela, Clarissa, and Harriet Byron live *for* their writing: their apparently endless scribbling is a means to an end, to a future denouement – marriage or disengagement from the world. Although the novel looks like a fictional autobiography, just as *Gulliver's Travels* looks like a traveller's tale, its purpose and its achievement are to question the very assumptions of its existence.

Progress for Tristram is not linear but digressive: pulling one strand from the carpet, he unravels a host of interconnected patterns. In order to understand the present he goes backwards and finishes up proceeding sideways: for Tristram there is no way of writing except 'to the moment'. The stories of characters other than Tristram himself are not neatly packaged interpolated narratives subservient and explanatory in function. In Sterne's fiction everything is connected with everything else, and constantly overwhelms the assumption that a single life may be seen as detachable from the world around it, and that it may in some simple way be 'represented' in the shape of an art form. Tristram remarks that John Locke's *Essay Concerning Human Understanding* (1690) is 'a history-book . . . of what passes in a man's own mind'.[2] Locke doubtless assumed that his analysis of the proper and improper processes of the mind had universal application, but Tristram shows that the bridge between an individual's mind and those of his fellow men was not to be exclusively and empirically constructed through words and ideas, nor even through a common epistemology. The question is, whether the oddity which generations of readers have marked in this novel is unique to Tristram and Sterne, or more generally applicable as Sterne's considered view of human personality and, more particularly, of Sterne's view of *literary* images of personality.[3]

However bizarre this novel may seem, it nevertheless relates organically to its time and to previous works of prose fiction. We may label it a fictional autobiography, with a first-person narrator. But it is nothing like Defoe's novels. Tristram addresses the reader approximately three hundred and fifty times during the course of the book, as 'My Lord', 'Jenny', 'Madam', 'your worship', 'my dear anti-Shandeans, and thrice able critics, and fellow labourers . . . subtle statesmen and discreet doctors', 'Julia', 'your reverences', and 'gentry', for example.[4] It is as though the reader has invaded the book and Tristram's confidence in a single communicable statement rests on *determining* the unknown readership. Tristram begins at the beginning, but this means in his case with the sexual act which procreates him and generates the cause of the novel's writing. He finishes when there is nothing more to be said and no way in which to say it, having covered only a fraction of his life. In spite of its apparently unfinished state, the idea of flight from mortality in the last three books is thick with pathos: the novel has, in every meaning of the term, a sense of an ending. Formally speaking, it is overwhelmed with the technical machinery of the novel form. There are volumes and chapters; there is a Dedication (I, 9), a Preface (III, 20), plot diagrams (VI, 40) which indicate in graphic form but not in actuality the notion of progress; and there is learned commentary in text and footnotes throughout. In other words, the relationship between the form of *Tristram Shandy* and the narrative conventions of the novel thus far established by Defoe, Richardson, and Fielding, is ironic and self-conscious.

There is, of course, no specific intention to mock Defoe's fictional autobiographies, Richardson's epistolary creation of individual and momentary psychology, and Fielding's manipulative comic–epic strategies. Sterne's criticism of literary narrative goes much deeper than such 'local' allusions, and may not depend at all on prior knowledge of the novel *per se*.[5] The literary formation of Tristram's *Life and Opinions* is the narrator's particular hobby-horse, his governing obsession, and the obvious example of Swift's *A Tale of a Tub* (1704 and 1710) alone would indicate that problems of presenting the self in literary terms pre-dated and were independent of the rise of the novel. Swift's *Tale* has gaps in the manuscript, an apparently incompetent narrator who, like Tristram, is obsessed with the need to impose literary form on his insignificant experience. Sterne needed to look no further than the work of Rabelais, Cervantes, and Fielding for books which direct irony against the expectations of a sequential narrative structure, and in John Dunton's *Voyage Round the World* (1691: reprinted in 1762 as *The Life, Travels, and Adventures of Christopher Wagstaff, Grandfather to Tristram Shandy*), the author plays games with the reader's assumptions about authorial control and frustrates the assumption of an organic connection between form and content. In *Tristram Shandy*, likewise, it is the digressions which contain Tristram's opinions, and more than a third of the novel elapses before Tristram is even born. Sterne's comic rationale depends on the established devices of literary presentation being known. *Tristram Shandy* thus has the *potential* form of a fictional autobiography but the *actual* shape of a novel in first draft, a work in continual progress and regress. For what Sterne and Tristram have to say, think, and feel, other men's narrative modes are inadequate and inappropriate simply because they are other men's properties. The comic ironies are therefore not merely textual jokes at the expense of the well-made novel but (as in the analogous case of Swift's *Tale*) the only way of defining Tristram and Sterne's *difference* as individuals and as authors.

The 'literariness' of *Tristram Shandy* is a physical fact. Yorick's death is represented by a black page (I, 12); the marbled page (III, 36) is, in its random patterning, a 'motley emblem of my work'; IV, 10 is the long-delayed 'chapter upon chapters'; IV, 24 is completely missing (it would have described the bastardy signalled on the Shandy coat of arms: the chapter and the fact need to be 'blotted out', as the following chapter explains); further sport with volumes and chapters occurs in IX, 25, where Tristram explains the necessity for writing Chapter 25 before Chapters 18 and 19. This self-conscious and self-reflecting textual comedy literally stands in the way of conventional fictional expectations, and many readers have found the novel tiresome and intensely frustrating. But Sterne forestalls this misunderstanding of his narrative purposes. In I, 20 Tristram tetchily demands that his female reader ('Madam') reread the last chapter in order to understand it better, and states that this is a penance imposed, 'to rebuke a vicious taste which has crept into thousands beside herself, – of reading straight forwards, more in quest of the adventures, than of the deep erudition and knowledge which a book of this cast, if read over as it should be, would infallibly impart with them' (48).

Sterne thus signals a particular relationship between story as a temporal sequence of events, and plot as a sequence of events connected by causation. If the significance of *Tristram Shandy* does not reveal itself in its action, which continually turns back on itself in search of causes, where then are we to look for its meaning? Does the book add up to no more than a random accretion of details unconnected by theme or intelligible pattern? In VIII, 2, Tristram seems to reveal no control whatsoever:

> That of all the several ways of beginning a book which are now in practice throughout the known world, I am confident my own way of doing it is the best – I'm sure it is the most religious – for I begin with writing the first sentence – and trusting to Almighty God for the second. (436)

In IX, 8, however, it is the prospect of not writing at all which elicits Tristram's most solemn response:

> Time wastes too fast: every letter I trace tells me with what rapidity Life follows my pen; the days and hours of it, more precious, my dear Jenny! than the rubies about thy neck, are flying over our heads, like light clouds of a windy day, never to return more – every thing presses on – whilst thou art twisting that lock, – see! it grows grey; and every time I kiss thy hand to bid adieu, and every absence which follows it, are preludes to that eternal separation which we are shortly to make. – Heaven have mercy on us both! (498)

Thus the most prominent 'significance' in *Tristram Shandy* is the act of writing. The self is defined in the act of writing about it, and life continues for as long as there is time, paper and ink, health, and a sympathetic reader. Tristram's near-emasculation by the sash window (IV, 17) leads directly to the act of authorship. His sexual disability means that he will never father a child, but the compensation is that he will create an autobiographical book, engendered from his own mind: 'the credit, which will attend thee as an author, shall counterbalance the many evils which have befallen thee as a man' (269). Uncle Toby's compensation for his innocence of women in general and Mrs Wadman in particular takes another form, but also originating in pain. He inhabits an entirely masculine world, dominated by the re-creation of the battlefield of Namur, where he received a wound in the groin. Toby is so far removed from self-consciousness that the place where he was wounded is, in his own mind, a matter of co-ordinates on a map, not a part of his anatomy at all. Tristram's father, Walter, is between fifty and sixty years old when Tristram is born (the child of exhausted loins), and Walter is too old to escape his obsession with allegories, metaphors, patterns, and schemes. His judgement has become the dupe of his wit, and he too prefers to live through the printed word. Instead of actively involving himself with Tristram's upbringing he devotes himself to compiling a book about it, the *Tristrapaedia*. All three retreat from the pain of living into a textual substitute. Each is an alienated character, whose selves have been externalized, narrowed, rigidified, 'textualized'.

If this were the whole truth about *Tristram Shandy*, the book would appear to be tragic, or at least absurd. But for Sterne there is no simple separation between laughter and tears. Indeed, the separation of mind and body provides the essential ingredient of a healing comedy. In the battle for psychic freedom neither scientific materialism nor the prison of language are allowed to prevail. In iv, 22, Tristram informs the gentle reader of his intention:

> If 'tis wrote against any thing, – 'tis wrote, an'please your worships, against the spleen; in order, by a more frequent and a more convulsive elevation and depression of the diaphragm, and the succussations of the intercostal and abdominal muscles in laughter, to drive the *gall* and *bitter juices* from the gall bladder, liver and sweet-bread of his majesty's subjects, with all the inimicitous passions which belong to them, down into their duodenum. (239)

This passage is, in miniature, an emblem of the expressive form of the novel as a whole. Its parody of cumbrous medical pedantry is self-reflexive: it generates the reaction (laughter) which it is trying desperately to describe through purely anatomical mechanisms. Equally, Sterne's own philosophical irony was a matter of laughing and weeping at the same time. In the last two paragraphs of the fourth book (published in January 1761), Sterne celebrates the joyous and liberating nature of '*True Shandeism*', which 'opens the heart and lungs . . . and makes the wheel of life run long and chearfully round' (270), but in the next paragraph he can also imagine a whole kingdom of 'hearty laughing subjects' which he knows he will not live to create: 'I take my leave of you till this time twelve-month, when (unless this vile cough kills me in the mean time) I'll have another pluck at your beards, and lay open a story to the world you little dream of' (270). Sterne's allusion to his own mortality adds poignancy to comedy, just as his cheeky irony qualifies any incipient sentimentality.

In such a passage it is unprofitable to attempt a separation between Sterne as author and Tristram as narrator. In real life the former was happy to be known as 'Tristram Shandy' or 'Parson Yorick' (the narrator of *A Sentimental Journey*).[6] In life and in fiction the problem of Time confronts both. In the final three volumes Tristram escapes from narrow self-concern into extreme sociability (a process of psychological healing most clearly articulated in the later novel), as if to slow down the passage of time by speeding up the rate of experience.

Tristram claims that the novel is also about what he calls 'small incidents'. We might best understand these as epiphany-like revelations of character and motive which though trivial nevertheless reveal the determinants of an individual life. The fact that Walter Shandy has forgotten to wind the clock (I, 1) means that the sexual act which will eventually produce the unfortunate Tristram is interrupted and that the homunculus takes a disordered and discontinuous route towards conception. It is also an emblem of that mechanism in human life which the novel so radically abhors. In this book everything deemed worthy escapes classification. Uncle Toby's apparently trivial gesture in refusing to swat the fly ('This world is surely wide enough to hold both thee and me', III, 4), reveals Toby's virtue as a compound of disinterested benevolence and humane tolerance, somewhat paradoxical in one who devotes his life to re-enacting the carnage of warfare. To the Widow Wadman's evident relief and delight, Uncle Toby's obsession with war games eventually gives way to the game of love. He sees in her what the reader is asked to see in him: HUMANITY (IX, 21) – the sum total of everything admirable, the capital virtue, the undefinable essence. But equally, the world of chance, of contingency incarnate, also operates through small incidents, and with sometimes disastrous consequences.

For most of the novel each character is as self-imprisoned as any of Samuel Beckett's characters. Sterne's phrase for this epistemological imprisonment is 'Hobby-horse'. One can ride a hobby-horse or, as in Walter Shandy's case, be ridden by it. Walter bends the world to fit his own preconceived theories, packaging awkward and baffling experience inside a comprehensive and, to him at least, a comprehensible abstract theory. The value of this theory is that it removes the necessity for coping with the demands and the pains of the flesh: the mind suppresses the body. There is no more frequent dichotomy in eighteenth-century literature. It is the causative disequilibrium of Fielding's absent-minded Parson Adams, of Swift's mad philosopher at the end of *The Mechanical Operation of the Spirit*, of Johnson's arrogant astronomer in *Rasselas*, and of the alienated Gulliver. To Uncle Toby's annoyance, Walter libels 'the desires and appetites of the lower part of us' (471), whereas Tristram's own hobby-horse functions not as a suppressant but as a distraction and as a substitute:

> 'Tis the sporting little filly-folly which carries you out for
> the present hour – a maggot, a butterfly, a picture, a
> fiddle-stick – an Uncle Toby's siege – or *any thing*, which
> a man makes a shift to get astride on, to canter it away

from the cares and solicitudes of life – 'Tis as useful a
beast as is in the whole creation – nor do I really see how
the world could do without it. (471)

Yet both are forms of escape, a narrowing down of the incompre-
hensible or threatening outside world until an elegant substitute model
(a toy battlefield, an encyclopaedia of child-rearing, a novel) may be
constructed. Intrinsically harmless, such a process of self-delusion may
have disastrous comic results when such an individual is obliged to
rejoin the human race in social interaction. When one obsession collides
with another, as in Walter's attempt to explain his (or rather Locke's)
theory of the association of ideas to Uncle Toby (whose mind is locked
into military strategies), the result is like matter colliding with anti-
matter: a linguistic black hole is created from which no light escapes:

> Now, whether we observe it or no, continued my
> father, in every sound man's head, there is a regular
> succession of ideas of one sort or other, which follow each
> other in train just like – A train of artillery? said my uncle
> *Toby*. – A train of a fiddle stick! – quoth my father, –
> which follow and succeed one another in our minds at
> certain distances, just like the images in the inside of a
> lanthorn turned round by the heat of a candle. – I declare,
> quoth my uncle *Toby*, mine are more like a smoak-jack. –
> Then, brother *Toby*, I have nothing more to say to you
> upon the subject, said my father. (151)

For all three characters some form of sexual inadequacy has led to
a compensatory obsession, and it is primarily the imagination and only
secondarily the libido which may provide the key to unlock the prison
of the self's identity. A more balanced relationship between their own
mind and body, and between themselves as individuals and the world
outside, is only a potentiality within the covers of the novel, however.
Sterne's often bawdy sexual comedy is a way of involving the reader
in this therapeutic process, eliciting his or her repressed sexual awareness, and it is also an emblem of his argument against the notion that
man's essential characteristic is his rationality. The novel begins with
an interrupted heterosexual act and ends with a sexual ambiguity, a
metaphorical elbow in the ribs: 'A COCK and a BULL' is what the
novel is about. For most of the novel sex is a fantastic and anarchic
joke, a priapic rebellion against social proprieties and intellectual preoccupations. In the central episode, the monstrously phallic nose of Slaw-
kenbergius (Volume IV) provokes sexual hysteria among the women
of Strasburg and logical disputes among the philosophers, theologians,

and academicians. It is a proof, as Sterne points out, of the principle that 'Heat is in proportion to the want of knowledge'. Sexual ignorance arises from sexual fear: all the references to whiskers, noses, chestnuts, nightcaps, chamber-pots, and the hobby-horse itself, represent escape from sex into comic metaphor, a means whereby anxiety is metamorphosed into the manageable.[7]

And yet, the most obvious truth about this complex novel is that it is *about* the act of writing, of inscribing an image of a disordered self on paper. Tristram's life is writing, and his writing is his life. But in attempting to account for his personality (i.e. his life and his opinions) through a re-creation of its influences, his literary personality dissolves in the very act of self-construction. He writes in the present moment about actions already past, but no pattern emerges which he can understand. His narrative failure becomes *the* principle of fictional (dis)organization: 'my reader has never yet been able to guess at any thing' (63). Sterne thus takes the reader into his confidence, as Fielding had done, but only to reveal that *neither* is in control. The reason for this is not incompetence. Tristram's fictional problem is that the life of the inner imagination bears an inverse relationship to his external and physical life. He will always be trapped in time. If every thought, impression, memory, and opinion must be committed to paper he will never finish the writing of the novel. As soon as one sentence is written, it is already history, and in the meantime new thoughts crowd in demanding to be written down and explained. It is the sheer connectedness of experience which defeats the attempt to impose a single, elegant, and entirely fictional shape. Writing itself becomes an aspect of the human comedy. More than a substitute for living, it is also an *intensification* of it: 'Time wastes too fast: every letter I trace tells me with what rapidity Life follows my pen' (498).

Technically, Tristram's problem is with what he calls 'Duration'. Clock time measures experience only in terms of arbitrary segments – minutes, hours, days, months, years – but psychological time measures experience only in terms of its intensity. Under clock time Tristram's narrative is constantly digressive, but under psychological time the 'digressions' reveal the core meanings. In ix, 8, for example, Tristram not only sees writing as an intensification of life's processes but also connects human transience with the theme of love. In ii, 9, similarly, Tristram remarks that 'Writing, when properly managed (as you may be sure I think mine is), is but a different name for conversation' (87), but the act of communion with the reader reveals the impossibility of enmeshing so many individual minds both within and outside the novel. The conversations between Walter and Toby, as in iii, 18, where Walter tries to explain his theories in relation to time, infinity, and duration, effect unbridgeable gaps between the conversational participants. Language reveals their difference; it fails as the medium of communication because a single consciousness perceives only one facet of reality. Tristram says of his progenitor:

> his road lay so very far on one side, from that wherein
> most men travelled, – that every object before him
> presented a face and section of itself to his eye, altogether
> different from the plan and elevation of it seen by the rest
> of mankind. – In other words, 'twas a different object, –
> and in course was differently considered: This is the true
> reason, that my dear *Jenny* and I, as well as all the world
> besides us, have such eternal squabbles about nothing –
> She looks at her outside, – I, at her in——. How is it
> possible we should agree about her value? (306)

Tristram is able to transcend the limits of his own consciousness by digressions because he can see everything except himself from different angles. The digressions have a double function: they enable Tristram to escape from his own incoherence as a man and as an author, but they also characterize his mind in the most extraordinarily precise way. Tristram may fail as an author of a conventional novel, but he succeeds brilliantly as a writer of his own unique intellectual biography. Unlike his father, who is mired in the world of words (a 'Logomachia', as he puts it), Tristram explores the gaps between words and systems of thought and becomes the exponent of discontinuities. As the analyst of misunderstanding, the expert in verbal escapology, Tristram stumbles into a relativistic world as complex and as 'modern' as Faulkner's *The Sound and the Fury*, Proust's *Remembrance of Things Past*, Joyce's *Ulysses*, and Virgina Woolf's *To the Lighthouse*. By inverting or parodying the narrative conventions of the novel form Sterne subverts the assumptions that individual experience can be 'contained' in a literary form and that there is a common perspective on reality. When Virginia Woolf faced a similar dilemma in 1929 she outlined a new direction for fiction which Sterne had already explored:

> Admitting the vagueness which afflicts all criticism of
> novels, let us hazard the opinion that for us at this
> moment the form of fiction most in vogue more often
> misses than secures the thing we seek. Whether we call it
> life or spirit, truth or reality, this, the essential thing, has
> moved off, or on, and refuses to be contained any longer
> in such ill-fitting vestments as we provide. Nevertheless,
> we go on perseveringly, conscientiously, constructing our
> two and thirty chapters after a design which more and

more ceases to resemble the vision on our minds. . . . Life
is . . . a luminous halo, a semi-transparent envelope
surrounding us from the beginning of consciousness to the
end.[8]

A Sentimental Journey through France and Italy and Journal to Eliza

Virginia Woolf's image of life as a 'luminous halo' is peculiarly apt for
an understanding of Sterne's second novel, *A Sentimental Journey*,
published three weeks before his death in 1768. Again, Sterne's animus
is directed against everything that is mechanical, life-denying, centred
upon the self-image. His subject is the communicability of charity and
love in spite of barriers erected by language, race, culture, and gender,
not to mention the physical barriers of doors, fences, national frontiers,
and so on: 'Tis so ordered, that from the want of languages, connections, and dependencies, and from the difference in education,
customs, and habits, we lie under so many impediments in commu-
nicating our sensations out of our own sphere, as often amounts to a
total impossibility.'[9]
    Like *Tristram Shandy*, this novel is a process novel, a chronological
account of an individual's changing moral and emotional self-interpret-
ation. Just as the former novel inverts the formal assumptions of the
conventional novel form, the latter displaces the conventional travel
book's concern with physical topography. Parson Yorick sets off for
France blithely unaware that England is currently at war with her
neighbour across the Channel. He is indifferent to public and political
sectarianism because Sterne's real concern is to show the potential
means of human community, not their actual difference. Yorick moves
from an initial state of self-absorbed introversion and inhibiting patriotism towards a generosity of spirit, an empathic sociability, and an
expression of love by means of a liberated sexual instinct. Imprisonment is the theme and escape by means of self-analysis is the plot.
Yorick's first action is to deny the monk's request for charity when
he lands at Calais, and then to choose a means of transport designed
to exclude all but himself (the *désobligeant* literally disobliges him from
all social duties). At the end of this short novel Yorick has experienced
a sea-change: he finds himself (in every sense of the phrase) in a dark-
ened bedroom, which he must share with a lady. The *fille de chambre*

creeps out of her closet, moves protectively between her lady's bed and that of Yorick. Already sexually aroused, Yorick stretches out his hand, and Sterne once more absorbs a textual convention into (erotic) textual meaning (125):

> So that when I stretch'd out my hand, I caught hold of the Fille de Chambre's
>
> END

Even though we are not *shown* what met Yorick's outstretched hand, we *know* that Eros has worked hand in hand with Chance not merely to transcend the social decorums but to conjoin a desire and an action in a moment of emotional bliss. Sterne's word for this liberation of the spirit from social and sexual imprisonment is Sensibility, and one of the valuable elements in *A Sentimental Journey* is that the notion of sensibility provides another way of understanding *Tristram Shandy's* comedy of isolation. Yorick defines sensibility as 'generous joys and generous cares beyond myself' (117). This emotional expansionism is an aspect of the European Enlightenment to which he refers in the Preface: 'It is an age so full of light, that there is scarce a country or corner of Europe whose beams are not crossed and interchanged with others' (12). Beyond Europe itself, it becomes a cosmic principle of benevolent love, 'thy divinity which stirs within me', emanating from 'thee, great – great SENSORIUM of the world!' (117). Sensibility is the great liberator of the human spirit, the medium of human communication, and the means through which its operation is perceived. A few lines after Yorick's hymn to an abstract Sensibility, Yorick depicts its human exemplar in a secular communion among a French farmhouse family at supper:

> The family consisted of an old gray-headed man and his wife, with five or six sons and sons-in-law and their several wives, and a joyous genealogy out of 'em.
>   They were sitting down together to their lentil-soup; a large wheaten loaf was in the middle of the table; and a flaggon of wine at each end of it promised joy thro' the stages of the repast – 'twas a feast of love. (118)

Yorick responds instinctively to this vision of social communion because it elicits something which he has been searching for on an unconscious level. It is both what he seeks and what he has so far denied. By contrast, SMELFUNGUS (i.e. Smollett, in *Travels through France and Italy*, 1766) had 'set out with the spleen and jaundice, and every object he pass'd by was discoloured or distorted – He wrote an account of them, but 'twas nothing but the account of his miserable feelings' (28–29).[10] Sterne implies here an argument similar to Tom's rejoinder to the Man of the Hill in *Tom Jones*, and also interpolates a conviction that a dialogue is itself a means towards psychic health: 'when your eyes are fixed upon a dead blank – you draw purely from yourselves' (16). An optimistic view of a benevolent world in harmony with itself depends upon a preliminary willingness to cultivate a receptive empathy. A man can see the world as a reflection of his own mind, for good or ill, and *Tristram Shandy* reaches this conclusion by a process of parody and irony. The breakdown of verbal communication in the Shandy household is caused by the imposition of a single mental set on the world of experience, thus reducing dialogue to a conflict of hypotheses or hobby-horses. Toby and Walter speak at rather than to each other, and yet their mutual affection is patently clear. Toby's humanitarian eccentricity in refusing to kill the fly reverberates through Tristram's soul as the larger cosmic echoes respond to the French family in *A Sentimental Journey*. Toby's action thus 'instantly set [Tristram's] whole frame into one vibration of most pleasurable sensation' (91). The philosophic rationale for each of these unheroic incidents is clear only to those who divest themselves of impersonal conventional and therefore obstructive ways of thinking: 'I think I can see the precise and distinguishing marks of national characters more in these *nonsensical minutiae*, than in the most important matters of state; where great men of all nations talk and stalk so much alike, that I would not give ninepence to chuse amongst them' (50).

A critical analogy for Sterne's nexus between significant, sentimental detail and empathic reception by the reader had been elaborated one year before the publication of *Tristram Shandy*. Edward Young's *Conjectures on Original Composition* (1759) – addressed to Samuel Richardson as author of *Grandison* – argues that 'Applause is not to be given, but extorted; and the silent lapse of a single tear does the writer more honour than the rattling thunder of a thousand hands. Applauding hands and dry eyes . . . are a satire on the writer's talent, and the spectator's taste'. Addison, in spite of the 'moral prudery' which prevented full expression of his 'warm and feeling heart', is now to be preferred to the satire of Swift and Pope, and Young includes an account of Addison's death, a sentimental Christian *memento mori* soon to be elaborated by Sterne and Mackenzie. A particular man with a particular sensibility is to become the central subject for the moral imagination. Sir Walter Scott was to label Mackenzie 'the northern Addison'. In relation to Sterne, however, Clara Reeve wrote in 1785 that 'Where *Sterne* attempts the Pathos, he is irresistible . . . though he affected humour and foolery, yet he was greatest in the pathetic style. – His *Maria* and *Le Fevre*, and his *Monk*, are charming pictures, and will survive, when all his other writings are forgot'.[11] Reeve's comment signalled a preference among contemporary readers (barely concealing a moral censoriousness) for Sterne's 'sentiment' rather than for his irony, sexual comedy, and verbal wit. But the whole point about Sterne's comedy, of course, is that each is inextricably connected to all the others. Sterne's 'epicureanism of emotion', which has been seen as his 'significant contribution to the development of sentimentalism in the eighteenth century',[12] is never without corrective irony. It is this which separates Sterne's novels not only from subsequent examples of the novel of sensibility, but also from all other novels written in the twenty years after 1760. After Sterne it is as though novelists such as Goldsmith and Mackenzie are forced to look at the now limitless formal dimensions of the novel through the diminishing end of a telescope.

There was no school of Sterne because Sterne had left no novelistic stone unturned. He radically destabilized the whole genre of fictional prose narrative, and *Tristram Shandy* is a terminal parody of all the known narrative orthodoxies, forms, and structures, a dissolution of truth into subjectivism, and a reduction of philosophy to questions of the self's identity. But yet the final paradox of this eccentric and quintessential novel is that in showing the limits of narrative fiction it also immeasurably expanded its potentialities, and far ahead of its time. As Patricia Meyer Spacks has said: 'Constantly stating what narrative cannot do, it simultaneously demonstrates what it can. It shows how language creates the meaning Tristram denies it, how story declares identity, though the teller barely believes in his continuing existence.'[13] In the vile and profligate town of Abdera it is a performance of the *Andromeda* of Euripides, which includes an invocation to 'Cupid! prince of God and men' (*A Sentimental Journey*, 35), that stimulates an outbreak of Love, Friendship and Virtue. The power of Art to reshape the mind is limitless, and there seems no reason to doubt that for Sterne fiction itself could have a profoundly recuperative moral purpose. As in his fiction, so in his life: there is a passage in *The Journal to Eliza* (1768), which Sterne apparently called his 'Work of Redemption',[14] which shows precisely how Sterne transmutes intractable facts (an intolerable marriage, a painful separation from a young Anglo-Indian married lady, loneliness, and mortality) into a *historical* account which is as entirely fictional as it is entirely happy:

> I have brought your name *Eliza*! and Picture into my
> work – where they will remain – when You and I are at
> rest for ever – Some Annotator or explainer of my works
> in this place will take occasion, to speak of the Friendship
> which Subsisted so long and faithfully betwixt Yorick and

the Lady he speaks of – Her Name he will tell the world
was Draper – a Native of India – married there to a
gentleman in the India Service of that Name – who
brought her over to England for the recovery of her health
in the Year 65 – where She continued to April 1767. It
was about three months before her Return to India, That
our Author's acquaintance and hers began. Mrs. Draper
had a great thirst for Knowledge – was handsome –
genteel – engaging – and of such gentle dispositions and so
enlightend an understanding, – That Yorick, (whether he
made much Opposition is not known) from an
acquaintance – soon became her Admirer – they caught
fire at each other at the same time – and they would often
say, without reserve to the world, and without any Idea of
saying wrong in it, That their Affections for each other
were *unbounded* – Mr. Draper dying in the Year ★★★★ –
This Lady return'd to England, and Yorick the year after
becoming a Widower – They were married – and retiring
to one of his Livings in Yorkshire, where was a most
romantic Situation – they lived and died happily. – and are
spoken of with honour in the parish to this day –
  June 18
  How do you like the History, of this couple, Eliza?
(166)

Sterne's ancient consolation is to re-create the brazen world of the
actual into the golden world of the ideal, but yet to look at the result
with a knowing irony, and to ask his reader (in this case Eliza Draper)
to co-operate in the conscious illusion. Time and social conventions
are obliterated by an act of imaginative self-projection. The result is
a triumph of art over reality, history is rewritten, and Time defeated.

Notes

1. David Hume, *Treatise of Human Nature* (1739–40), Book I, Part IV, Chapter 6, 'Of Personal Identity'.

2. *The Life and Opinions of Tristram Shandy, Gentleman*, edited by Ian Campbell Ross (Oxford, 1983), p. 71. All references are to this edition and are given in the text.

3. The Russian Formalist critic Viktor Shklovsky, in a discussion of 'the general

laws of novelistic form', remarks that *Tristram Shandy* is 'the most typical novel of world literature'. Originally published in Moscow in 1929, this essay is translated in *Laurence Sterne: A Collection of Critical Essays*, edited by John Traugott (Englewood Cliffs, New Jersey, 1968), pp. 66–89.

4. Mary S. Wagoner, 'Satire of the Reader in *Tristram Shandy*', *TSLL*, 8 (1966–67), 337.

5. Robert Burton's *Anatomy of Melancholy* and Rabelais are discussed as generic models by Northrop Frye, *The Anatomy of Criticism: Four Essays* (Princeton, 1957), pp. 311–13, and by D. W. Jefferson, '*Tristram Shandy* and the Learned Tradition of Wit' (1951), reprinted in *Sterne: Collection of Essays*, pp. 148–67. See also Wayne C. Booth, 'The Self-Conscious Narrator in Comic Fiction before *Tristram Shandy*', *PMLA*, LXVII (March, 1952), 163–85.

6. Unprofitable and inappropriate: compare John Preston's reading, that 'Tristram, the fictional author, turns real life, real books, real people (John Hall-Stevenson, for instance, or Dr. Burton) into fictions. He invents them, in just the way that he invents his own family, to populate his fictional world. What is more, Tristram, invented to be the author of Sterne's novel, turns Sterne himself into the fictional Yorick. Sterne invents the conditions in which he can invent himself' (*The Created Self: The Reader's Role in Eighteenth-Century Fiction* (London, 1970), p. 188).

7. For an excellent discussion of the idea that the novel is 'organized [*sic*] to reveal the pervasiveness of male fear, demonstrating in form and substance how the terror of impotence spreads through every endeavor', see Patricia Meyer Spacks, *Imagining a Self: Autobiography and Novel in Eighteenth-Century England* (Cambridge, Mass., and London, 1976), pp. 158 and 127–57.

8. Virginia Woolf, 'Modern Fiction', in *The Common Reader*, first series (1925; reprinted London 1957), pp. 188–89. In her introduction to the World's Classics edition of *A Sentimental Journey* (London, 1928), Woolf remarks that 'the very punctuation is that of speech, not writing, and brings the sound, the associations, of the speaking voice in with it. The order of the ideas, their suddenness and irrelevancy, is more true to life than to literature. . . . Under the influence of this extraordinary style the book becomes semi-transparent. The usual ceremonies and conventions which keep reader and writer at arm's length disappear. We are as close to life as we can be' (vii). This essay was reprinted in the second series of *The Common Reader* (1932; reprinted London, 1959), pp. 78–85.

9. *A Sentimental Journey through France and Italy*, edited by Ian Jack (London, 1968), p. 9. All references are to this edition.

10. Smollett is thus classified as a Splenetic Traveller: see Sterne's typology of Travellers on p. 11. Yorick, of course, is the antithetical Sentimental Traveller. Sterne's first choice of soubriquet for Smollett was Smeldungus, and Philip Thicknesse remarked in *Useful Hints to Those Who Make the Tour to France* (1768, p. 4) that Smollett's *Travels* should 'more properly . . . be intitled, "QUARRELS through France and Italy for the cure of a pulmonic disorder"'. See *Travels through France and Italy*, edited by Frank Felsenstein (Oxford, 1981), p. xii.

11. Clara Reeve, *The Progress of Romance*, 2 vols (1785), II, 31. Reeve's preference for the morally educative sort of novel is clear, not only from her reluctance to mention the 'scandal' novels of Aphra Behn, Mrs Manley, and Eliza Haywood, but from the words of the duke in her posthumously published

novel *Fatherless Fanny, or the little Mendicant* (1839): 'Novels . . . are a kind of reading universally in vogue . . . yet, I believe, I may safely assert, that they have corrupted the morals of more than they have improved.' See *Eighteenth-Century British Novelists on the Novel*, edited by George L. Barnett (New York, 1968), p. 133.

12. *Tristram Shandy*, edited by James A. Work (New York, 1940), p. lxx.

13. Spacks, p. 128.

14. This remark was reported by Richard Griffith, and is cited in *A Sentimental Journey through France and Italy*, Introduction, p. xv.

Chapter 7

Transition and Transformation: Society, Sentiment, and the Self in the Novel, 1764–1789

Most critical studies of the novel in the eighteenth century stop after Sterne. There are clear reasons for this. The fifth volume of Ernest Baker's ten-volume study of the English novel has a double focus, 'The Novel of Sentiment and the Gothic Novel', and its first marginal note sets an unpromising tone: '*The next half century comparatively dull*'.[1] Adding Smollett to what Baker calls the 'Great Four' (Defoe, Richardson, Fielding, and Sterne) does not solve the problem of apparent discontinuity in the novel after Sterne, after whom the most significant single novelist in the last quarter of the century is Fanny Burney. Indeed, there could be no more startling contrast than that between *Tristram Shandy* and *Evelina* (1778). In the words of Patricia Meyer Spacks,

> Committed to propriety as he to its opposite, apparently
> unaware of the formal possibilities or implications of her
> conventional plots, feeling that the most important
> question about novels concerned their moral influence,
> [Fanny Burney] reminds the reader that Tristram Shandy's
> conviction of the impossibilities of art does not represent
> the only conceivable viewpoint. The moral and
> psychological organization of her fiction and her diaries
> insists on the order of life itself.[2]

Between these two novels there were hundreds of others published, so many in fact that for the first time in the history of the genre of prose fiction it is possible to speak with confidence of a middle-class readership as an instrumental force in determining literary production.[3] Whether the enormous numerical increase in novels and readers itself led to a qualitative decline, or whether the demise of the 'Great Four or Five' exposed a novelistic vacuum filled with minor talents, the history of the novel between Sterne and Jane Austen is a matter of undercurrents, not high tides. Very few of the novels in this period emerged with the triumphant novelty of Sterne, none with the consummate artistic shape of Fielding or with the pioneering energy of Defoe's lust for realism. The acidic social satire of Smollett's novels is the single greatest deletion in the novel's repertoire. If there is a single immediate influence, it is Richardson, and in a group of novels variously known as 'novels of sensibility', 'novels of sentiment', and 'Gothic' novels. They are all transitional, not simply because they are difficult to label – in this sense most of the novels discussed so far are characterized by generic instability – but because they lift the curtain on a pre-Romantic phase of literary history which, to a greater or lesser extent, stands in opposition to the world of Augustan values and its imaginative priorities.

The novels of Brooke, Goldsmith, Walpole, Beckford, and Mackenzie attempt new subjects and exploit different imaginative resources. This new 'shift in sensibility' in England was only a part of a complex European phenomenon.[4] Just as Defoe would not have been aware of his historical significance as the first exponent of 'formal realism' in prose fiction, so these novelists write in response to and as causes of a changing intellectual and moral climate without brandishing their historical significance. Indeed, their individuality of approach is equalled only by their artistic diffidence. Goldsmith remarked of his only novel, *The Vicar of Wakefield* (1766), that 'There are an hundred faults in this Thing'; Walpole spoke of *The Castle of Otranto* (1764) as originating in a recurrent dream, and as a distraction from politics, an escape from the complications of a distasteful present, an example of automatic writing, a 'trifle' dealing with 'preternatural events', and therefore needing an apology; Beckford's *Vathek* (1786) was published without its author's permission at all, having been translated from its original French through a breach of confidence; Mackenzie's *The Man of Feeling* (1771) is described as 'a bundle of little episodes, put together without art, and of no importance on the whole'. There is more here than the familiar convention of commercially motivated disingenuousness, or the old ploy of a newly discovered manuscript. Each in its own way is moving away from the public Augustan modes towards a revelation of private imagined worlds. The paradox of all authorship was revealed in a particularly acute form by Fanny Burney when her first novel appeared: 'It is now in the power of *any* and *every* body to read what I so carefully hoarded even from my best friends, till this last month or so.'[5]

The novel hero may now be an outsider, a man of exceptional sensitivity, solving moral problems not for society but for himself, and exclusively through emotion (Harley); he may be a marginal man drawn to retirement and innocent of the world's corruption (Dr Primrose), existing uneasily within an artistic parable; he may live out of contemporary time altogether, in an exotic 'historical' metaphor of the present (Manfred); or he may be an antidote to the new sensibility, an epic exemplar of staggering arbitrary power and sheer ego in the world of medieval Islam (*Vathek*). Brooke's *The Fool of Quality* was to illustrate the perils of elevating the individual outsider from an Epicurean marginality to the status of national exemplar. Taking risks is, however, a measure of these novels' separation from the first major wave.

The absence of a theory of the novel was doubtless a factor in the proliferation in quantity and artistic variability of novels after 1765, although it is doubtful that this alone is ever the single determinant of composition. Richardson's prolixity was, in his own mind, a measure of his own commitment to authenticity and a disincentive to others. Fielding's theory of the novel as a comic epic poem in prose had served his own purposes brilliantly, but no other major writer followed his example. The simple facts of chronology suggest another reason for discontinuity. Fielding had died in 1754, Richardson in 1761, Sterne in 1768, and nine years elapsed between Smollett's penultimate novel and his last, *Humphry Clinker*, published in the year of his death (1771). The range of such idiosyncratically strong influences as these doubtless produced a generic uncertainty in their followers. One possible reason for the structural awkwardness of *The Vicar of Wakefield* is the residual influence within it of Fielding's confident satiric and parabolic techniques at a time when contrary and Richardsonian strains of sensibility were becoming a major influence. As for Sterne, it might be argued that he had never been properly understood in his own time. Regarded as wildly eccentric, his novels were inimitable. Johnson's famous judgement on *Tristram Shandy*, 'Nothing odd will do long. Tristram Shandy did not last',[6] was true for its time, if not for its critical future, and if we look at the subsequent generation of novels themselves we can see that in both theme and form they defy any claim to neat chronological development: the sentimentalism of Goldsmith's novel (1766) is as close to the sensibility of *The Man of Feeling* (1771) as both are distant from the exotic horrors of *The Castle of Otranto* (1764) and *Vathek* (1786), and each is distinct again from the social comedy of *Evelina* (1778).

By the 1780s, if we can take Clara Reeve's remarks as representative, there was a reaction against the immodesty of realistic fiction, and particularly against its depiction of women, which drew both writers and readers away from Defoe, Fielding, and Smollett, back to the romance tradition as a more appropriate vehicle for moral education. If anything, Reeve's claim comes twenty years after the event. In 1764 Walpole had clearly stated his own frustration with the imaginative strait-jacket of realism and wrote in defiance of his age's rationalism. Reeve's own Gothic novels were written to show that Walpole's

Gothic story had gone too far from reasonable probability. She also accounted for the decline of the novel by blaming the institution of the circulating library, cheaper book prices, and the 'swarm of imitators'.[7]

Finally, we must also reckon with the continuing low esteem of the novel as a species of literature inferior to its literary cousins, history, poetry, travel literature, popular journalism, and the sermon. In 1750 Johnson had remarked that novels were written for the intellectually inert, 'chiefly to the young, the ignorant, and the idle. . . . They are the entertainments of minds unfurnished with ideas . . . not fixed by principles . . . not informed by experience'.[8] In her corrective satire of the excesses of Gothic fiction, *Northanger Abbey* (written in the last decade of the century), Jane Austen both confirmed and rejected Johnson's criticism by a careful discrimination between irresponsible and responsible novels, and between popular taste and critical dogma. She referred to the reviewers who 'abuse such effusions of fancy at their leisure, and over every new novel . . . talk in threadbare strains of the trash with which the press now groans . . . no species of composition has been so much decried'.[9] As always, the novel had taken no notice of its critics. Johnson's stern warnings against sentimental optimism in *Rasselas* (1759) was a precise diagnosis of exactly the path that some novelists were to take. Neither did novelists of the last quarter of the century (with the exception of Fanny Burney) prepare themselves to receive the professional accolade bestowed on them in Austen's definition of the novel as 'some work in which the most thorough knowledge of human nature, the happiest delineation of its varieties, the liveliest effusions of its wit and humour are conveyed to the world in the best chosen language'.

Social optimism and the self: Brooke and Goldsmith

The first volume of Henry Brooke's *The Fool of Quality* appeared in 1764, the fifth and final volume appearing in 1770. His long life (1703?–83) included friendship with the leading Augustan satirists, Swift and Pope, and the year of his death saw the publication of Blake's *Poetical Sketches*. This would seem to suggest that he is in some ways a 'transitional' figure. But although *The Fool of Quality* repeats many of the formal ingredients of the earlier novelists, its particular fusion of moral teaching and visionary social optimism would have

seemed anathema, even embarrassing, and certainly euphoric, to the
satirists. Addressing himself to the novel's three essential characteristics, piety, sentiment, and prolixity, John Wesley reissued the novel
in 1781 'with retrenchments', remarking that it was 'one of the most
beautiful pictures that ever was drawn in the world; the strokes are so
delicately fine, the touches so easy, natural, and affecting, that I know
not who can survey it with tearless eyes, unless he has a heart of
stone'.[10] Ostensibly, it is the story of the education of an idealized
nobleman by a surrogate father, but in large part it is a miscellany of
essays on everything from childhood superstitions to prisons, blushing,
physiognomy, benevolence, and the spiritual and economic benefits of
inland navigation, tied loosely and episodically to a Rousseauesque
theory of natural education. It clearly exhibits the new sensibility. It
is lachrymose fiction. When Mr Clinton is relating to the Countess the
loss of both children and his wife Matty through smallpox, the
exquisite pleasure of grief is elaborated:

> There is surely, my cousin, a species of pleasure in
> grief, a kind of soothing and deep delight, that arises with
> the tears which are pushed from the fountain of God in
> the soul, from the charities and sensibilities of the human
> heart divine.
>
>   True, true, my precious cousin, replied the countess,
> giving a fresh loose to her tears. O Matilda! I would I
> were with thee! – True, my cousin, I say; even now I sink
> under the weight of the sentiment of your story. (206)

The heart is elevated above the head (hence, perhaps, the meaning
of the title), and the implausibilities of romantic fiction are both
occasionally ironized and finally (even preposterously at times)
affirmed. In a sense *The Fool of Quality* is a synopsis of the novel's
development thus far. Its overwhelmingly didactic and overtly Christian message awkwardly combines Bunyan's purpose and Richardson's
morality. Its formal incoherence is caused largely by an exhausting
repetition of the *récit*, whereby forward action (the education of Henry
Earl of Moreland) is regularly interrupted in order to permit each new
character to narrate his or her life-history (the present thus loops back
to the past). There is also an equally implausible equivalence maintained between Chance and the strong arm of Providence. Its minority
status as a novel is assured by its uncritical recycling of some novelistic
commonplaces and some familiar Augustan topoi: nature versus
nurture in the contrast between Henry and his brother Richard's
education; the corruption of the city, the 'mausoleum of dead souls
. . . full of rottenness and reeking abominations' (309) versus the

'innocence' of the country; the heroism of the heart as opposed to the heroism of martial or political prowess; the evils of self-love as opposed to the warming joys of human benevolence. Technically, also, it relies on an uneasy combination of social realism (the prison scenes, for example, as well as Mr Fielding's essay on the bottomless pit of the law (148–54), fable and emblem (as in the use of numerous biblical types such as Job, David and Jonathan, etc.), and character-types already embedded in previous English fiction. Aspects of Harry remind one of Tom Jones, Mr Fenton (Harry's exceedingly rich and wholly benevolent patron and father-substitute) reminds us of Allworthy, whereas the moral characteristics of others are merely sketched from their nomenclature in the tradition of Jonsonian 'humours' characters (Mr Meekly, like Parson Adams, our hero's guide and Christian philosopher; Fanny Goodall, whose battle with Virtue and Passion towards the end of Ch. 12 can have only one outcome; and Mr Vindex, the Thwackum-like schoolmaster who teaches morality through fear).

Although the sentimental piety of *The Fool of Quality* will not readily recommend itself to the modern reader, there is some evidence that Brooke himself tried to moderate its enthusiastic idealism. The first half of the novel, chiefly devoted to the childhood of Harry, and as such a distinctly new *subject* in the novel thus far, is framed by a dialogue between *Author* and *Friend*, a critical distancing which is unfortunately dropped as the novel proceeds. Initially, this interpolated dialogue elaborates the broad moral significance of an episode (as for example the educational value of toys, in Ch. 2, or the nature of heroism in Ch. 4, or on the 'established arbitrators of genius and litera-ture', the critics, in Ch. 6). The *Friend*, however, is allowed too few opportunities to tone down the increasingly euphoric text. When Arabella is declared innocent of Lord Stivers's murder (he had in fact tried to rape her), she is described as possessing 'a harmony and beati-tude of motion and aspect, as though she had instantly dropped from . . . heaven' (109). The *Friend* remarks, with a nice but all too infre-quent piece of self-entrapping irony:

> Your story of Clement, my friend, is truly interesting, and in some passages may be edifying also. I have only to observe that it is too long for an episode, and that the character of your heroine-milliner is constrained and unnatural; it is elevated above the fortitude and virtues of man himself, but quite out of the sight and soaring of any of her weak and silly sex. Had she been a princess – an empress – she could not have figured in your history with greater dignity. (119)

Brooke's purpose is to show, of course, that 'royalty or station was [not] necessary to Christian resignation and lowliness of temper' (119), and that neither sex has the prerogative on tender feeling. If Brooke had continued the device of the interpolated dialogue the implications of his novel's analysis of feeling would have been much clearer and less mawkish. As it is, the novel's meaning is too often reduced from enactment to the baldest doctrine. Indeed, at one stage we are invited to skip ten pages devoted to Mr Fenton's encomiastic analysis of the 'beauties and benefits' of the British constitution. No such invitation is necessary to treat similarly Mr Meekly's expositions of Christian doctrine. In such episodes all artistic considerations are subsumed under the doctrinal imperative and the novel becomes a tract, without either Bunyan's keen sense of the drama of Christian eschatology or Fielding's ironic awareness that even the well-meaning singer may distort the song by his own pomposity. Like Joseph Andrews and Tom Jones, Harry is a naive hero whose education lies in the hands of a benevolent and paternalistic tutor; also like them his intuitive moral sense is naturally benevolent and needs only the opportunity to reveal itself. Harry, like Joseph and Parson Adams, is a sensitive soul in a muscular body. He duels, fights with his fists, and kills a mad dog, in a world too often bent on exploiting the apparently weak and vulnerable. The moral core of the novel, as in the novels of Sterne and Mackenzie, consists in laying open 'the very horrible and detestable nature of Self in your soul', as Mr Clinton says to Harry:

> Self appears to us as the whole of our existence; as the
> sum-total of all in which we are interested or concerned. It
> is as a Narcissus, self-delighted, self-enamoured. It desires,
> it craves, and claims as its right, the loves, attachments,
> and respects of all mankind. But does it acquire them, my
> Harry? O never, never! Self never was beloved, never will
> be beloved, never was honourable or respectable in the eye
> of any creature. And the characters of the patriot, the
> hero, the friend, and the lover, are only so amiable, so far
> reverable, as they are supposed to have gone forth from
> the confines of self. (399)

Having learned and enacted this principle, Harry, as in all good romantic fiction, acquires a princess for a wife (of mixed African–English parentage, a point not lost in the novel's propagation of universal brotherhood), an earldom, an enormous fortune, and the adulation of his feudal dependants. The reader will anticipate, from the many clues about the Providential basis of the novel's plotting, that such extravagant rewards are only to be expected for a hero who is so extravagantly benevolent. But what the reader cannot so easily credit is the limitless optimism and the jingoistic vision which accompany it. When the novel of individual sensibility attempts to create a whole national psyche and a vision of endless commercial expansion based on *British* Christian benevolence, we have a bizarre compact of Utopian wish-fulfilment based on a naive idealism which can only flourish in the novel in a context of lost, abandoned, or temporarily fatherless children who are permitted to exercise their benevolence in a privileged environment of great wealth. Harry's bounty creates a microcosmic social pastoral. He can enjoy the banquet because he can afford to pay for it with his uncle's money. Just as the emotional landscape is reduced to only two responses, joy and grief, so the social vision is reduced to a one-eyed patriotism. Sexual relationships within the novel are, inevitably, confused and ambiguous because they threaten the adolescent world. Thus, Harry is first in love with a male blackamoor (Abenamin) and then in love with his 'sister' (Abenaide). The former is in fact merely a disguise of the latter, and the reader need have no suspicion that when male relationships in this novel are described (as they often are) in what conventionally passes for heterosexual terms Brooke is proposing something revolutionary. In this example the confusion is caused by an awkward and implausible piece of plotting, even though we see that Brooke wishes to liberate personal relationships between and within the sexes. And yet, in the episode in which Maria disguises herself as Pierre in order to enjoy Harry's company, and in deliberately taking the bullet that was meant for him (402–04), one wonders to what extent Brooke was aware of sublimating and therefore disguising sexual realities by sexual fantasies.

Essentially, *The Fool of Quality*, as all the novels in this sub-genre, exhibits an argument for mutual sympathy and tolerance, for charity and an emotional expansion of the individual universe in which the boundaries and possibilities have nothing to do with gender, birthright, social place, or culture. As such, these novels attempt a brave argument for a much-needed human compassion in a brutalizing world characterized by class, privilege, social deprivation, and the kind of institutionalized cruelty depicted by Hogarth which we would find intolerable today. In concentrating on childhood, however, the traps of sentimentality and naive idealism prove fatal. Both the naivety and the social gaucherie of *The Fool of Quality* continue to dog such novels not only because they lack the controlling and corrective ironies of Fielding and Sterne, but because however admirable their moral programme may be, without psychological probability they remain inert and merely programmatic. It is as if a way has yet to be rediscovered, in artistic terms, of unifying a socially desirable compassion normally associated with Christian teaching and a credible psychology of character beyond mere allegorical types. A novel published in 1766, one year before the reprinting of Brooke's first two volumes, almost solved this problem by making its hero a member of the clergy; but it too failed to move cleanly between allegory and realism.

A contemporary reviewer of Goldsmith's only novel set the tone for much subsequent critical difficulty when he wrote in *The Monthly Review* (1766):

> Through the whole course of our travels in the wild of romance, we were never met with any thing more difficult to characterize than the Vicar of Wakefield; a performance which contains beauties sufficient to entitle it to almost the highest applause, and defects enough to put the discerning reader out of all patience with an author capable of so strangely under-writing himself.[11]

Essentially, arguments revolve around the extent to which Goldsmith's narrative intentions synchronize with narrative control. Is the *Vicar of Wakefield* consistently or only intermittently an ironic novel?[12] Is it a sentimental romance, or a parody of romance, or both? Does its schematic balancing of idyllic happiness, great disaster, and great rewards for patient suffering make it a domestic parable of the Book of Job? To what extent is the theme of Providence an integral part of the book's moral argument, or merely an organizational device within which to contain a wide range of narrative modes: pastoral, romance, essay, dialogue, interpolated narrative, theological tract, social satire? Undoubtedly a novel of mixed modes, *The Vicar* also poses problems for the reader's role. Goldsmith has carefully provided a narrative margin, a space within which the attentive reader can enjoy both the sentimental comedy and the satire of the Vicar's folly, and in ways which are invisible to the narrator. It is a sophisticated intellectual comedy, but it is balanced uneasily between Richardsonian sentiment and Fieldingesque satire.

Towards the end of the fourth chapter Mr Burchell (in reality, Sir William Thornhill) makes a grammatical slip: his account of the benevolent Sir William Thornhill momentarily switches from the third person to the first. The narrator of the novel is Dr Charles Primrose, and although he narrates the slip he does not notice its significance. The attentive reader has been warned. Further clues, not necessarily importing anything particular at this stage, are provided by the naming of three of Primrose's children: two are taken from romance (Olivia and Sophia), and one from the Bible (Moses). The action of the novel, or rather its larger emblematic significance, will be bounded by these two 'texts'. In addition, the novel opens with a rural idyll, and with a family of but one character: 'all equally generous, credulous, simple, and inoffensive'.[13] No reader familiar with the generic history of the novel, and with *Tom Jones* in particular, can believe that Primrose's literary Eden can survive contact with the post-lapsarian world for very long. Moses sells the family horse at the fair and is immediately duped into buying a gross of tinted spectacles (green, not rose). A travelling painter does a family portrait, with Mrs Primrose as Venus, Olivia as an Amazon (that Augustan code-word for female pride and gender-crossing), Sophia as a shepherdess, the Squire as Alexander the Great, and the Vicar himself as a theological disputant. The portrait proves too big for any doorway, and is propped up in the kitchen. Exactly half-way through the novel the lurking ironies emerge to generate actual disaster: news of Olivia's abduction by Squire Thornhill arrives immediately after the Vicar's complacent eulogy on the civilized marriage modes of the English.

It is as though everything the Primrose family sees and does in the first half of the novel is to be placed by the reader within quotation marks, suggesting provisional truths, half-truths, one-eyed distortions of reality, and downright errors of foolish credulity. In each example the alert reader sees a gap between Primrose's trusting interpretation of the world and the probability of betrayal, both from within Primrose and from without (chiefly through the sophisticated and patronizing villainy of Squire Thornhill). However admirable for his high moral tone, Primrose is living neither in the real world, nor in the world of romance or theological myths. And yet Goldsmith demurs at a corrective social realism. Is it no more than a gracious complement, one wonders, that during Primrose's pursuit of the abducted Olivia he meets the real-life printer of children's books, John Newbery, 'the friend of all mankind' (91), and the man who probably bought the manuscript of *The Vicar of Wakefield* for publication? The complex implications of this incident are symptomatic: autobiography, an example of benevolence, children's fiction, and all of marginal relevance to the situation at hand. Admittedly, Primrose's errors are follies, not vices, and the snake in his garden is Imprudence rather than Pride, but one wonders whether the real source of the Vicar's anxieties lies in his own immaturity, and perhaps in Goldsmith's attraction to fairy-tale. Whatever the case may be, the reader is confused. The Vicar is both an ironized target and a morally admirable mouthpiece. The plot, not the psychological dynamics within the Vicar, will determine the outcome, and we are required only as spectators. We witness the accumulation of dangers, but we are not required to censure. The novel is therefore (like *Moll Flanders*) not consistently ironic, but ironic situations are triggered almost constantly. Mr Burchell, already revealed to the reader as 'a man whose character for every virtue was universal' (108), promises to limit the disastrous effects of Primrose's folly as soon as the villainy of his nephew is known. But why, then, does he not forestall his nephew's marriage subterfuge with the Vicar's daughter? And how can he move freely among his tenants without being once recognized? Again, the effect is that of a provisional psychology: probability is entirely subject to the machinery of an external plot. Goldsmith delays implementing Burchell's role as *Plutus ex machina*[14] until the Vicar has been re-educated in the ways of the world, and also because romances must end happily.

Olivia's 'bigamous' marriage to Squire Thornhill is the first in a chain of disasters which threaten not merely to counteract the earlier pastoral bliss but obliterate it, not merely chastening the Vicar but driving him to distraction. The thematic and structural symmetry of the Book of Job, with its sudden and disproportionate calamities, is an undeniable paradigm for the novel.[15] The problem lies in the obviousness with which it determines meanings, however, and its stranglehold on the psychology of character. Primrose is imprisoned for debt, but institutes a reformation of the inmates on the principle that the law should reward virtue as well as punish vice. He is both the exponent and (eventually) the beneficiary of this principle. Providence is at work through the agency of Jenkinson as well as Burchell, it seems, to vindicate the ways of God to Man and the Vicar to his fellow men. Remembering Parson Adams's sermon to Joseph on immoderate grief, and its aftermath when Adams is told of the loss of his own favourite son, the reader marvels either at Primrose's insouciance or at his stupidity: when his dearest daughter, Sophia, is abducted and his son imprisoned, he discourses on 'the equal dealings of providence' (161). The Vicar's response is that of Job, 'the Lord gave, and the Lord hath taken away; blessed is the name of the Lord' (Job 1.21). But unlike Job the Vicar neither curses the day he was born, nor is he the pawn in God's contest with Satan. Again, our only reaction is to defer judgement until the stylized parable has worked its way.

The symmetry of the novel mechanically underpins the moral argument: there is a group of thirteen comedic chapters before Olivia's disappearance, another group of thirteen after her disappearance, whose tone is increasingly parabolic, and both are framed by three introductory chapters and three concluding chapters. Goldsmith's chapter titles (like those in Johnson's *Rasselas*) signal a series of illustrative parables: 'Seeming calamities may be real blessings', or 'Happiness and misery rather the result of prudence than of virtue in this life', and so on. The effect is to emphasize the novel's emblematic artifice. Knowing in advance that Burchell has, in his own words (170) 'long been a disguised spectator of [Primrose's] benevolence', the reader can accept the sentimental passages and the 'tragic' episodes because neither requires psychological probability. If nothing is accidental, all must be planned, as Primrose himself points out in Ch. 31: 'Nor can I go on, without a reflection on those accidental meetings, which though they happen every day, seldom excite our surprize but upon some extraordinary occasion. To what a fortuitous concurrence do we not owe every pleasure and convenience of our lives' (177).

The final confrontation of Sir William Thornhill and Squire Thornhill has all the contrived artifice of the last scene in Gay's *The Beggar's Opera*. Olivia is returned to her parents; Thornhill has been deceived by Jenkinson into a *legal* marriage to her; and the novel ends (like all good comedies *and* the Book of Job) with marriage and financial settlements all round. The point is not the occasional incoherence of details but the pattern, not the artifice of the plot but what that artifice signifies. The Vicar remarks of his son George's sufferings: 'The greatest object in the universe, says a certain philosopher, is a good man struggling with adversity; yet there is still a greater, which is the good man that comes to relieve it' (169). The reader, of course, is free to savour the irony of the Vicar himself being the unconscious example of his own maxim. The Providential pattern moves behind and through the Vicar, and the wisdom which comes to Primrose is the wisdom that the reader is already assumed to possess. Primrose finally recognizes something which has always been true, not something new and unexpected. In this sense the novel is in the mould of Fielding's first two novels, except that the theatrical detachment of Goldsmith's narrative stance does not permit overt authorial comment, nor that intimacy between reader and narrator so crucial to preserve the comic and moral poise of *Joseph Andrews* and *Tom Jones*. In both novelists a life of high moral principle is valid only if compatible with the actualities of a fallen world, and the presiding spirit of both is comic and Providential. Irony sabotages the pretensions of the inflated ego in each, but in Goldsmith the moral framework and the parabolic detachment collide with a sentimental content and an uncontrolled emotional sympathy. His eye was on the larger pattern, not the principle of probability, and the novel has too much sentiment for satire, too little plausibility for realism, and too much realism for a moral parable.

Social pessimism and the self: Mackenzie and Graves

Mackenzie's short fragment of a novel *The Man of Feeling*, published in 1771, is historically important, a kind of handbook of sensibility which

owes something to Fielding, Richardson, Sterne (a debt which Mackenzie denied), and Goldsmith, but which also stands out from all of
its predecessors in its particular psychology of emotion. It is described
as 'a bundle of little episodes, put together without art, and of no
importance on the whole, with something of nature, and little else in
them'.[16] Even though nothing essential to our understanding of the
novel is actually missing, it is passed off as a fragmentary manuscript.
Twenty-two chapters and a conclusion are all that survive the sporting
curate's use of the manuscript as gun-wadding. The world seems to
be a callously indifferent place for fragile human emotions. It is a novel
in which the hero dies of joy, in which a dog drops dead from grief,
and in which true sensibility is revealed by the shedding of tears.
Harley is in love with Miss Walton, but his love is entirely disem-
bodied; his love is a feeling, not a principle of action. Love, when
uttered, comes in the same moment as his death, and Harley dies as
if shamed by Miss Walton's innocence and his own presumption.
Characteristically, the love poem which Harley writes is a melancholic
pastoral elegy. Its seventh stanza (115) tells of a love for which there
exists no language: 'On words it could never rely;/It reigned in the
throb of my heart,/It gleam'd in the glance of my eye', and stanza 20
indicates that Harley's desire and his future lie not on the wings of Eros
but beneath the cloak of Thanatos:

> Oh! give me the dubious light
> That gleams thro' the quivering shade;
> Oh! give me the horrors of night,
> By gloom and by silence array'd!
>
> (117)

Anything less like the exuberant sexual ironies and comic pathos of
Sterne and Fielding could hardly be imagined. Moreover, it is a novel
in which the commitment of the novelist to social realities through
satire is specifically rejected. Though acknowledged to be real enough,
social injustice, materialism, and moral corruption are no longer to be
counteracted by the moral conscience. As the pseudo-author writes:

> I have observed one ingredient, somewhat necessary in a
> man's composition towards happiness, which people of
> feeling would do well to acquire; *a certain respect for the*
> *follies of mankind*: for there are so many fools whom the
> opinion of the world entitles to regard . . . that he who
> cannot restrain his contempt or indignation at the sight,
> will be too often quarrelling with the disposal of things, to
> relish that share which is allotted to himself.
>
> (113: my emphasis)

The problem for the modern reader of *The Man of Feeling* lies in determining its tone. Harley is a passive hero, 'a child in the drama of the world', whose Primrose-like idealism is sometimes ridiculed in the novel as self-delusion and as the product of a 'romantic imagination'. On the other hand, his compassionate response to the inmates of Bedlam, for example, or his charity towards Miss Atkins and old Edwards, conventional casualties of an impassive world, is not only commended but programmatically displayed as a refinement of sensibility for which the world of 1771 is not ready: 'The world is in general selfish, interested, and unthinking, and throws the imputation of romance or melancholy on every temper more susceptible than its own' (128). Whereas Goldsmith's Vicar must learn from the world in order to go on living in it, Harley is always above its cruelty and eventually leaves it. Harley is an enfeebled romantic hero, Primrose is a member of a protected species of Augustan.

Unlike Goldsmith, Mackenzie has no over-arching parable inside which the narrative may operate: the lachrymose Harley's emotional Epicureanism is linked only tenuously to the business of actual living, his sentimentality is energized by thoughts of a lost childhood and the prospect of future reunion with his deceased mother. He sees life not, like Parson Adams, through the spectacles of books, but inside the framework of art. The scene of his meeting with old Edwards (85) is recomposed as a painting by Salvator Rosa, and its natural scenery is made up of 'wildness' and 'fantastic shrub-wood'. Fifty years before, Defoe had found the mountainous landscape of the English Lake District full of 'inhospitable terror . . . all barren and wild, of no use or advantage either to man or beast'.[17] In 1739 Thomas Gray was searching out the thrills of such a landscape, finding in the Grande Chartreuse 'the most romantic and the most astonishing scenes I ever beheld . . . not a precipice, not a torrent, not a cliff, but is pregnant with religion and poetry'.[18] Edmund Burke had generated a whole aesthetic theory based on ideas of pain and terror in his *Philosophical Inquiry into the origin of our Ideas of the Sublime and Beautiful* (1757–59), and well before Mackenzie's novel appeared poets had turned for inspiration to the graveyard and the wilderness for their objective correlatives.[19] If there is more significance in this novel than the slight and unoriginal plot would appear to sustain, it is because Mackenzie is capitalizing on this new taste. He encodes feelings rather than explains them in a series of affective sentimental tableaux. Midway through old Edwards's tale of distress he pauses for breath: 'He eyed Harley's face; it was bathed in tears: the story was grown familiar to himself; he dropped one tear and no more' (89).

Harley's sensibility, his 'moral weeping', is more than a matter of shedding tears, more than a crude feminization of standard male insouci-

ance. In 1755 an anonymous but representative statement on this shift
in sensibility was published in a periodical aptly entitled *Man*:

> Moral weeping is the sign of so noble a passion, that it
> may be questioned whether those are properly men, who
> never weep upon any occasion. They may pretend to be as
> heroical as they please, and pride themselves in a stoical
> insensibility; but this will never pass for virtue with the
> true judges of human nature. What can be more nobly
> human than to have a tender sentimental feeling of our
> own and others' misfortunes? This degree of sensibility
> every man ought to wish to have for his own sake, as it
> disposes him to, and renders him more capable of
> practising all the virtues that promote his own welfare and
> happiness.[20]

Except for Harley's death, which comes in the same moment as
confirmation of Miss Walton's love for him, thus making his reward
of empathic benevolence somewhat short-lived, this comment accurately foreshadows Mackenzie's moral scheme for *The Man of Feeling*.
Harley is like a man without skin, his moral conscience is constantly
abraded by the world, and he thus lives only briefly and in a series of
intense moments. If satire of the world's ways is a species of wasted
pride, then the only alternative seems to be an emotional élitism
purified by retreat: 'the feelings are not yet lost that applaud benevolence, and censure inhumanity. Let us endeavour to strengthen them
in ourselves; and we, who have lived sequestered from the noise of the
multitude, have better opportunities of listening undisturbed to their
voice' (104).

Like the novel itself, true sensibility is a minor fragment of the
human psyche, rubbed, chipped, broken by exposure to a callous
world. Sensibility becomes a secular religion. Robert Burns called *The
Man of Feeling* 'a book I prize next to the Bible', as Byron was similarly
to estimate Beckford's *Vathek*. For a less enraptured view, we should
turn to Jane Austen's satire of the Man of Feeling in *Sanditon* (a fragment
unpublished in her lifetime), which shows that Mackenzie's appeal to
'affections deeper than mere argument or moral reasoning'[21] was an
evasion of moral responsibilities. As the enervated Harley slips away
at the close of the novel it is a question as to whether his mind is more
on heaven than on childhood: 'My mind expands at the thought I shall
enter into the society of the blessed, wise as angels, with the simplicity
of children' (128). Sterne's *fille de chambre* has undergone a final apotheosis. The prevailing tone of *The Man of Feeling* is elegiac, not affirm-
ative, its fragmentary form is blamed on the world's barbarity, not a

triumph of the will and of Eros over an intransigent reality.

Before Sterne and Mackenzie the minor novelists exploited a wide range of fictional categories, the memoir, secret history and scandal chronicle, the moralizing romance, and various uses of the epistolary form. In the period after 1771 the frequency of sentimental fiction and imitations of the major novelists bespeak an authorship bent on exploiting a book-buying public characterized by a taste for intertextual repetition and a narrowing emotional range. Titles of novels signal a preferred subject and a particular obsession among readers, especially among the patrons of the circulating library. As the bookseller in *The Adventures of a Bank-Note* (1770–71) by Thomas Bridges remarks, 'A crying volume . . . brings me more money in six months than a heavy merry thing will do in six years' (III, 5). From the enormous output of such lachrymose fiction we might notice (if not actually read): Pierre Treyssac de Vergy's *The Palinode: Or, the Triumph of Virtue and Love* (1771); the anonymous *Feelings of the Heart: Or, the History of a Country-Girl* (1772); one of the novels sought out by Lydia in *The Rivals*, Murdoch's translation of d'Arnaud's *The Tears of Sensibility* (1773); Henry Brooke's *Juliet Grenville: Or, the History of the Human Heart* (1774); Alexander Bicknell's *The Benevolent Man: Or, the History of Mr Belville* (1775: an imitation of *Clarissa*); Samuel Jackson Pratt ('Courtney Melmoth'), *Travels for the Heart* (1777: an imitation of Sterne's *Sentimental Journey*); and Mrs Adela Burke's *Ela: Or, the Delusions of the Heart* (1787).

Henry Mackenzie's second novel, *The Man of the World* (1773), clearly illustrates both the narrowing emotional field of the sentimental genre, and its frequently enervated impatience with conventions of form and probabilities of plotting. It includes tableaux of a tearful father parting with son and daughter, family ruin, death-bed repentance, scenes of wild grief, natural desolation, nostalgic memories of dead mothers and lost childhood, and a repetition of the commonplace opposition between idylls of rural retirement and dehumanized urban corruption. Its essential characteristics of plotting reach back to Richardson: a female innocent is assailed by a predatory aristocrat; and to Fielding's use of secret births, kidnapped babies, and sudden reunions. Sir Thomas Sindall, like Lovelace, is the spoilt child of an over-indulgent mother. He corrupts Harriet Annesley's brother as a prelude to abducting, imprisoning, drugging, and raping Harriet herself. Part II begins to repeat Part I in that Sindall attempts to seduce the 'orphan' Lucy Sindall (in reality his own illegitimate daughter by the deceased Harriet). Actual incest and complete literary repetition are prevented by the fortuitous reappearance of Harriet's brother (who has not returned from the dead but from a sojourn among the noble savages, in this case the Cherokee Indians). Mackenzie also repeats his own previous fiction. The most obvious example is the reappearance from *The Man of Feeling* of Miss Walton, now the custodian and next inhabitant of Harley's tomb, 'in whose bosom resided every gentle excellence that adorns humanity' (II, 48).[22] Mackenzie's apologetic motive for indulging in this episode of moral iconography is as follows: 'The reader will pardon the digression I have made; I would not, willingly, lead him [*sic*] out of his way, except into some path, where his feelings may be expanded, and his heart improved' (II, 54). Underlying the whole novel, but remaining inchoate, there is the theme of Shakespeare's last plays, i.e. the reparation of parental sins by their children. Mackenzie's title-page contains the motto from Horace, *Virginibus Puerisque Cano*.

The logic of Mackenzie's novel, and of the sentimental novel in general, does not depend on a complex psychology which determines action, but on the public exhibition of simple dichotomies between innocence and corruption, virtue and vice, naivety and hypocrisy, benevolence and malice. It depends least of all on an original plot. Moreover, the narrative which connects the moments of sentimental pageantry is often, as it is in *The Fool of Quality*, flat, mechanical, or homiletic. Mackenzie's narrator disarmingly remarks at one point: 'I am not in a disposition to stop in the midst of this part of my recital, solicitous to embellish, or studious to arrange it. My readers shall receive it simple, as becomes a tale of sorrow, and I flatter myself, they are at this moment, readier to feel than to judge it' (I, 316). The reader, accordingly, is instructed that artlessness means authenticity, and that fictional shaping would mean a contamination of genuine feeling. But the reader is also prevented from using his own critical intelligence. No secret of the plot is sustained for very long because Mackenzie cannot resist letting the motivational cat out of the narrative bag. For example, in I, 18, Harriet mistakes gratitude for love of Sir Thomas Sindall. He has rescued her brother from his life of debauchery, although she is unaware that he has also been the direct cause of it:

> At sight of him, her cheek was flushed with the
> mingled glow of shame for her brother, and gratitude
> towards his benefactor. He advanced to salute her; when,
> with the tears starting into her eyes, she fell on her knees
> before him, and poured forth a prayer of blessings on his
> head. There could not perhaps be a figure more lovely, or
> more striking, than that which she then exhibited. The
> lustre of her eyes, heightened by those tears with which
> the overflowing of her heart supplied them; the glow of
> her complexion, animated with the suffusion of tenderness
> and gratitude; these, joined to the easy negligence of her

dark-brown locks, that waved in ringlets on her panting bosom, made altogether such an assemblage as beauty is a word too weak for. So forcibly indeed was Sindall struck with it, that some little time past before he thought of lifting her from the ground; he looked indeed his very soul at every glance; but it was a soul unworthy of the object on which he gazed, brutal, unfeeling and inhuman; he considered her, at that moment, as already within the reach of his machinations, and feasted the grossness of his fancy with the anticipation of her undoing. (I, 188–89)

Such a passage lacks the emotional depths, the syntactic energy, and the psychological tension of similar passages in Richardson. It frames, distances, and stylizes an emotional climax, rather than rendering the immediacy of experience; its ironies are obliterated by ritualized posturing.

In 1779 Richard Graves brought to English readers Goethe's *Sorrows of Werter: A German Story* (from a French translation of the 1774 original). This classic novel of sentiment is one of the earliest examples of cross-cultural intertextuality, and although Continental fiction is not the central concern here it would be a false distinction to claim it as an exotic. In the first place, the eighteenth-century reader of novels drew no clear line between English novels and novels translated from other European languages. Peter Wagner has pointed out how quickly French erotic fiction, for example, was translated into English in the first half of the century. One of Shamela's books, Barrin's *Venus in the Cloyster; Or, the Nun in her Smock*, went through three English translations (1692, 1724, and 1745) after its publication in France (1683 and 1702); *Le Sopha*, by Crébillon fils (1742) was also published in English in 1742 and went through eighteen editions by 1801.[23] Apart from Cervantes's *Don Quixote* and French romances, Clara Reeve and James Lackington's lists of 'English' novels include authors such as Voltaire, Marmontel, Le Sage, and Marivaux. Neither is German literature a rarity in English at this tme.[24] *Werter*, a cult book in continental Europe, was regarded as a dangerous commodity to place before English readers. Graves's Preface warns the reader that he is about to encounter abnormal psychological states: 'Those who expect a novel will be disappointed in this work, which contains few characters and few events; and the design of which is to exhibit a picture of that disordered state of mind, too common in our own country' (v). Such a comment would not be misdirected against the novels of Mackenzie or Beckford, and indeed Goethe's novel closely parallels *The Man of Feeling*, steering European taste into the deeper reaches of the individual personality. Like Harley, Werter is an emotional isolate, prone to interpret the world around him in terms of literary or pictorial art. As Harley's sensibility is 'framed' by the paintings of Salvator Rosa, so the imagination and passion of Werter are triggered and objectified by Lessing's *Emilia Galotti*, Goldsmith's *The Vicar of Wakefield*, the poetry of Klopstock, and the poetical prose of James Macpherson. His consuming, obsessional, and (like Harley) 'pure' love for Lotte is communicated by their common enthusiasm for the misty, romantic, and epic melancholy of the Ossian poems (forgeries of ancient Gaelic poetry published by Macpherson in *Fingal: An Ancient Epic Poem in Six Books*, 1762). Towards the end of the novel Werter's reading of his own translation of Ossian to Charlotte is the sole vehicle of their emotional transaction. In Letter xiv (Vol. ii, 75), he rails against the emotional inadequacies of language itself:

> I could tear open my bosom, I could beat my head against
> the wall, when I see how difficult it is to communicate
> our ideas, our sensations to others; to make them enter
> intirely into our feelings. I cannot receive from another the
> love, the joy, the warmth, the pleasure, that I do not
> naturally possess; nor with a heart glowing with the most
> lively affection, can I make the happiness of one in whom
> the same warmth and energy are not inherent.

Unlike Harley, Werter combines melancholy with an anti-bourgeois anger. He is hostile to all notions of social decorum, to bourgeois materialism, to the ordinary reliability of Charlotte's husband, Albert, and to the Prince who employs him: 'The Prince has some taste for the arts, and would have more if it was not cramped by cold rules and technical terms. I often lose all patience, when with a glowing imagination I am giving to art and nature the most lively expression, and he stops me with learned criticisms, upon which he highly values himself' (ii, 53–54). Charlotte points out that Werter's participation in life is too intense, and his emotional extremism eventually leads to suicide. Whereas Mackenzie separated and polarized benevolence (*The Man of Feeling*) and vice (*The Man of the World*), Goethe's novel contains epiphanies both of moral bliss and of a despairing personal waste land. Literature and landscape are the objective correlatives for both emotional states. Of Charlotte's devoted but dull businessman-husband, Werter remarks:

> Albert was not made for her: he wants a certain
> sensibility; he wants – in short their hearts do not beat in
> unison. Ah! my dear friend, how often in reading an
> interesting passage, where my heart and Charlotte's

> seemed to meet; and where our sentiments were unfolded
> by the story and situation of a fictitious character, how
> often have I seen and felt, that we were made to
> understand each other? (II, 56)

In theme and form the novel of sentiment establishes its opposition to the bourgeois world and its preferred kind of novel in absolute terms. There is now a new landscape for the emotions. When Werter describes his emotional crisis he encodes his disillusion in a shift from the classical world to the imagined world of tempestuous romantic epic:

> Ossian has taken the place of Homer in my heart and
> imagination. To what a world does the illustrious bard
> carry me! To wander in heaths and wilds, surrounded by
> impetuous whirlwinds, in which, by the feeble light of the
> moon, we discover the spirits of our ancestors; – to hear
> from the top of the mountains, amidst the roaring of the
> waters, their plaintive sounds issuing from deep caverns,
> and the sorrowful lamentations of a maiden who sighs and
> dies on the mossy tomb of the warrior by whom she was
> adored! (Letter LXI, II, 68)

Taken out of context, it would be difficult to know whether such a passage comes from either a novel of sensibility or a Gothic romance. But as a whole text *Werter* shares the formal characteristics of the English novel of sensibility: like Mackenzie and Sterne's fragmentary novels, it begins and ends abruptly; its syntax is sometimes inchoate; like *The Man of Feeling* it requires an 'editor' to complete the tragic narrative, as if to convey in formal terms the inadequacy of conventional means of containing new and fragile emotional experience; and its overriding thematic concern is with a barely expressible individual passion in opposition to the constraints of an emotionally illiterate and materialistic society. Convention is the enemy. If the individual is socially alienated, a confessional art form is the only liberator apart from death itself. As Werter sardonically remarks, 'We cultured ones – cultured until there is nothing left!'[25] In the earlier novels of Defoe, Richardson, and Fielding, there is a constant tension between the assertion of individualism and the necessary constraints of bourgeois society. The individual is of primary importance, but social duties are his or her context of self-definition. The choice lies between accommodation or opposition: anarchy is never an option. But in later fiction bourgeois social norms are ignored or transcended as inimical to the realization of the self. Harley's death, Werter's suicide, Manfred's feudal tyranny, and Vathek's massive hubris suggest a new kind of heroic individualism which is asocial, anti-social, and ultimately self-destructive. Whereas Moll, Pamela, and Tom Jones evolve socialized selves in order to go on living in established society, their later counterparts (like Clarissa and Werter) may sacrifice everything to the realization of their own integrity. Society and the self are radically opposed.

Gothic transformations: Walpole and Beckford

Fielding and Smollett's use of the Cervantic romance for satire did not exhaust the potential of the romance as a narrative mode. As we have seen, Mackenzie had rehabilitated the term 'romantic' and turned it from a synonym for exaggerated and unrealistic fictionality into a code-word for the genuinely sympathetic. Without risking Mackenzie's preciosity, Clara Reeve saw in the tradition of romance a chance for rescuing the novel from the embarrassments of realism:

> Notwithstanding the absurdities of the old Romance, it seems calculated to produce more favorable effects on the morals of mankind than our modern Novels. If the former did not represent men as they really are, it presented them better. Its heroes were patterns of courage, truth, generosity, humanity, and the most exalted virtues, – its heroines were distinguished for modesty, delicacy, and the utmost dignity of manners. The latter represent mankind too much what they really are, and paint such scenes of pleasure and vice as are unworthy to see the light, and thus in a manner hackney youth in the ways of wickedness before they are well entered into the world; they expose the fair sex in the most wanton and shameless manner to the eyes of the whole world, by stripping them of that modest reserve, which is the foundation of grace and dignity, the veil which nature intended to protect them from too familiar an eye, in order to be at once the greatest incitement to love, and the greatest security to virtue.[26]

Thirteen years later she was to follow the example of Walpole's *Castle of Otranto* in *The Champion of Virtue, a Gothic Story* (1777), written 'upon the same plan, with a design to unite the most attractive and interesting circumstances of the ancient Romance and modern Novel'.[27] When this novel was reissued in 1778 as *The Old English Baron* it was dedicated to Samuel Richardson's daughter. Horace Walpole, by contrast, had no such didactic intentions. In the Preface to the second edition of his novel he wrote that 'It was an attempt to blend two kinds of romance, the ancient and the modern. In the former all was imagination and improbability: in the latter, nature is always intended to be, and sometimes has been, copied with success. Invention has not been wanting; but the great resources of fancy have been dammed up, by a strict adherence to common life.'[28] The first edition of the novel had nevertheless adopted the ancient ruse of a 'real' discovered manuscript, in this case a pseudonymous translation from the original Italian, found in the library of an ancient Catholic family in the north of England, and printed in black letter in 1529. The new is thus passed off as the very old, and at a stroke Walpole triggered every contemporary Protestant's instinct for authentic mystery from the dark age of medieval Catholic superstition and violence. In what is perhaps the classic Gothic horror novel, Matthew Lewis's *The Monk* (1796), the epigraph similarly hints at the timeless origins of the narrative: it cites the lines from Horace's *Epistles*, II, ii, 208–09, and offers a synopsis of the Gothic novel's ingredients:

> Dreams, magic terrors, spells of mighty power,
> Witches, and ghosts who rove at midnight hour.

Walpole's novel was a major stimulus to, if not the prime cause of, a new genre, and overtly written against what Walpole took to be the prevailing taste in prose fiction: 'I have not written the book for the present age, which will endure nothing but *cold common sense* . . . I have composed it in defiance of rules, critics, and of philosophers; and it seems to me just so much better for that reason.'[29] Its fictional elements (*unlike* those of Clara Reeve, and of course Mrs Radcliffe's novels, as well as Jane Austen's *Northanger Abbey*) celebrate *inexplicable* mysteries and supernatural causation in a way quite alien to the Providential plots of Defoe, Fielding, and Goldsmith. Its 'Gothic' mechanics include a portrait which comes to life, secret passages and concealed trapdoors, *Hamlet*-like ghosts, giants in armour, a bleeding statue, an enchanted castle, a speaking skeleton, the clanking of armour, thunder and lightning, and a vague toying with the theme of incest. *The Castle of Otranto* does for the novel what the graveyard poets had done for poetry: each begins a new phase in the sociology of the imagination. Walpole's windows are Gothic, not Palladian, but the architecture is as yet only skin-deep: what we see is a decorative pilaster, not yet a supporting pillar.

The Castle of Otranto is the story of the usurper, Manfred, Prince of Otranto, whose private guilt and insecurity are suddenly sparked into a fierce and feudal arbitrary tyranny by the melodramatic death of his second heir, Conrad, who is crushed to death on the eve of his marriage to Isabella by a gigantic helmet. Manfred's desperate need for an heir leads him to plot divorce from his wife Hippolita and pursue Isabella. The latter escapes with the help of a young peasant, eventually identified as Theodore, the long-lost son of Father Jerome, who in turn is revealed as the grandson and legitimate heir of Alfonso the Good. Manfred's usurpation drives him to murder his daughter Matilda in the mistaken belief that she is Hippolita, the barrier to his plan to unite the competing dynastic claims of Isabella's father, Frederic, with his own family. Manfred abdicates and, with Hippolita, retires to a religious order. When he has recovered from his grief at the death of Matilda, the rightful heir to Otranto, Theodore, will marry Isabella. Although the action of the novel occupies less than three days, the springs of its human plot lie hidden several generations in the past. This necessitates retrospective explanations from Manfred (59, 64–66) and from Jerome (109–10), which provide genealogical history but which do not explain away the supernatural horrors of the narrative present. The novel's frequent, indeed pervasive allusions to Shakespeare's tragedies (*Hamlet, Macbeth, Julius Caesar, Cymbeline,* and *Romeo and Juliet*) reveal the models and literary precedent for Walpole's imagination. The garrulous maid Bianca provides a comic chorus to the Gothic mystery and terror, and she clearly descends from the nurse in *Romeo and Juliet*. The Shakespearean allusions also suggest a theatrical structure in the novel, its five chapters and its time-scheme roughly corresponding to the 'probability' theory of the Unities.

Beneath its Gothic crenellations, however, there lurk the plain lineaments of a conventional fiction. The exotic is built on a series of imaginative transformations of the realistic bourgeois novel. For Walpole's theme of an innocent virgin imprisoned by a patriarchal and feudal materialism, precedent existed in *Pamela* and *Clarissa*. Indeed, it is Hippolita herself who says that 'It is not ours to make election for ourselves; heaven, our fathers, and our husbands, must decide for us' (88) The imprisoning houses of Mr B and Lovelace are metamorphosed into a real medieval castle; tyrannical parents have become feudal princes; family secrets have become real skeletons in the cupboard; arguments in letters materialize into actual duels; contemporary England and the uncivilized barbarities of the Augustan metropolis have become the threatening precincts and tenebral cavities of a late medieval Italian fortress; a Providential universe has been translated into a world of dynastic feuding and historical determinism. It is tempting, of course, to draw the obvious analogy between the Gothic confectionery of Walpole's Strawberry Hill, the house in which

[handwritten margin note: A parody of contemporary moral standards.]

he wrote the novel, and the plain Georgian villa which it concealed. Both the house and the novel were hypostatized products of his imagination, and both were a matter of surfaces. Walpole's novel betrays no psychological interest: the plot is pre-eminent. This provides, paradoxically, an imaginative strength which Clara Reeve, among others, misunderstood. Since there is no rational explanation for the gigantic helmet, the speaking portrait, the portentous plumes, and so on, the novel's *frissons* are repeatable. Reading to the end of the book will not 'explain' everything. Reasonable explanations are fatal to the genre of Gothic fiction, which reassures the reader that mystery remains, that the Enlightenment still contained corners of impenetrable darkness, and that the imagination will always be the master of reason. Walpole's decision to leave the inexplicable unexplained was a stroke of fictional genius.

Theodore (as his name implies) is the one character in the book untouched by guilt, fear, and superstition. In the caves he 'had no apprehension that good men were abandoned without cause to the malice of the powers of darkness. He thought the place more likely to be infested with robbers, than by those infernal agents who are reported to molest and bewilder travellers' (72). This is the mark of Walpole's transitional status, since even such a minority confidence in the rational norms is soon to disappear in the later examples of Gothic fiction, nowhere more unnervingly than in Lewis's *The Monk*. In 1764 Walpole's gratuitous injection of anxiety and apprehension into the fictional diet of the contemporary reader was unprecedented, a quantum leap away from the authorially controlled vicarious experience common to all fiction. The fact that Walpole set his novel in late-medieval Italy rather than contemporary England suggests that history could be used as an escape from social realities and exploited as the imaginative repository of fantasy. But in shifting the reader's interest from character to setting, from the known to the inexplicable, and from present to past, Walpole also sacrificed a wide range of psychological necessities. In spite of its horrors there is an odd kind of chastity in Walpole's novel. There is no sensuous or sensual perspective, and the reader is reduced to an observer, not a participant. Walpole toys with the powerful, dominating will of Manfred, and deploys the sentimentalist's conviction that, in the end, justice will triumph. For all its dream-like and synthetic darkness, *The Castle of Otranto* says infinitely less about man's irrationality and cruelty than Fielding's *Amelia*. *Northanger Abbey* was to show that ordinary irrationality could be just as vexing in a brightly lit English country house.

Like Johnson's *Rasselas* and Goldsmith's *Citizen of the World*, Beckford's *Vathek* belongs to the genre of the oriental tale. But its generic similarity stops there. Johnson's *Rasselas* in particular is a philosophical essay on the vanity of human wishes, heavily didactic and almost incidentally novelistic. His characters are no more than pegs on which to hang an argument which is already displayed in the opening sentence, an anticipatory recapitulation which removes all suspense at a single stroke: 'Ye who listen with credulity to the whispers of fancy, and persue with eagerness the phantoms of hope; who expect that age will perform the promises of youth, and that the deficiencies of the present day will be supplied by the morrow; attend to the history of Rasselas prince of Abissinia.' Beckford reverses Johnson's emphasis, gives absolute priority to the historical and imaginative creation of his Muslim prince, and tacks on the moral conclusion almost as an afterthought:

> Such was, and such should be, the punishment of unrestrained passions and atrocious deeds! Such shall be the chastisement of that blind curiosity, which would transgress those bounds the wisdom of the Creator has prescribed to human knowledge; and such the dreadful disappointment of that restless ambition, which, aiming at discoveries reserved for beings of a supernatural order, perceives not, through its infatuated pride, that the condition of man upon earth is to be – humble and ignorant.[30]

Allowing for the difference between Johnson's stately prose rhythms and this somewhat perfunctory and conventional piety, the two books reach similar conclusions. If only by implication, Johnson included imaginative fiction *per se* in his list of intellectual delusions. Beckford's *Vathek*, by contrast, celebrates the rococo imaginings of the mind with a virtuoso delight in the magic of words. Like Walpole, Beckford hypostatized his imagination into a novel and into a building, but in both cases his achievements dwarfed Walpole's attempts. Fonthill Abbey had a spire (constructed of wood and plaster, initially, it is true) higher than that of Salisbury Cathedral, whereas Walpole's Gothic tracery was made from cardboard. *Vathek* is a warning against hubris, but it is the hubris that attracts and energizes the narrative, not the trite moral of Vathek's inevitable failure. The hero is a Faustus figure set in the context of medieval Islam, who turns from massive self-indulgence of the flesh to the lusts of the spirit. Carathis, Vathek's mother, drives him onward to acquire the throne and the riches of the pre-Adamite kings through a landscape populated by the bizarre and the grotesque – a gigantic *giaour*, female Negroes, mutes, mummies, abominable drugs, dwarfs, eunuchs, human sacrificial pyres, tigers, devils, serpents, secret passages, and oracular fish. As a plaything of the gods, Vathek's progress is accompanied by streaks of sardonic commentary which ironize the hero's presumption until the final descent into a hell of 'unabating anguish' in the 'very entrails of the earth, where breathes the sansar, or the icy wind of death' (253). Nothing in the previous history of the English novel, except the allegorical visions of Bunyan, prepared Beckford's English readers for such voluptuous writing. The chief resources of Beckford's tale were Galland's French translation of *The Thousand and One Nights* (1704–12), the Koran, oriental tales, and dictionaries. Its immediate predecessors were also French, Voltaire's *Contes Philosophiques*, Montesquieu's *Lettres Persanes*, and although Beckford's story is original his translator, Samuel Henley, provided a somewhat obtuse battery of footnotes, deconstructing the fantastic into literary precedents by referring the reader to French and Arab sources, to the poetry of Akenside and Milton, Aeschylus, collections of voyages and travels, the Koran, *Arabian Nights*, Lucretius, Plutarch, the Psalms, Pliny, histories of the Ottoman Empire, Xenophon, Virgil's *Aeneid, Don Quixote*, Ariosto, Shakespeare, and Spenser. *Vathek* is an image of Beckford's own gargantuan appetite for knowledge, an exotic token of an esoteric hobby-horse, but it also includes an undercutting facetiousness. For all its extraordinary megalomania, there is an occasional irony revealing a rationalist's scepticism:

> [Vathek] then descended from the litter with Nouronihar. They sauntered together in the meadow; and amused themselves with culling flowers, and passing a thousand pleasantries on each other. But the bees, who were staunch Mussulmans, thinking it their duty to revenge the insult offered to their dear masters the santons, assembled so zealously to do it with good effect, that the Caliph and Nouronihar were glad to find their tents prepared to receive them. (238)

Two pages later, wry comedy turns to the psychology of guilt:

> Vathek and Nouronihar turned pale in their litter; and regarding each other with haggard looks, reproached themselves – the one with a thousand of the blackest crimes, a thousand projects of impious ambition; the other with the desolation of her family, and the perdition of the amiable Gulchenrouz. Nouronihar persuaded herself that she heard, in the fatal music, the groans of her dying father; and Vathek, the sobs of the fifty children he had sacrificed to the Giaour. (240–41)

Like Faustus pleading with Mephistopheles, Vathek pleads with the Giaour for mercy, and among Vathek's catalogue of 'sins' there is pride, avarice, curiosity, and the love of women. Vathek's love for Nouronihar turns to loathing, Carathis curses the day she was born and her heart becomes 'a receptacle of eternal fire' (254). *Vathek*'s social irrelevance is directly proportionate to its imaginative power, drawing its resources not from realism but from pathology.

The self socialized: Fanny Burney

Fanny Burney's first novel is her best. It is also the first novel by a woman to challenge the artistic pre-eminence of Richardson and Fielding in the eighteenth century. *Evelina* was published three years after de Sade's *Justine* and one year before the French Revolution: neither convulsions in the European body politic nor revolutions in fiction played the slightest part in her novel. *Evelina* is incontestably the first novel exclusively concerned with social manners, written from within the orthodox social proprieties and not from outside. Fanny Burney affirms the social status quo and affirms the guardianship of social and moral codes as the prerogative of a patriarchal social system, to which the aspiring woman must accommodate herself. Nor is there in her novels the slightest interest (as there is in Beckford, Walpole, and Sterne) in the use of fiction to create autonomous, fantastic, or imagined worlds, or minutely individualized psychological states. For Burney the previous history of the novel offered the potential for using fiction as the public vehicle of moral education. Her Preface to *Evelina* shows an intention to rehabilitate the form by using the models provided by Rousseau's *Eloise*, Johnson's *Rasselas*, Marivaux's *Marianne* and, in an unequal proportion, the examples of Fielding, Richardson, and Smollett. More particularly, Burney continues the Richardsonian campaign to reform the reading habits of women who indulged themselves in the 'fantastic regions of Romance', described as a 'distemper' spread by the kind of novels read by 'our young ladies in general, and boarding-school damsels in particular'.[31]

Evelina also borrows the Richardsonian variant of the epistolary novel and some elements of *Grandison*'s moral scheme. What is missing is Richardson's profound social criticism of sexual politics and the internalized dramatic conflict between social pressures and individual integrity. Like Emily and Harriet in *Grandison* Evelina is an *ingénue* who moves from the parochial shelter of country life to the public and private temptations of the city, there to confront and eventually choose between the rake (Sir Clement Willoughby and Lord Merton in *Evelina*, Sir Hargrave Pollexfen in *Grandison*) and the ideal husband (Lord Orville in *Evelina* is a type of the male paragon as much as Grandison and Mr Knightley in Jane Austen's *Emma*). The novels of Fielding may have provided Burney with the confidence to depict a social panorama within a firm concept of social place, together with a patrician confidence with which to ridicule the *nouveau riche* snobberies and social gaucheries of the Branghtons (Evelina's cousins) – bourgeois shopkeepers by trade and mentality.

Evelina is neither the victim like Pamela of would-be rapists, nor is she actually seduced like Clarissa. The momentous and eventually tragic anguish of Clarissa is here turned to a series of social embarrassments and a steady accumulation of moral wisdom protected from real danger by a comic tone and a morally responsible patriarchy. Whereas Richardson had exposed the institutionalized sexual and moral hypocrisies of a materialistic society in relation to the position of women, Burney's social and sexual vision remains conservative and static. Though central in the novel, her heroines happily embrace marginality within marriage. As for her debt to Smollett, there is sometimes an awkward and gratuitous liking for grotesque comic types, as in the surrealistic pageant of types who cavort before Harrel's suicide in her second novel, *Cecilia* (1782), and in the figure of Captain Mirvan, the coarse but honest practical joker who injects a farcical comedy of tone and incident in *Evelina*. The latter's clowning is a world apart from Smollett's fiercely subversive social satire. Just as Burney writes as a social insider rather than a social outsider, so her novel's heroine is a natural member of the class to which she aspires and to which she is eventually admitted. At the beginning of the novel Evelina is *de facto* if not yet *de jure* high-born. As in *Tom Jones*, the trick of fate which has robbed Evelina of her patrimony and social position is a device which, when exposed and corrected, will underwrite the status quo. It is thus a fictional technique, not an opportunity to expose any radical social injustices.

Before the novel begins, Evelina's father (Sir John Belmont) has deserted his wife, disowned Evelina, destroyed the marriage certificate, and recognized Polly Green as his daughter (she is in fact the child of Evelina's mother's maid). Evelina becomes the ward of the Reverend Mr Villars, who agrees to her visit to London in the company of Mrs Mirvan and her daughter. There she compiles her 'town journal', an epistolary record of her social progress and setbacks which is sent to Mr Villars. He responds to her letters with a mixture of delight at her increasing sophistication and anxiety at her unrecognized social dangers. Evelina's dilemma pivots on the love and duty theme, i.e.

'the weakness of my heart' and 'uprightness and propriety' (336). Whereas Pamela had to battle with her own naivety as well as the predatory Mr B, Evelina's strong social and moral instincts carry her through temptations without destabilizing uncertainties. She is, for example, immediately attracted to the fashionable opera, and well able to defend it against the reductive barbarianism of the Branghtons, whose bourgeois materialism she deplores. The prospect of marrying one of them would be grotesque mismatching, rendered possible only because of her (temporary) social misplacement. Evelina is constantly worrying about the impression she is making on the aristocratic Lord Orville. He is the immovable certainty against which her ambiguous social position and her wavering romantic dilemma are to be measured. Like Mr Knightley he is poised to rescue Evelina from social embarrassments or, by his very presence, compound them. Evelina's first dilemma is to choose which of two carriages to ride in, Orville's or Willoughby's (95–96), and after Willoughby's precipitate declaration of love for her she reflects on the alternatives. Attracted neither by Willoughby's title nor flattered by his hauteur, she decisively prefers the graceful ease and *sprezzatura* of a natural gentleman:

> In all ranks and all stations of life, how strangely do characters and manners differ! Lord Orville, with a politeness which knows no intermission, and makes no distinction, is as unassuming and modest, as if he had never mixed with the great, and was totally ignorant of every qualification he possesses; this other Lord, though lavish of compliments and fine speeches, seems to me an entire stranger to real good-breeding; whoever strikes his fancy, engrosses his whole attention. He is forward and bold, has an air of haughtiness towards men, and a look of libertinism towards women, and his conscious quality seems to have given him a freedom in his ways of speaking to either sex, that is very little short of rudeness. (113–14)

As in the case of *Emma*, social admiration precedes and also obscures less disinterested motives for liking. Yet Austen's interpolation of this knowing irony seems absent from Burney's passage. At the end of the second volume, Evelina is still at the stage of testing her own preferences: social *savoir-faire* and civilized poise (once achieved) provide knowledge but no engagement. Evelina's social status is the immediate problem, not her own identity. Her sexual awareness of others is, however, acute, though a matter of external judgement at this stage. Her admiration for Orville is 'as a sister': she admires his 'honour, so *feminine* delicacy, and so amiable . . . nature' (261), just as her companion, the satirical Mrs Selwyn, is described by Evelina as regrettably *'masculine'* in both mind and manners. These elisions of sexual identity are not resolved in psychological terms but by social and theatrical events. Orville expresses his love for Evelina by an appropriately romantic and, for once, an unstiffened condescension on his knees, just as Evelina drops to her knees in another sentimental tableau to beg her father's filial recognition (383). There is a report of her marriage to Lord Orville on the last page of the novel (the shortest letter in the book), but the intimacy and the sentiment are swept aside by the broad and farcical comedy of Captain Mirvan's reductive foolery. He introduces the foppish Mr Lovel to his 'twin-brother', a monkey, 'full dressed and extravagantly *à la mode*' (400), deflating phoney graces and fake-gentlemanliness in order to assert the difference between the fashionable and the real, and between intolerable social role-playing and the accepted feudal structures. Evelina's patrimony is, of course, restored, and propriety is vindicated.

Burney's middle-class boarding-school readers no doubt would have delighted in the glimpses she affords of fashionable and sophisticated London life and the manners of the aristocracy. They might also have been chastened by her cutting satire of the Branghtons and the vulgar gentility of Mr Smith. Evelina's success comes from conforming to the demands of an aristocratic manner without trading either her virtue or her moral convictions. Even to put it in such crudely materialistic terms emphasizes the delicacy and selectivity of Burney's social analysis. Her concern is for social education, for manners rather than morals, embarrassment rather than anguish. Burney's novel does not dare disturb the universe as Defoe, Richardson, and Smollett had done, and perhaps this is why the most vocal and, for Burney herself, the most gratifying praise of *Evelina* came from the leading male intellectuals in her circle (Johnson, Reynolds, Burke, as well as her father Dr Burney). All of deeply conservative convictions, they could each rejoice in the pre-structured social comedy of her writing, in the assertion of a masculine high-mindedness enacted through the mentor-father-figure Villars and the mentor-lover Lord Orville, as well as in the triumphant social vindication of the despised novel for a serious moral purpose. Evelina learns the value of prudence without the sexually compromising escapades of Tom Jones; she grows up socially without the radical individualism and amoral street wisdom of a Roxana; she has no need of Clarissa's proud demand for self-definition and, of course, runs no risk of her tragic isolation. There is no cause for social and sexual anxieties in *Evelina* because no injustice is confirmed, only a corrigible deception. Burney's social poise, together with her sharp social observation, prepares the way for that famous opening sentence of Austen's *Pride and Prejudice*. The self is socialized and the novel is now presentable in the best company.

Notes

1. Ernest A. Baker, *The History of the English Novel*, 10 vols (1924–36; reprinted New York, 1961), v, 11. Of the 1300 or more novels published in the years 1770–1800, Baker remarks: 'All we need to know is that these novels existed, and were produced in large numbers; it would be a waste of the reader's time to pay them much individual attention' (p. 13). For a survey, see J. M. S. Tompkins, *The Popular Novel in England, 1770–1800* (London, 1932), especially pp. 92–112, for a discussion of the popular novelist's highly developed awareness of the consumer's taste for the 'sweet emotion of pity', and 'the luxury of grief'.

2. Patricia Meyer Spacks, *Imagining a Self: Autobiography and Novel in Eighteenth-Century England* (Cambridge, Mass. and London, 1976), p. 158, and also pp. 158–92.

3. Although much more evidence is needed to measure the extent and the implications of this claim, it seems more likely that readers' preferences steered the novel's progress in the post-1740 period than in the period before. See D. T. Laurenson and A. Swingewood, *The Sociology of Literature* (London, 1972), pp. 184–85: 'An urban middle class simply did not exist as a cohesive and significant social class until well into the eighteenth century, some time after the publication of *Pamela, Tom Jones,* and *Clarissa.* Indeed, it may be possible to link the actual decline of the English novel after 1760 with the growth of a middle class, through its insatiable need for entertainment which resulted in the development of circulating libraries, women novelists [*sic*] and the remarkable popularity of the Gothic horror novels. Yet Ian Watt argues for a direct causal relation between the novel and the rise of a specifically middle class public consisting of wealthy shopkeepers, tradesmen, administrative and clerical workers, etc.' Lennard C. Davis, in *Factual Fictions: The Origins of the English Novel* (New York, 1983), pp. 192–93, argues similarly against Watt's assumption of a necessity and 'intentionality' in the rise of the novel.

4. For discussion of its European context, see Mario Praz, *The Romantic Agony* (1933; reprinted New York, 1960); for some definitions, see R. S. Crane, 'Suggestions Toward a Genealogy of "The Man of Feeling"', *ELH*, 1 (1934), 205–30; reprinted in *Studies in the Literature of the Augustan Age*, edited by Richard C. Boys (Ann Arbor, 1952), pp. 62–87, and in *Backgrounds to Eighteenth-Century Literature*, edited by Kathleen Williams (Scranton, Pennsylvania, 1971), pp. 322–49. For some account of parallel social and philosophical movements, see A. R. Humphreys, '"The Friend of Mankind" (1700–1760) – An Aspect of Eighteenth-Century Sensibility', *RES*, 24 (1948), 203–18.

5. Fanny Burney to her cousin, 26 March 1778: cited in *Evelina; or, The History*

of a Young Lady's Entrance into the World, edited by Edward and Lillian Bloom (Oxford, 1982), p. xv. All quotations are from this edition.

6. Boswell's *Life of Johnson,* Wednesday, 20 March 1776. For the contemporary reputation of Sterne, see Alan B. Howes, *Yorick and the Critics: Sterne's Reputation in England, 1760–1868,* Yale Studies in English, 139 (New Haven, 1958), and the same author's *Sterne: The Critical Heritage* (London, 1974).

7. Clara Reeve, *The Progress of Romance,* 2 vols (1785), II, Chapter 7.

8. *The Rambler,* no. 4 (31 March 1750).

9. *Northanger Abbey* (1818), Chapter 4. Austen here argues that critical dogma is out of step with the unofficial critical standards of the general reader. Compare Charles Jenner, *The Placid Man: or, Memoirs of Sir Charles Beville* (1770), IV, 1, for a similar complaint, and also Fanny Burney's Preface to *Evelina* (1778) and her Dedication to *The Wanderer, or Female Difficulties* (1814).

10. All quotations are taken from *The Fool of Quality; or, The History of Henry Earl of Moreland* (reprinted London, 1906, with E. A. Baker's biographical introduction and Charles Kingsley's Preface of 1859). Kingsley cites Wesley's opinion on p. liii. Wesley's edition was issued with Brooke's permission, but without the name of Brooke on either title-page or in the Preface. About a third of the original was cut out, and 'a great part of the mystic divinity as it is more philosophical than spiritual', in Wesley's words. He also remarked to a female correspondent, in relation to this novel, 'I would recommend very few novels to young persons for fear they should be too desirous of more. – The want of novels may be supplied by well chosen histories.' See F. Louis Barber, 'John Wesley Edits a Novel', *The London Quarterly and Holborn Review,* 172 (January 1946), 50–54. Kingsley's edition also made substantial cuts, including a 125-page section about adventures in Africa.

11. Quoted in Ricardo Quintana, *Oliver Goldsmith: A Georgian Study* (London, 1967), p. 100.

12. See Robert H. Hopkins, *The True Genius of Oliver Goldsmith* (Baltimore, 1969). Hopkins argues for the (minority) view that the novel shows Goldsmith is 'a master of comic satire and refined irony'.

13. *The Vicar of Wakefield,* edited by Arthur Friedman (Oxford, 1981), p. 12. All quotations are from this edition.

14. This apt phrase is used by Brian Vickers in the Introduction to his edition of Mackenzie's *The Man of Feeling* (London, 1967), p. xxi, in a detailed comparison of the similarities of sentiment and episode in both novels. See also W. F. Galloway, 'The Sentimentalism of Goldsmith', *PMLA,* 48 (1933), 167–81.

15. The most extensive treatment of this theme is Martin Battestin's chapter, 'Goldsmith: The Comedy of Job', in *The Providence of Wit,* pp. 193–214. In his '*The Vicar of Wakefield*: Goldsmith's Oriental Job', *ELH,* 46 (1979), 97–121, James H. Lehmann argues that the Job analogy is 'often invoked only to be toyed with'.

16. *The Man of Feeling,* edited by Brian Vickers (London, 1967), p. 117. All quotations are from this edition. Mackenzie wrote three novels. *The Man of the World* (1773) is the antithesis of *The Man of Feeling,* its hero being a

monster of vice (see discussion below); *Julia de Roubigné* (1777) is an epistolary novel which, in Walter Scott's words, plots 'the excess and over-indulgence of passions and feelings in themselves blameless . . . but which, encouraged to a morbid excess . . . lead to the most disastrous consequences'.

17. Defoe, *A Tour through the Whole Island of Great Britain* (1724; Everyman edition, 1928; revised edition, London, 1962; reprinted 1974), p. 269.

18. Gray to Mr West, 16 November 1739, *Gray's Poems, Letters and Essays*, Everyman edition (1912; reprinted London, 1966), pp. 101, 106.

19. See Young's *Night Thoughts* (1742–45), Blair's *The Grave* (1743), Percy's *Reliques of Ancient English Poetry* (1765); and in prose, Hervey's *Meditation among the Tombs* (1745–47) and Thomas Warton's *Pleasures of Melancholy* (1747), for examples. For a discussion of the new psychological context for such writing, see Samuel Holt Monk, *The Sublime: A Study of Critical Theories in XVIII-Century England* (1935; reprinted Ann Arbor, 1960), pp. 101–33.

20. Quoted in Crane, *op. cit.*, p. 206, note 4 above.

21. This phrase is used by Mackenzie in a series of letters (1769): see H. W. Thompson, *A Scottish Man of Feeling* (London, 1931), pp. 107–11.

22. All quotations from *The Man of the World* are from the first edition.

23. See Peter Wagner's edition of Cleland's *Fanny Hill* (Harmondsworth, 1985), pp. 8–9, 23–27, 33–34, and the same author's *Eros Revived: A Study of Erotica in Eighteenth-Century England and America* (London, 1985).

24. See *New Cambridge Bibliography of English Literature*, Volume II, *1660–1800*, edited by George Watson (Cambridge, 1971), columns 151–86 and 1537–42.

25. This remark does not appear in Graves's translation, although there are similar sentiments throughout his version. See *The Sorrows of Young Werther and Selected Writings*, translated by Catharine Hutter (New York, 1962), p. 87. All quotations are from the 1779 edition.

26. Reeve, II, 86. Reeve's words are in fact a quotation from John Gregory's *Comparative View of the State and Faculties of Man with those of the Animal World* (1766), which Reeve is using to add (male) authority to her argument.

27. Preface to *The Old English Baron*, second edition, 1778: Reeve describes her novel as 'the literary offspring' of Walpole's book, but criticizes the latter because 'the machinery is so violent that it destroys the effect it is intended to excite', as well as going beyond 'the utmost *verge* of probability'.

28. Preface to the second edition, see *The Castle of Otranto*, edited by W. S. Lewis (Oxford, 1982), p. 7.

29. Walpole to Mme du Deffand, 13 March 1767: see *The Yale Edition of Horace Walpole's Correspondence*, III, p. 260 (in French).

30. *Three Gothic Novels (The Castle of Otranto, Vathek, Frankenstein)*, edited by Peter Fairclough (London, 1968), p. 254. *Vathek* is printed on pp. 151–255: all references are to this edition.

31. *Evelina*, p. 8.

Postscript

The novel is the most natural literary form because in a
sense it has no form; it is the nearest thing to a
conversation, whether between friends or acquaintances.
. . .

Genre and convention free the writer from the whims of
his private impulses and allow him to draw on the funds
of a long tradition even if he inverts or distorts the
tradition in the process.[1]

If the first of these two comments were entirely true one would have
expected to see the novel emerge long before the early eighteenth
century, and if the second were true the early novelists would have
much more to say than they do about their antecedents. In general,
the earlier novelists discussed in this present book did not enjoy the
literary luxury of repeating forms established by their predecessors,
and spent most of their criticism on defining what their novels were
not. With the exception of the parodic *Shamela* they each write prose
fiction as if none of the other novelists existed, repeating his own
individual experiments but not following the models of contemporaries. Denying critics any role at all, each novelist appeals to the
common reader. Apart from developing different strategies for narrative fiction, each of them creates a different role for their respective
readers. Just as an author makes a contract with a publisher, so an
author is bound to postulate a certain type of reader. In both cases the
final result may turn out to be something other than originally
planned.

Defoe's contract with the reader stipulates that the prose medium
is to be regarded as transparent. We are asked to look through the
window of narration in order to see real life. To this extent Defoe
abolishes the shaping function of the imaginative artist and gives
absolute priority to an autonomous narrative ego, the autobiographical
I. His overt intention is to show the pattern in an individual life, not
the means by which fiction can shape reality. But the problem of

fictional shaping was not so easily ignored, and Defoe's rough artistry is a symptom of a thematic and artistic individualism locking horns not only with intractable social imperatives but also with the uncertain public form of the novel itself. Even a first-person confessional autobiography needs an audience. In absolute isolation Robinson Crusoe enters into transactional dialogues, either by means of his diary or through impositions of his will and needs on the sometimes cooperative and sometimes resistant island itself. God is Robinson's ultimate and far from inscrutable conversational partner. Defoe's own contract with the reader invites us to confront the harsh realities of an intractable and ruggedly inelegant reality. However morally appalling his people may be, their alienated lives may yet be regarded usefully as negative exemplars. The mysteries of Moll's moral muddle, paradoxically, create a genuine sense of individual psychological turmoil which becomes a crucial part of the reading experience. Defoe's failure to explain away Moll's moral ambiguity puts the burden of interpretation on the reader himself. Plot and meaning converge exactly at the same point, that is, when Defoe is obliged to show his social outcasts re-entering society and when Defoe's own didactic promise is to be superimposed upon the individual life-history. Defoe's art is exploratory and provisional, his difficulties associated not only with the uncertain handling of a radically new literary form but also with the permanent anguish of a disenfranchised, dynamic, and restless individualism at odds with a static social structure, a materialistic and an exacting ethic of religious imperatives which demand that an individual must represent in his or her own life the virtues of the society which surrounds them.

One thematic link between Defoe and Richardson is clear. Both are obsessed with the subject of moral and social definition of the self, and with the existential implications of loneliness. Again, Richardson's contract with the reader stipulates that there has been no authorial intervention and that what we read is an authentic individual memoir. Nothing has been invented or shaped. The reader is, as it were, given direct access to a private confession, and the only artistic principle involved is that of documentary authenticity. The reader's relationship with the text is the most intimate imaginable. We watch Pamela and Clarissa as they write words on a page in a continuous present. Richardson also writes exemplary fiction, but at least in *Clarissa* there is no urge to validate the individual self by social approval. *Clarissa* is the literary testament of opposition: it deals with the psychology of isolation. Whereas Defoe's people are outside respectable society, as criminals or rebels, Richardson's middle-class heroine writes a deeply subversive novel. Here we are asked to identify with a heroine for whom the prevailing social codes are intolerable, corrupting, and destructive of individual integrity. In Defoe's *Roxana* the harrowing guilt is entirely the heroine's, in *Clarissa* the cause of the tragedy is laid squarely at the door of the bourgeois materialism of society in conflict with its own spiritual claims. Both characters end as outsiders but Clarissa's death is a triumph, a kind of freedom, a defeat for her society. In neither Defoe's nor Richardson's work are we obliged to see characters as representing anything but themselves, but it is the prerogative of the novel to insinuate profound social themes through the lives of individuals. Its characteristic is to hint that what seems to be an individual case is nevertheless a symptom of wider public perception. In Defoe's prefaces and journalism and in Richardson's letters and prefaces we can observe this process of the individual case-history being converted into social myth. Richardson's post-*Pamela* fiction opened up vast areas of concern, and his questions about sexual politics were not fully taken up until our own time.

Fielding's novels reverse the relationship between individualism and social imperatives. If Defoe's and Richardson's stylistic claims require authorial absence and stylistic transparency, Fielding's style is the essential medium of his moral argument. Whereas Crusoe and Clarissa represent nobody but themselves, Fielding's characters are consistently seen as human representatives, types of moral being and states of mind. Everything in Fielding's novels is seen through a selective filter, often rearranging material which already exists in mythic or emblematic form. He watches us watching the stage on which his people speak their lines, unaware that they enact timeless stories. Fielding makes no pretence whatever to formal realism. His authorial presence is manipulative, ostentatious, authoritative, and definitive. His style obtrudes itself between what is taking place and the means of its description in order to determine the reader's response to its moral significance. Fielding's art both contains and controls the individual, just as comedy as a genre asserts the needful conformity of the disruptive individual to social manners and values. Whereas *Roxana* is a psychological tragedy and *Clarissa* both an actual tragedy and a Christian triumph, *Joseph Andrews* and *Tom Jones* finally assert a faith in the social status quo impervious to individual disruption. After Defoe's naturalism and Richardson's depiction of social and sexual antagonisms, Fielding's fundamental concern is with the fictional representation of moral choice. Reading Fielding successfully depends on perceiving the large and comprehensive patterns (social, emblematic, religious) which will eventually constrain and accommodate the individual. Even for the moral rejects there is an established place – Blifil is exiled to northern Methodism. Fielding's art is therefore not exploratory or oppositional, but illustrative and confirmatory. His fiction, too, is exemplary, but in a different way from that of his predecessors. *Amelia* is the single and exceptional Fielding novel which, apart from its happy ending, repeats the discovery of Defoe and Richardson that the individual is not necessarily at home in the society which has created him or her. This novel, by contrast with all the others, fails to provide a satisfactory relationship between its social horrors and its Providential moral basis, drawing a *merely* stylistic veil across its revelation of oppressive social ugliness. It goes beyond the confirmation of a consoling pattern, although not ultimately to the point where Defoe's and Richardson's perception of life as a battleground inimical to individual self-definition turns into tragic social realism.

Even *Amelia*, however, continues the examination, fundamental to all novels, of the interface between the individual and society. Sterne turns the screw and pins down the individual to a prior *self-examination* in which escape into social life is virtually impossible and in which the shaping function of fiction is revealed as what it always must be, a piece of role-playing. For Sterne literary form cannot 'contain' meaning: this is the central subject and Tristram's central error. *Tristram Shandy* sets up all the formal structures for a 'conventional' autobiography, including chapters, prefaces, books, chronology, and plots, and each proves inadequate except as a brilliant illustration of life as a continuous succession of changes. As Clarissa battles with Lovelace and Crusoe with his isolation, so Tristram battles with the act of writing down the self. Thirty-two chapters in the novel begin with the word 'I', and time after time chapters begin with the grammatical promise to move forwards from a conditional syntax to a conclusion (If, When, Though, Whether, Now, Then, But, As, And now, And so, Whilst, etc.).[2] An autobiography is an image of the self, and although Tristram has the public syntax by which to step outside the self, he is, as much as Clarissa, destined to a solipsistic fate. Sterne's novels penetrate to the very heart of literary narrative. We do not go to Sterne to find out what eighteenth-century society was like. We learn from his novels how one unique individual thought, and how wide the gap between the unique world of the individual and the public world can be.

Regarded as conversations between author and reader, the eighteenth-century novel offers a new range of relationships. The most intimate relationship is offered by Richardson. As Ian Watt puts it, Richardson 'does not analyse Clarissa, but presents a complete and detailed behavioural report on her whole being: she is defined by the fullness of our participation in her life'.[3] Defoe's characters are less articulate, and markedly unable or unwilling to analyse themselves in anything other than 'public' forms of discourse alien to or separable from their own individual beings (Sin, Rebellion, Repentance, Forgiveness). They better understand the language of Material Success and

Material Bankruptcy, and often the language of one penetrates the other. Fielding's sociable art is sufficiently public to base the reader's education on the condition that each share the other's friendship: hence the imagery of guest and host at a public ordinary at the beginning of *Tom Jones*. The condition of membership is that we are to agree on the civilized rules of common behaviour and defer to our patron's hospitality. Fielding's public hospitality also rules out (as indecorous) any access to private and intimate knowledge of individual characters. The novel is a public form and a public forum, and individual experience is admissable and authentic only in so far as it conforms to general truths. Fielding thus withholds both his approval and his narrative presence when Tom tumbles Molly Seagrim into the bushes, in the full knowledge that a mature reader has no need to be informed of the obvious, nor to have the positive, morally healthful social tone damaged by baser instincts being analysed too scrupulously.[4]

Fielding's intimacy of tone with his reader is entirely absent from the work of Smollett, the outstanding example of the satirical novelist who holds up a wilfully and negatively distorted image of life which requires neither authorial validation nor the reader's sympathy. Apart from *Humphry Clinker*, Smollett's novels are the antidote both to *politesse* and to formal considerations of meaning and form. His single-plot principle is the tyranny of a single character plundering society for his own satisfaction, and Smollett has as much need of a friendly contract with his reader as Hobbes has need of philanthropy. If Fielding establishes the ties that bind humanity together, Smollett dangles a noose in front of us all. In short, he ignores all fictional structures except that of a continuous and linear series of incidents strung together by an individual life and a satirist's rage to reveal physical and moral squalor beneath established appearance. Of all the major novelists he has least to say about the medium of his message. Smollett's prose bends under the weight of an emotional monotone and an almost purely phenomenal world. As John Barth has said of Smollett's first novel, Smollett's special organ is not the head or the heart, but the spleen: 'What hunger is to Lazarillo de Tormes and lust to Don Juan Tenorio, resentment is to Roderick Random: more than a drive; almost an organizing principle. Odysseus wants to get home; Jason, to get the Fleece; Roderick, to get even.'[5] Relative to this, Defoe's characters undergo traumatic psychological strains when their rapacious self-sufficiency collides with their need for social recognition.

The novel is neither intrinsically conservative nor intrinsically subversive, and after Sterne the novel temporarily turns away from the individual/social interaction altogether in order to investigate alienation as a theme or fictional contexts which are at least remote from the demands of social realism. It is as though the hyperdevelopment of the imagination stems from a temporary surfeit of social realism: there is now no fictional pleasure in reporting the facts of actual living in a known and accepted context. The Gothic and the sentimental novel exploit fictionality for its own sake, as if to test and assert the ability of the prose imagination to define areas of experience previously associated with the poet (or in some cases, the priest). Thus, the novels of Mackenzie and of Walpole and Beckford create substitute imagined worlds antipathetic to the moral didacticism of Richardson and Fielding, downgrading or rejecting common social values for the sake of an exquisite individualism, pushing aside dull norms in favour of marginal states of excitement or lyrical expression. This second wave of lesser novelists certainly indicates the range of experimental possibilities ignored by the Big Five, and yet as subsequent novelists were to go back over the achievements of their eighteenth-century predecessors, they were to add surprisingly little either to the moral aims or the literary methods of the first pioneers in the form. Most novels, then and now, simply expand the choice available to those who read only to occupy their leisure moments. This audience, too, was a creation of the eighteenth century, and it was to provide Jane Austen with the opportunity to establish the novel as 'some work in which the greatest powers of the mind are displayed, in which the most thorough knowledge of human nature, the happiest delineation of its varieties, the liveliest effusions of wit and humour are conveyed to the world in the best chosen language'.[6] In retrospect, Jane Austen tames the tiger of rough life which courses through the formally inelegant novels of Defoe and Smollett; she narrows the social vision of Fielding, suppresses the psychological relativities of Sterne, and marginalizes the fictional fantasies of the Gothic and sentimental novel. For her, the normal and accepted social realities – in all their irrationality and folly – were a sufficient source of human variety and fictional models.

Notes

1. Gabriel Josipovici, *The World and the Book: A Study of Modern Fiction* (London, 1971), pp. 286, 288–89.

2. See Martin Battestin, '*A Sentimental Journey* and the Syntax of Things', in *Augustan Worlds*, edited by J. C. Hilson and others (Leicester, 1978), pp. 223–39.

3. Ian Watt, *The Rise of the Novel: Studies in Defoe, Richardson and Fielding* (London, 1957), p. 272.

4. Compare the remark in Fielding's only extant literary prose manuscript, a pseudonymous letter to the editor of the Opposition organ *Common Sense* (1 April 1738): 'I am at length thoroughly convinced, that the utmost Perfection of human Wisdom is Silence; and that when a Man hath learnt to hold his Tongue, he may be properly said to have arrived at the highest Pitch of Philosophy.' See M. C. and R. R. Battestin, 'A Fielding Discovery, with some Remarks on the Canon', *SB*, 33 (1980), 131–43.

5. *The Adventures of Roderick Random*, Signet Classics edition (New York, 1964), 'Afterword', p. 473.

6. *Northanger Abbey* (written 1797–99, published 1818), Chapter 5.

Chronology

Note: Dates refer to first publication of works, whether in volume or serial form, and only short titles are given. Some minor novels and significant translations are included. An asterisk indicates novels discussed in the text.

DATE	WORKS OF FICTION	OTHER WORKS	HISTORICAL/CULTURAL EVENTS
1700	Motteux trans. Cervantes's *Don Quixote (−1703) Behn The Dumb Virgin		John Dryden d.
1701		Swift Discourse of the Contests and Dissensions in Athens and Rome	Act of Settlement establishes Protestant Succession after death of James II War of the Spanish succession
1702	Anon. The Adventures of Lindamira	Clarendon History of the Rebellion (−1704) Defoe Shortest Way with the Dissenters	Death of William III (March) Accession of Queen Anne Declaration of war on France and Spain Dampier, Voyage to New Holland
1703	Russen Iter-lunare: or a Voyage to the Moon	Defoe Hymn to the Pillory Edward Ward The London Spy (collected edn)	John Wesley b.

DATE	WORKS OF FICTION	OTHER WORKS	HISTORICAL/CULTURAL EVENTS
1704	Swift *A Tale of a Tub*, etc.	Defoe *A Review* (−1713) Newton *Optics*	John Locke d. Battle of Blenheim
1705	Manley ★*The Secret History of Queen Zarah*	Steele *The Tender Husband* Mandeville *The Grumbling Hive*	
1706	Antoine Galland trans. *The Arabian Nights Entertainments*	Defoe *Apparition of Mrs Veal* Farquhar *The Recruiting Officer*	
1707	Manley *The Lady's Pacquet of Letters*	Echard *History of England* (−1718)	Act of Union with Scotland Charles Wesley b. Henry Fielding b.
1708	Motteux and others trans. *Rabelais Works*	Shaftesbury *Letter Concerning Enthusiasm*	
1709	Manley ★*New Atalantis* Anon. *The Life and Adventures of Captain Avery*	Berkeley *New Theory of Vision* Pope *Pastorals* Steele *The Tatler* (−Jan. 1711)	First Copyright Act (14-year term renewable during author's life) Samuel Johnson b.
1710	Manley ★*Memoirs of Europe*	Bayle *Historical and Critical Dictionary* (first English edn) Bolingbroke, Swift, and others *The Examiner* (−1712) Leibnitz *Théodicée*	Academy of Ancient Music established Handel arrives in England Fall of Whigs. Tory Ministry formed under Robert Harley, later Lord Oxford

DATE	WORKS OF FICTION	OTHER WORKS	HISTORICAL/CULTURAL EVENTS
1711		Addison *The Spectator* (−1712) Dennis *On the Genius and Writings of Shakespeare* Pope *Essay on Criticism* Shaftesbury *Characteristics of Men and Manners* Swift *Argument Against Abolishing Christianity* *The Conduct of the Allies*	Occasional Conformity Bill David Hume b.
1712		Arbuthnot *History of John Bull* Pope *The Rape of the Lock* *Messiah* Swift *Proposal for Correcting the English Tongue* Woodes Rogers *A Cruising Voyage Round the World*	J.-J. Rousseau b.
1713	Jane Barker *Love's Intrigues* Smith, Alexander *History of the Lives of the most noted Highwaymen*	Addison *Cato* Pope *Windsor Forest* Steele *The Guardian* (12 March–1 October) *The Englishman* (6 October–11 February 1714)	Treaty of Utrecht ends War of Spanish Succession Pope, Swift, Gay, and others form the Scriblerus Club Laurence Sterne b.

DATE	WORKS OF FICTION	OTHER WORKS	HISTORICAL/CULTURAL EVENTS
1714	Manley *The Adventures of Rivella*	Gay *The Shepherd's Week* Locke *Collected Works* Mandeville *The Fable of the Bees Inquiry into the Origin of Moral Virtue* Swift *The Public Spirit of the Whigs*	Queen Anne dies; accession of George I, who dismisses Tories; Bolingbroke flees to France, Swift installed as Dean of St Patrick's, Dublin George Whitefield b.
1715	Jane Barker *Exilius, or the banish'd Roman*	Pope trans. Homer's *Iliad* (−1720) Watts *Divine Songs for Children* Richardson, Jonathan *An Essay on the Theory of Painting*	First Jacobite Rebellion Death of Louis XIV
1716	Le Sage *Gil Blas of Santillane*	Gay *Trivia* Defoe *Mercurius Politicus* (−1720)	Septennial Act Leibnitz d. Gray b.
1717	Theobald *History of the Loves of Antiochus and Stratonice*	Pope *Collected Works*	Horace Walpole b. David Garrick b.
1718	Anon. *The Double Captive: or chain upon chains*	Gildon *Complete Art of Poetry* Prior *Poems*	Refoundation of Society of Antiquaries

DATE	WORKS OF FICTION	OTHER WORKS	HISTORICAL/CULTURAL EVENTS
1719	Defoe *Robinson Crusoe *Further Adventures of Robinson Crusoe Haywood Love in Excess: or the Fatal Enquiry		Joseph Addison d. Jacobite uprising in Scotland
1720	Defoe *Memoirs of a Cavalier *Captain Singleton *Serious Reflections of Robinson Crusoe Manley The Power of Love, in Seven Novels	Swift A Proposal for the Universal Use of Irish Manufacture	South Sea Bubble
1721		Gildon Laws of Poetry	Walpole's Ministry, 1721–42 ('Prime Minister'/Lord Treasurer) Tobias Smollett b.
1722	Defoe *Journal of the Plague ·Year *Moll Flanders *Colonel Jacque		
1723	Haywood Idalia: or the Unfortunate Mistress	Burnet History of my Own Time (–1735) Mandeville The Fable of the Bees Essay on Charity Steele The Conscious Lovers	Sir Christopher Wren d. Adam Smith b. Joshua Reynolds b.

DATE	WORKS OF FICTION	OTHER WORKS	HISTORICAL/CULTURAL EVENTS
1724	Defoe *Roxana* Mary Davys *The Reform'd Coquet* Pseud. *Authentic Memoirs of John Sheppard*	Defoe *Tour through the Whole Island of Great Britain* (−1726) *General History of the Pirates* Swift *The Drapier's Letters*	Immanuel Kant b.
1725	Defoe *Jonathan Wild* Humphreys (?) trans. Bussy-Rabutin's *Amorous History of the Gauls*	Defoe *Complete English Tradesman* (−1727) *A New Voyage Round the World* Pope *Shakespeare Works* *Odyssey* (trans. −1726) Young *Universal Passion*	
1726	Swift *Gulliver's Travels* Smith, Alexander *Memoirs of the famous Jonathan Wilde*	Bolingbroke *The Craftsman* (−1736) Thomson *Winter*	Voltaire in England for three years Handel naturalized
1727	Longueville *The Hermit*	Dyer *Grongar Hill* Gay *Fables* (−1738) Thomson *Summer* Motte trans. Newton's *Principia* (first English trans.)	Accession of George II Sir Isaac Newton d.

DATE	WORKS OF FICTION	OTHER WORKS	HISTORICAL/CULTURAL EVENTS
1728	Elizabeth Rowe *Friendship in Death*	Fielding *Love in Several Masques* Gay *The Beggar's Opera* Pope *The Dunciad* (−1729)	Ephraim Chambers, *Cyclopaedia Britannica*, the first national encyclopaedia
1729	Haywood *The Fair Hebrew*	Gay *Polly: an Opera* Oldmixon *History of England* (−1730) Swift *A Modest Proposal* Thomson *Britannia*	Edmund Burke b. Richard Steele and William Congreve d.
1730	Haywood *Love Letters on all Occasions*	Fielding *The Author's Farce Rape upon Rape Tom Thumb* Thomson *The Seasons*	Oliver Goldsmith b.
1731	Prévost d'Exiles *Life of Mr Cleveland, natural Son of Oliver Cromwell*	Pope *Epistle to Burlington*	Edward Cave starts *The Gentleman's Magazine* (−1907) Daniel Defoe d.
1732	Anon. *Memoirs of Love and Gallantry*	Fielding *Covent Garden Tragedy Modern Husband Mock Doctor* Pope *Epistle to Bathurst* Milton's *Paradise Lost* ed. Bentley	William Hogarth: *The Harlot's Progress*

DATE	WORKS OF FICTION	OTHER WORKS	HISTORICAL/CULTURAL EVENTS
1733		Bolingbroke *Dissertation upon Parties*	
		Fielding *The Miser*	
		Pope *Essay on Man* *Epistle to Cobham*	
		Swift *On Poetry a Rhapsody*	
		John Lockman trans. Voltaire's *Letters Concerning the English Nation*	
1734		Fielding *Don Quixote in England*	
		Sale trans. *The Koran*	
		Shakespeare Works ed. Lewis Theobald	
1735	Marivaux *Le Paysan Parvenu: or the Fortunate Peasant*	Johnson trans. *Voyage to Abysinnia*	William Hogarth: *The Rake's Progress*
	Lyttelton *Letters from a Persian in England*	Pope *Epistle to Arbuthnot*	
		Wesley *Journals* (–1798)	
1736	Haywood *Adventures of Eovaai, Princess of Ijaveo*	Fielding *Historical Register for 1736*	
		Thomson *Liberty*	
1737		Pope *Horatian Epistles*	Theatrical Licensing Act
		Shenstone *Poems*	Queen Caroline d.
		Wesley *Psalms and Hymns*	

DATE	WORKS OF FICTION	OTHER WORKS	HISTORICAL/CULTURAL EVENTS
1738		Johnson *London* Swift *Collection of Genteel Conversation*	
1739		Hume *Treatise of Human Nature* (−1740) Swift *Verses on the Death of Dr. Swift* Fielding and James Ralph *The Champion* (15 November−June 1741)	Foundling Hospital established War declared on Spain
1740	Richardson *Pamela*, Vols I−II	Cibber *Apology for the Life*	James Boswell b. War of Austrian Succession
1741	Fielding *Shamela* Richardson *Pamela*, Vols III−IV *Familiar Letters* Haywood (?) *Anti-Pamela* Kelly *Pamela's Conduct in High-Life*	Arbuthnot, Pope, Gay and others *Memoirs of Scriblerus* Hume *Essays Moral and Political* (−1742)	Handel's *Messiah*, first performed in Dublin Garrick acts Richard III
1742	Fielding *Joseph Andrews*	Collins *Persian Eclogues* Pope *New Dunciad* Young *The Complaint, or Night Thoughts* (−1745)	Walpole resigns

DATE	WORKS OF FICTION	OTHER WORKS	HISTORICAL/CULTURAL EVENTS
1743	Fielding *Jonathan Wild (in Miscellanies)	Blair The Grave Pope The Dunciad (4 Books)	Battle of Dettingen
1744	Fielding, Sarah *David Simple	Akenside Pleasures of Imagination Johnson Life of Savage	Alexander Pope d.
1745		Akenside Odes Fielding The True Patriot (5 November–17 June 1746) Johnson Observations on Macbeth Swift Directions to Servants	Second Jacobite Rebellion, led by Charles Edward, the Young Pretender Henry Mackenzie b. Swift d.
1746		Collins Odes Upton Critical Observations on Shakespeare Warton, Joseph Odes	Battle of Culloden
1747	Richardson *Clarissa (–1748) Fielding, Sarah *Familiar Letters between the Characters in 'David Simple'	Gray Ode on Eton College Johnson Plan of a Dictionary Warton, Thomas Pleasures of Melancholy Fielding The Jacobites Journal (5 December–5 November 1748)	Biographia Britannica (–1766) the first biographical dictionary

DATE	WORKS OF FICTION	OTHER WORKS	HISTORICAL/CULTURAL EVENTS
1748	Smollett *Roderick Random Cleland *Memoirs of a Woman of Pleasure	Anson Voyage Round the World Gray Ode to Spring Hume Philosophical Essays Thomson Castle of Indolence	Peace of Aix-la- Chapelle Jeremy Bentham b.
1749	Fielding, Sarah The Governess, or Little Female Academy Fielding *Tom Jones Smollett trans. Le Sage's Gil Blas	Hartley Observations on Man Johnson Vanity of Human Wishes Buffon Histoire Naturelle (−1804)	Goethe b.
1750	Lennox The Life of Harriot Stuart	Johnson The Rambler (20 March−14 March 1752)	Excavation of Pompeii begins
1751	Paltock Peter Wilkins Smollett *Peregrine Pickle Fielding *Amelia Cleland Memoirs of a Coxcomb Coventry *History of Pompey the Little	Fielding Late Increase of Robbers Gray Elegy in a Country Churchyard Hume Enquiry Concerning Principles of Morals	Gin Act

DATE	WORKS OF FICTION	OTHER WORKS	HISTORICAL/CULTURAL EVENTS
1752	Lennox *The Female Quixote	Hume *Political Discourses* Smart *Poems* Fielding *The Covent-Garden Journal* (4 January–25 November)	The calendar is changed Frances Burney b.
1753	Smollett *Ferdinand Count Fathom* Richardson *Sir Charles Grandison* (–1754)	Lennox *Shakespeare Illustrated*	Reconstruction of Walpole's Strawberry Hill
1754		Hume *History of England* (–1762) Warton, Thomas *Observations on the Faerie Queene*	Henry Fielding d.
1755	Smollett trans. Cervantes's *Don Quixote* Haywood *The Invisible Spy*	Fielding *Voyage to Lisbon* Hutcheson *System of Moral Philosophy* Richardson *Collection of . . . Moral and Instructive sentiments* Johnson *English Dictionary* Swift *Collected Works* Rousseau *Discours sur Inégalité*	Lisbon earthquake

DATE	WORKS OF FICTION	OTHER WORKS	HISTORICAL/CULTURAL EVENTS
1756	Amory *The Life of John Buncle*	Smollett *Compendium of Authentic Voyages* Warton, Joseph *Essay on the Genius and Writings of Pope* (−1782) Smollett *The Critical Review* (−1763) Voltaire *Désastre de Lisbonne*	Pitt–Devonshire Ministry William Godwin b.
1757	Fielding, Sarah *The Lives of Cleopatra and Octavia*	Collins *Oriental Eclogues* Burke *The Sublime and Beautiful* Hume *Four Dissertations* Smollett *History of England* (−1758)	Walpole sets up printing press at Strawberry Hill William Blake b.
1758	Lennox *Henrietta*	Johnson *The Idler* (15 April–5 April 1760) Swift *Four Last Years of the Queen*	
1759	Johnson *Rasselas* Voltaire *Candide* Fielding, Sarah *History of the Countess of Dellwyn*	Goldsmith *Present State of Polite Learning* *The Bee* (6 October–24 November) Smith *Theory of Moral Sentiments* Young *Conjectures on Original Composition*	Opening of the British Museum Death of Handel Robert Burns and William Beckford b.

DATE	WORKS OF FICTION	OTHER WORKS	HISTORICAL/CULTURAL EVENTS
1760	Sterne ★*Tristram Shandy* (−1767) Fielding, Sarah *History of Ophelia* Johnstone *Chrysal: the Adventures of a Guinea* (−1765) Riccoboni *Letters from Juliet*	Goldsmith *The Citizen of the World* (in *The Public Ledger*, 24 January to 14 August 1761) Lyttelton *Dialogues of the Dead* Macpherson *Fragments of Ancient Poetry* (the 'Ossian' poems) Sterne *Sermons of Yorick* (−1769) Diderot *La Religieuse*	Accession of George III
1761	Smollett *et al.* trans. *Voltaire Works* (−1744) Rousseau *Eloisa: or a Series of Letters*	Smollett *Continuation of the Complete History of England* (−1765)	Samuel Richardson d.
1762	*Fielding Works* ed. Murphy Smollett ★*Sir Launcelot Greaves* Anon. *The Life, Travels and Adventures of Christopher Wagstaff* Leland *Longsword, Earl of Salisbury* Lennox *Sophia*	Goldsmith *Life of Richard Nash* Hurd *Letters on Chivalry and Romance* Kames *Elements of Criticism* Macpherson *Fingal and Other Poems by Ossian* Walpole *Anecdotes of Painting* Rousseau *Contrat Social*	Samuel Johnson granted a pension J. C. Bach arrives in England

DATE	WORKS OF FICTION	OTHER WORKS	HISTORICAL/CULTURAL EVENTS
1763	Brooke, Frances *The History of Lady Julia Mandeville* Marmontel *Moral Tales* (−1765)	Percy *Five Pieces of Runic Poetry* Smart *Song to David*	The Wilkes Affair Boswell meets Johnson for the first time
1764	Gentleman *A Trip to the Moon* Ridley *Tales of the Genii* Brooke, Henry ★*The Fool of Quality: or the History of Henry Earl of Moreland* (−1770)	Goldsmith *History of England* Reid *Enquiry into the Human Mind* Smollett *Present State of all Nations* Rousseau *Émile* Voltaire *Dictionnaire Philosophique*	Ann Radcliffe b.
1765	Walpole ★*The Castle of Otranto* Scott, Sarah *The Man of Real Sensibility* (−1766)	Blackstone *Commentaries on the Laws of England* (−1769) *Shakespeare's Works* ed. Johnson Percy *Reliques of Ancient English Poetry* Smart *The Psalms of David*	
1766	Newbery (?) *The History of Little Goody Twoshoes* Goldsmith ★*The Vicar of Wakefield*	Anstey *New Bath Guide* Smollett *Travels through France and Italy* Lessing *Laokoon*	Death of Old Pretender Rousseau in England

DATE	WORKS OF FICTION	OTHER WORKS	HISTORICAL/CULTURAL EVENTS
1767	Boswell *Dorando: A Spanish Tale*	Ferguson *History of Civil Society*	
1768	Sterne ★*A Sentimental Journey*	Boswell *Account of Corsica* Goldsmith *The Good-Natur'd Man* Gray *Poems* Walpole *Historic Doubts on Richard III* *Encyclopaedia Britannica*	Foundation of Royal Academy Joshua Reynolds as President, Gainsborough a member J. C. Bach introduces the pianoforte as a solo instrument Laurence Sterne d.
1769	Smollett *Adventures of an Atom*	Goldsmith *Roman History* Reynolds *Discourse* to the Royal Academy	Shakespeare Jubilee conducted at Stratford-upon-Avon by David Garrick Josiah Wedgwood opens pottery factory, 'Etruria'
1770	Bridges ★*The Adventures of a Bank-Note* (–1771)	Beattie *Essay on Truth* Goldsmith *The Deserted Village*	William Wordsworth b. General Dispensary founded in London
1771	Mackenzie ★*The Man of Feeling* Smollett ★*Humphry Clinker*	Beattie *The Minstrel* (–1774) Wesley, John *Collected Prose Works* (–1774)	Walter Scott b. Smollett d.
1772	Reeve *The Phoenix*	Akenside *Poems* 'Junius' Letters collected	Samuel Taylor Coleridge b.

DATE	WORKS OF FICTION	OTHER WORKS	HISTORICAL/CULTURAL EVENTS
1773	Mackenzie ★ *The Man of the World* Graves ★ *The Spiritual Quixote* d'Arnaud *The Tears of Sensibility*	Cook *Voyage Round the World in 1768–71* Goldsmith *She Stoops to Conquer* Monboddo *Origin and Progress of Language* (–1792) *Edinburgh Review* (–1799)	
1774	Brooke, Henry ★*Juliet Grenville: or the History of the Human Heart* (trans. German, 1774)	Chesterfield *Letters to his Son* Goldsmith *History of Earth and Animated Nature* Kames *Sketches of the History of Man* Walpole *Description of Strawberry Hill* Warton, Thomas *History of English Poetry* (–1781 Goethe *Werther*	Goldsmith d.
1775	Bicknell *The Benevolent Man, or the History of Mr. Belville* Young *Julia Benson: or the Sufferings of Innocence*	Johnson *Journey to the Western Islands of Scotland* Sheridan *The Rivals* Sterne *Letters from Yorick to Eliza*	War of American Independence Jane Austen b.

DATE	WORKS OF FICTION	OTHER WORKS	HISTORICAL/CULTURAL EVENTS
1776	Smollett trans. Fénelon's *Télémaque*	Beattie *Essays on Poetry and Music* Campbell *Philosophy of Rhetoric* Gibbon *Decline and Fall of the Roman Empire* (–1788) Hawkins *History of Music* Smith *The Wealth of Nations*	Declaration of American Independence David Hume d.
1777	Mackenzie *Julia de Roubigné* Reeve *Champion of Virtue*	Chatterton *Poems* Cook *Voyage towards the South Pole and Round the World, 1772–5* Hume *Two Essays* on Suicide and the Immortality of the Soul Morgann *Essay on the Character of Falstaff*	
1778	Burney ★*Evelina*	Chatterton *Miscellanies in Prose and Verse*	Voltaire and Rousseau d.

DATE	WORKS OF FICTION	OTHER WORKS	HISTORICAL/CULTURAL EVENTS
1779	Combe *Letters supposed to have been written by Yorick and Eliza* Graves trans., Goethe's ★*The Sorrows of Werther*	Cowper *Olney Hymns* Gibbon *Vindication of the 15th and 16th chapters of the Decline and Fall* Hume *Dialogues Concerning Natural Religion* Johnson *Prefaces, Biographical and Critical* (reissued in 1781 as *Lives of the Poets*)	
1780	Holcroft *Alwyn: or the Gentleman Comedian*	Crabbe *The Candidate* Paine *Public Good*	Gordon Riots (June) Beginning of Sunday Schools
1781	Combe *Letters of an Italian Nun and an English Gentleman*	Jefferson *The Rights of British America* Sheridan *The Critic*	
1782	Burney *Cecilia*	Cowper *Poems* Nichols *Biographical and Literary Anecdotes*	Sarah Siddons at Drury Lane theatre

DATE	WORKS OF FICTION	OTHER WORKS	HISTORICAL/CULTURAL EVENTS
1783	Reeve *The Two Mentors* Thomson, William (?) *The Man in the Moon*	Beattie *Dissertations Moral and Critical* Beckford *Dreams, Waking Thoughts and Incidents* (suppressed, partly published in 1834) Blair *Lectures on Rhetoric* Blake *Poetical Sketches* Crabbe *The Village* Sheridan *The School for Scandal*	Peace of Versailles Pitt Ministry (−1801)
1784	Godwin *Imogen* Laclos *Dangerous Connections* (trans.)	Cook *Voyage to the Pacific Ocean* (−1780)	Samuel Johnson d.
1785	Anon. *The Aerostatic Spy: or Adventures with an Air-Balloon* Genlis *Tales of the Castle*	Boswell *Tour to the Hebrides* Johnson *Prayers and Meditations* Mackenzie *The Lounger* (February, to January 1787) Reeve *The Progress of Romance* Reid *Essay on the Intellectual Powers of Man*	

DATE	WORKS OF FICTION	OTHER WORKS	HISTORICAL/CULTURAL EVENTS
1786	Beckford *Vathek* Lee *The Errors of Innocence*	Burns *Poems Chiefly in Scottish Dialect* Gilpin *Observations on Cumberland and Westmorland* Piozzi *Anecdotes of Samuel Johnson* Tooke *Diversions of Purley* (−1798, 1805)	Samuel Taylor, 'Universal System of Stenography' (later adapted by Isaac Pitman)
1787		Burns *Songs* Hawkins *Life of Johnson* Wollstonecraft *Thoughts on Education of Children*	American Constitution signed
1788	Reeve *The Exiles: memoirs of the Count de Cronstadt* Smith *Emmeline: or the Orphan of the Castle* Wollstonecraft *Mary: a fiction*	Johnson *Sermons* Reid *Essay on the Active Powers of Man* Wollstonecraft *Original Stories from Real Life*	*The Daily Universal Register* becomes *The Times* Death of the Young Pretender Byron b.

DATE	WORKS OF FICTION	OTHER WORKS	HISTORICAL/CULTURAL EVENTS
1789	Radcliffe *The Castles of Athlin and Dunbayne* Smith *Ethelinda: or the Recluse of the Lake*	Bentham *Principles of Morals and Legislation* Blake *Songs of Innocence* *Book of Thel* Darwin, Erasmus *Loves of the Plants* Gilpin *Observations on the Highlands of Scotland* White *Natural History of Selborne*	French Revolution

General Bibliographies

Note: *Each section is arranged alphabetically. Place of publication is London unless otherwise stated.*

(i) English fiction: history and criticism

Altick, R. D. — *The English Common Reader: A Social History of the Mass Reading Public 1800–1900* (Chicago and London, 1957). (Ch. 2 on the period 1699–1790s.)

Baker, E. A. — *The History of the English Novel*, 10 vols (1924–36; reprinted New York, 1950–67), with supplement (XI) by L. Stevenson (1967). (The most comprehensive survey, including accounts of lesser-known novels: IV and V on the eighteenth-century period.)

Booth, W. C. — *The Rhetoric of Fiction* (Chicago and London, 1961). (A standard introduction to reading and interpretation: broad chronological scope.)

Davis, L. J. — *Factual Fictions* (New York, 1983). (On the origins of the novel in the 'news/novel' discourse: critical of Ian Watt's thesis – see below section C.)

Donovan, R. A. — *The Shaping Vision: Imagination in the English Novel from Defoe to Dickens* (Ithaca, 1966). (Chapters on Defoe, Fielding, Sterne, Smollett.)

Josipovici, G. — *The World and the Book: A Study of Modern Fiction* (1971). (Ch. 5, on the 'truth' and 'fiction' of the early novel.)

Kettle, A. — *An Introduction to English Novel* (1951–53). (The novel as a product of social history: close reading of passages from selected novels, but eccentric readings of Richardson and *Tom Jones*.)

Laurenson, D. and Swingewood, A. — *The Sociology of Literature* (1966). (On the social significance of the novel and readership: critical of Watt's assumptions.)

Leavis, Q. D. — *Fiction and the Reading Public* (1932; reprinted 1965). (Pioneering study of readership.)

Mendilow, A. A. — *Time and the Novel* (London and New York, 1952). (Chapter on Sterne, pp. 165–99.)

Spearman, D.   *The Novel and Society* (1966). (Parts 1 and 2 on the rise of the novel; provides debating points against Watt, but through views rather than analysis and evidence.)

Van Ghent, D.   *The English Novel: Form and Function* (1953; reprinted New York, 1961). ('Essays in Analysis', from *Don Quixote* to Sterne and beyond.)

(ii) Eighteenth-century background: historical, intellectual, cultural

Abrams, M. H.   *The Mirror and the Lamp: Romantic Theory and the Critical Tradition* (1953). (Broad discussion of Augustan critical theories.)

Allen, B. S.   *Tides in English Taste (1619–1800): A Background for the Study of Literature*, 2 vols (Athens, Georgia, 1977). (General aesthetic background.)

Bate, W. J.   *From Classic to Romantic: Premises of Taste in Eighteenth-Century England* (1946: reprinted New York, 1961). (Study of aesthetic theories: cogent and brief.)

Battestin, M. C.   *The Providence of Wit: Aspects of Form in Augustan Literature and the Arts* (Oxford, 1974). (The meaning of 'Augustanism' in Fielding, Goldsmith, and Sterne.)

Clark, K.   *The Gothic Revival, an Essay in the History of Taste* (1928). (Architecture, chiefly.)

Dobree, B.   *English Literature in the Early Eighteenth Century, 1700–1740* (Oxford, 1959): Volume VII of The Oxford History of English Literature.

Foss, M.   *The Age of Patronage: The Arts in Society 1660–1750* (1971). (Survey of literature, politics, music, and painting.)

Fussell, P.   *The Rhetorical World of Augustan Humanism: Ethics and Imagery from Swift to Burke* (Oxford and New York, 1965). (Recurrent images and meanings in broad range of major works in prose and verse.)

George, D.   *London Life in the Eighteenth Century* (1925; reprinted 1965). (Classic social history.)

Greene, D. J.   *The Age of Exuberance: Backgrounds to Eighteenth-Century English Literature* (New York, 1970). (Highly readable introductory survey.)

Hagstrum, J. H.   *The Sister Arts: The Tradition of Literary Pictorialism and English Poetry from Dryden to Gray* (Chicago, 1958). (On the contemporary systematization of aesthetic theories.)

Humphreys, A. H.   *The Augustan World: Life and Letters in Eighteenth-Century England* (1954; reprinted New York, 1963). (Still one of the best general introductions to the cultural context: see Pat Rogers below.)

Lovejoy, A. O.   *The Great Chain of Being: A Study of the History of an Idea* (Cambridge, Mass., 1936). (Ideas of order and hierarchy.)

MacLean, K.   *John Locke and English Literature of the Eighteenth Century* (New Haven, 1936). (For Locke's influence on Sterne.)

Malins, E.   *English Landscaping and Literature, 1660–1840* (1966). (Mainly with reference to poetry.)

Milne, J. L.   *Earls of Creation: Five Great Patrons of Eighteenth-Century Art* (1962). (Especially useful for Shaftesbury and Burlington.)

Monk, S. H.   *The Sublime: A Study of Critical Theories in XVIIIth-Century England* (1935; 2nd edn, Ann Arbor, Michigan, 1960). (A study of the psychological bases of critical theories.)

Price, M.   *To the Palace of Wisdom: Studies in Order and Energy from Dryden to Blake* (New York, 1964). (Excellent on major figures.)

Rogers, K. M.   *Feminism in Eighteenth-Century England* (Carbondale, 1982). (Particularly useful for discussion of the early feminists Mrs Astell and Mrs Montagu.)

Rogers, P.   *The Augustan Vision* (1974). (A shrewd and popular general introduction.)

Stephen, L.   *History of English Thought in the Eighteenth-Century* (1876; reprinted 1902). (Detailed discussion of theological controversies in particular.)

Stone, L.   *The Family, Sex and Marriage in England, 1500–1800* (1977). (Social history, partly based on literary evidence from Pepys and Boswell.)

Turberville, A. S.   *Johnson's England: An Account of the Life and Manners of His Age*, 2 vols (Oxford, 1933; revised 1952). (Essays by divers hands on many aspects of contemporary life, profusely illustrated.)

Wellek, R.   *A History of Modern Criticism, 1750–1950*, Volume I, *The Later Eighteenth Century* (New Haven, 1955). (Not specifically on the novel, but useful and reliable critical mapwork.)

Willey, B.   *The Eighteenth-Century Background: Studies on the Idea of Nature in the Thought of the Period* (1940;

reprinted Harmondsworth, 1962). (The subtitle is the more accurate description of contents.)

Wittkower, R.   *Architectural Principles in the Age of Humanism* (1949; reprinted 1971). (Renaissance ideas of order, influence on eighteenth-century building.)

(iii) Eighteenth-century fiction

A. Bibliographies and reference guides (general)

Bell, F. I. and Baird, D.   *The English Novel 1578–1956: A Checklist of Twentieth-Century Criticisms* (Denver, 1958). (Useful for its broad purpose, but outdated by particular author bibliographis: see next section below.)

Glock, W. S.   *Eighteenth-Century English Literary Studies: A Bibliography* (New Jersey and London, 1984). (A major-author bibliography, with brief and sometimes evaluative remarks: not comprehensive and omits individual author bibliographies: see Section B below.)

McBurney, W. H.   *A Check-List of English Prose Fiction 1700–39* (Cambridge, Mass., 1960). (The standard check-list.)

Mayo, R. D.   *The English Novel in the Magazines 1740–1815* (Evanston and London, 1962). (Bibliography of short fiction published in non-newspaper British magazines in alphabetical order of title.)

Morgan, C. E.   *The Rise of the Novel of Manners* (1911; reprinted New York, 1963). (Chronological list of 653 prose narratives printed between 1600 and 1740.)

Rogers, K. M.   *Feminism in Eighteenth-Century England* (Brighton, 1982). (Chs 3 and 4 survey the early women writers; 36-page appendix of biographical and sociological detail on women writers 1660–1800.)

Watson, G., ed.   *The New Cambridge Bibliography of English Literature*, Volume II, *1660–1800* (Cambridge 1971). (The standard reference, and which lists minor fiction in chronological order of publication, columns 975–1014.)

Wiles, R. M.   *Serial Publications in England before 1750* (Cambridge, 1957). (Minor fiction and chronological list of titles.)

B. Special author bibliographies (major figures only)

Beckford

Gemmett, R. J.   'An Annotated Checklist of the Works of William Beckford', *PBSA*, 61 (1967), 243–58. (Beckford's published works, and editions thereof, 1780–1957.)

Burney

Grau, J. A.   *Fanny Burney: An Annotated Bibliography* (New York and London, 1981). (From 1778 to the late 1970s.)

Defoe

Moore, J. R.   *A Checklist of the Writings of Daniel Defoe* (1948; 2nd edn, Hamden, Connecticut, 1971). (The authoritative listing.)

Stoler, J. A.   *Daniel Defoe: An Annotated Bibliography of Modern Criticism* (New York and London, 1984). (From 1900 to 1980.)

Fielding

Morrissey, L. J.   *Henry Fielding: A Reference Guide* (Boston, 1980). (From 1755 to 1977).

Stoler, J. A. and Fulton, R. D.   *Henry Fielding: An Annotated Bibliography of Twentieth-Century Criticism 1900–1977* (New York and London, 1980)

Goldsmith

Friedman, A.   See: *NCBEL*, Volume II, *1660–1800*, columns 1191–1210, for Goldsmith's published works, and criticism up to 1971. (See Watson, Section A)

Woods, S. H.   *Oliver Goldsmith: A Reference Guide* (Boston, 1982). (From 1755 to 1978.)

Richardson

Hannaford, Richard Gordon   *Samuel Richardson: An Annotated Bibliography of Critical Studies* (Garland, N.Y. and London, 1980). (From 1740 to 1978.)

Sale, William Merritt, Jr.   *Samuel Richardson: A Bibliographical Record of his Literary Career with Historical Notes* (New Haven, 1936, reprinted Archon, 1969). (Bibliographical account of novels, edited works, pamphlets, collaborative works in chronological order, including Anti-Pamelas.)

Smollett

Cordasco, F.   *Tobias George Smollett: A Bibliographical Guide* (New York, 1978).

Spector, R. D.   *Tobias Smollett: A Reference Guide* (Boston, 1980). (Annotated, chronological listing, to 1978.)

Wagoner, M.   *Tobias Smollett: A Checklist of Editions of his Works and an Annotated Secondary Bibliography* (1983). (Includes translations, and starts at 1746.)

Sterne

Cordasco, F.   *Laurence Sterne: A List of Critical Studies published from 1896 to 1946* (Brooklyn, 1948).

Hartley, L.   *Sterne in the Twentieth Century: An Essay and a Bibliography of Sternean Studies 1900–1965* (1966; corrected, Chapel Hill, 1968). *Laurence Sterne: An Annotated Bibliography, 1965–1977* (Boston, 1978).

Walpole

Hazen, A. T.   *A Bibliography of Horace Walpole* (New Haven, 1948). (Books by and printed by Walpole.)

Sabor, P.   *Horace Walpole: An Annotated Bibliography* (New York and London, 1981). (From 1778 to the late 1970s.)

C. History and criticism (general)

Barnett, G. L., ed.   *Eighteenth-Century British Novelists on the Novel* (New York, 1968). (Reprints the prefaces of Richardson, Fielding, Manley, Walpole, Reeve, Burney, and others.)

Brooks, D.   *Number and Pattern in the Eighteenth-Century Novel: Defoe, Fielding, Smollett and Sterne* (1973). (Numerological structures related symbolically to meaning in most of the major novels.)

Foxon, D.   *Libertine Literature in England 1660–1750* (New York, 1965). (Final chapter on the publication and textual history of Cleland's *Memoirs of a Woman of Pleasure*.)

McKillop, A. D.   *The Early Masters of English Fiction* (Lawrence, Kansas, 1956). (Standard introduction to the five major novelists.)

Nuttall, A. D.   *A Common Sky: Philosophy and the Literary Imagination* (1974). (Ch. 2 on *Tristram Shandy*, and 3 on 'Sentiment and Sensibility'.)

Preston, J.   *The Created Self: The Reader's Role in Eighteenth-Century Fiction* (1970). (An excellent discussion of Defoe, Richardson, Fielding, and Sterne, as in subtitle.)

Shepperson, A. B.   *The Novel in Motley: A History of the Burlesque Novel in English* (1936; reprinted New York, 1967). (On *Shamela*, pp. 20–28, and *Joseph Andrews*, pp. 28–30.)

Sherbo, A.   *Studies in the Eighteenth-Century Novel* (East Lansing, 1969). (Six essays on aspects of Fielding's novels, one on Sterne, two on *Moll Flanders*, and one on physical description of characters in the novel.)

Spector, R., ed.   *Essays on the Eighteenth-Century Novel* (Bloomington and London, 1965). (A useful selection of modern criticism including Christopher Hill's essay on *Clarissa* and R. S. Crane on 'The Plot of *Tom Jones*'.)

Summers, M.   *The Gothic Quest: A History of the Gothic Novel* (1938). (For Walpole and Beckford.)

Tompkins, J. M. S.   *The Popular Novel in England, 1770–1800* (1932). (Particularly valuable for its social commentary on many minor novels.)

Watt, I.   *The Rise of the Novel: Studies in Defoe, Richardson and Fielding* (1957; reprinted Berkeley and Los Angeles, 1964). (The classic exposition of 'formal realism', widely influential: but cf. Davis, and Laurenson and Swingewood above.)

Williams, I.   *Novel and Romance 1700–1800: A Documentary Record* (New York, 1970). (101 extracts from contemporary reviews and author's prefaces, on the novel from 1691–1798.)

D. Forms and sub-genres

Adams, P. G.   *Travelers and Travel-Liars 1660–1800* (Berkeley, 1978).
Travel Literature and the Evolution of the Novel (Lexington, 1983). (Both examine the fusion of and the difference between the two cognate prose genres; the latter's scope is from the Renaissance to the eighteenth century.)

Conant, M. P.   *The Oriental Tale in England in the Eighteenth Century* (1908; reprinted 1966). (For discussion of *Rasselas, Candide, Vathek*.)

Day, R. A.   *Told in Letters: Epistolary Fiction Before Richardson* (Ann Arbor, 1966). (Contains a chronological list of English letter fiction; 1660–1740 – 203 items– and a list of letter fiction in periodicals – 35 items.)

Maresca, T. E.   *Epic to Novel* (Columbus, 1974). (Traces the replacing of the epic by the novel as the major literary form: pp. 181–233 on Fielding.)

Richetti, J. J.   *Popular Fiction before Richardson: Narrative Patterns 1700–1739* (Oxford, 1969). (Traces 'mythological' patterns, e.g. the persecuted maiden, and examines secular-religious antithesis in earlier fiction: Ch. 4 on Mrs Manley and Eliza Haywood.)

Singer, C. F.   *The Epistolary Novel: Its Origin, Development, Decline, and Residuary Influence* (1933; reprinted New York, 1963). (Ch. 4 on Richardson.)

Spacks, P. M.   *Imagining a Self: Autobiography and Novel in Eighteenth-Century England* (Cambridge, Mass. and London, 1976). (Relevant for each of the major novelists, and an excellent chapter on Burney.)

Würzbach, N.   *The Novel in Letters: Epistolary Fiction in the English Novel 1678–1740* (1969). (Reprints nine early epistolary novels.)

E. Themes, motifs, and conventions

Auty, S. G.   *The Comic Spirit of Eighteenth-Century Novels* (New York, 1975). (Essay on major novelists, pp. 55–102, Ch. 3 on Fielding's followers – Francis Coventry, Goldsmith, Lennox's *Female Quixote*, and Graves's *The Spiritual Quixote*.)

Bredvold, L. I.   *The Natural History of Sensibility* (Detroit, 1962). (Four essays, from Shaftesbury to Lewis's *The Monk*.)

Byrd, M.   *London Transformed: Images of the City in the Eighteenth Century* (New Haven and London, 1978). (pp. 8–43 on Defoe's London.)

Carnochan, W. B.   *Confinement and Flight: An Essay on English Literature of the Eighteenth Century* (Berkeley, 1977). (Includes commentary on *Robinson Crusoe*, Sterne, and *Vathek*.)

Dussinger, J. A.   *The Discourse of the Mind in Eighteenth-Century Fiction* (The Hague, 1974). (A study of the problem of knowledge for narrator, character, and reader in the new species of writing: *Pamela, Clarissa, The Vicar of Wakefield, A Sentimental Journey*.)

Flanders, W. A.   *Structures of Experience: History, Society and Personal Life in the Eighteenth-Century British Novel* (Columbia, South Carolina, 1984). (Discusses language, the family, women, crime, urban life, as reflected in the novels.)

Karl, F. R.   *The Adversary Literature: The English Novel in the Eighteenth Century. A Study in Genre* (New York, 1974). (A reading of the novel as a subversive and destabilizing force in society.)

Paulson, R.   *Satire and the Novel in Eighteenth-Century England* (New Haven, 1967). (Broad, stimulating survey, particularly in relation to Fielding and Smollett, and the form of the novel.)

Perry, R.   *Women, Letters, and the Novel* (New York, 1980). (Examines novels of Behn and Manley among others in the context of London and the fictional fantasies of 'ideal love situations'.)

Sacks, S.   *Fiction and the Shape of Belief: A Study of Henry Fielding, with Glances at Swift, Johnson and Richardson* (Berkeley, 1964). (On Fielding's successful artistic representation of his ideas.)

Seidel, M.   *Satiric Inheritance: Rabelais to Sterne* (Princeton, 1979). (The place of satire in the general context of narrative theory: relevant to Swift and Sterne, among others.)

Sheriff, J. K.   *The Good-Natured Man: The Evolution of a Moral Ideal, 1660–1800* (Alabama, 1982). (On Fielding, Goldsmith, Sterne, Mackenzie.)

Stubbs, P.   *Women and Fiction: Feminism and the Novel, 1880–1920* (Brighton, 1979). (First chapter argues that sexual inequality is the central theme in the English novel.)

Tave, S.   *The Amiable Humorist: A Study in the Comic Theory and Criticism of the Eighteenth and Early Nineteenth Centuries* (Chicago, 1960). (Comic theory in relation to the novel, and to Fielding in particular.)

Individual Authors

Notes on biography, major works, and criticism

Each entry is divided into three sections:
(a) *Outline of author's life and literary career.* Dates of novels are those of the first published form.
(b) *Selected biographies and letters.* Place of publication is London unless otherwise stated.
(c) *Selected critical works, etc.* Listed chronologically. Place of publication is London unless otherwise stated.

Collections of contemporary criticism are included in the volumes of the Critical Heritage series (Routledge and Kegan Paul), and selections of modern critical essays may be found in the Twentieth Century Views series (Prentice-Hall). Neither is listed below as a matter of course.

Many of the minor novels have been reprinted in the facsimile series published by Garland Publishing, Inc. (New York and London) under the series title 'The Flowering of the Novel: Representative Mid-Eighteenth Century Fiction 1740–1775', and some of the novels by Cleland, Sarah Fielding, Eliza Haywood, Charlotte Lennox, and Henry Mackenzie, for example, are only generally available in this series.

BECKFORD, William (1760–1844), born at Fonthill, 29 September, the son of Alderman Beckford (twice Lord Mayor of London), heir to a fortune made from Jamaica sugar plantations. Privately educated: Mozart at nine taught Beckford music at five, and Sir William Chambers taught him the principles of architecture. Travelled with his tutor to Geneva to complete his education in 1777, and to the Low Countries and Italy, 1780–82. His account of the tour was ready for publication in 1783 as *Dreams, Waking Thoughts, and Incidents*, but it was suppressed by his family; nearly all copies destroyed, and it was published in a diluted form in 1834 as *Italy: with Sketches of Spain and Portugal*. *Vathek* was already written at this time, in French, but it was his tutor, Samuel Henley, who surreptitiously and anonymously published it first in an English translation, with copious footnotes. The 'original' appeared at Paris, and then with Beckford's name on it at Lausanne (1787). He married Lady Margaret Gordon in 1783, who died three years later, leaving him two daughters (one of whom later became the Duchess of Hamilton). In 1784 the press charged him with homosexuality, and from 1786 to 1796 he was travelling in Portugal,

Spain, and in France where he witnessed the destruction of the Bastille. Back in Paris in 1791 and 1792, he then went to Lausanne and bought Gibbon's library. He was MP for Wells (1784–90) and Hindon (1790–94, 1794–1820). He published two burlesques of the sentimental novels written by his stepsister Elizabeth Hervey, *Modern Novel Writing, or the Elegant Enthusiast; and Interesting Emotions of Arabella Bloomville; A Rhapsodical Romance* (1796), and *Azemia: a Descriptive and Sentimental Novel* (1797). The latter adopts the Richardsonian principle of procrastinated rape. In 1796 he set about creating the Gothic extravaganza at Fonthill, where he spent twenty years in seclusion surrounded by books and *objets d'art*, until financial necessity made him put Fonthill on the market. Hazlitt described the place as 'a desert of magnificence, a glittering waste of laborious idleness, a cathedral turned into a toyshop'. Three suppressed episodes of *Vathek* were found after his death. In the *DNB* Richard Garnett calls him 'the most brilliant amateur in English Literature'.

> Brockman, H. A. N., *The Caliph of Fonthill* (1956). (Illustrated biography.)
> Mahmoud, F. M., ed., *Beckford of Fonthill: Bicentenary Essays* (Cairo, 1960).
> Alexander, B., *England's Wealthiest Son: A Study of William Beckford* (1962). (Not, strictly, a biography, but a study of Beckford's 'contradictory character'.)
> Alexander, B., trans. and ed., *The Journal of William Beckford in Portugal and Spain 1787–1788* (1954).
> Alexander, B., trans. and ed., *Life at Fonthill 1807–1822. With Interludes in Paris and London, from the Correspondence of William Beckford* (1957).

See:
> Hazlitt, W., 'Fonthill Abbey', *London Magazine*, 6, no. 35 (November 1822), 405–10.
> Conant, M. P., *The Oriental Tale in England in the Eighteenth Century* (1908; reprinted 1966).
> Fothergill, B., *Beckford of Fonthill* (London and Boston, 1979). (Critical and biographical.)

BROOKE, Henry (1703?–83) was born in Rantavan, County Cavan, Ireland, the second of three sons of the Rev. William Brooke. Reliable biographical details are scarce, but his early tutors included Dr Thomas Sheridan (Swift's close friend). He entered Trinity College Dublin in 1720 and then crossed to England to study law at the Temple in 1724. Back in Ireland he married his fourteen-year-old ward, clandestinely, and returned to England. In 1735 he published a poem 'Universal Beauty', possibly overseen by Pope, and enjoyed the friendship and patronage of Lyttelton, Pitt, and Frederick Prince of Wales. His translation of the first three books of Tasso's *Jerusalem Delivered* appeared in 1738, and his best-known play *Gustavus Vasa* the following year. It was printed but not performed, having been prohibited by the lord chamberlain on political grounds (Trollis being thought to reflect on Walpole). Swift subscribed to ten copies of the play and, with a different title, *The Patriot*, it was successfully produced in Dublin. Garrick was impressed by Brooke's theatrical talents. Brooke also turned his hand to religious and economic tracts, such as the anti-Catholic *Farmer's Six Letters to the People of Ireland* (1745; during the Jacobite Rebellion), and the pro-Catholic *Tryal of the Cause of the Roman Catholics* (1761), arguing for relaxation of the penal laws. He also wrote a satirical opera, *Jack the Giant-Queller* (1748), which was also banned after its first Dublin performance. The first two volumes of *The Fool of Quality* appeared in 1764 and sold well. The novel was completed in 1770. Wesley's abridgement was the form in which the novel was known until Charles Kingsley's two- volume edition of 1859. His last novel, *Juliet Grenville; or, The History of the Human Heart*, appeared in 1774. His daughter, Charlotte Brooke (d. 1793) published *Reliques of Irish Poetry* in 1789 and an edition of her father's poetical works, with a biographical memoir, in 1792. Other biographical details may be found in C. H. Wilson's *Brookiana: Anecdotes of Henry Brooke*, 2 vols, 1804 (including extracts from correspondence between Pope and Brooke), and in H. M. Scurr, *Henry Brooke*, Minneapolis, 1927.

BURNEY, Frances (1752–1840), later Mme D'Arblay, one of six children, born at King's Lynn, Norfolk, on 13 June, the daughter of Dr Charles Burney, then church organist but later to become one of the age's most outstanding musicologists. One of Fanny's brothers was to become a rear-admiral, another a Greek scholar. In 1760 the family moved to London, Mrs Burney dying in September 1761. The family was dispersed, but Fanny stayed at home with her father: she was self-educated. Dr Burney remarried in 1766. Fanny burnt all her juvenilia on her fifteenth birthday, including a novel about the mother of Evelina, *The History of Caroline Evelyn*, but she continued to write, eventually offering Dodsley two volumes of a publishable novel, which he declined. *Evelina* was accepted by Lowndes and published anonymously in January 1778, earning her a total of thirty pounds. Dr Burney leaked the identity of the anonymous author to Mrs Thrale, and it was much admired by Reynolds, Burke, and Johnson, into whose company Fanny was introduced. It went into four editions by 1779. She maintained a close, filial relationship with Samuel 'Daddy' Crisp, a friend of her father. *Cecilia, or Memoirs of an Heiress* was published in 1782, in five volumes, and the first edition sold out in three months. She met two of the age's great bluestockings, Mrs Montague and Mrs Delany. The latter had been assigned a house in Windsor by George III in 1785 and through her influence Fanny began to move in court circles. She was appointed to the Royal household as Second Keeper of the Robes, under the coarse and tyrannical Mme Schwellenberg (17 July 1786), a menial, time-consuming, and exhausting duty even for someone in good health, which Fanny was not. Kept a diary, which contained descriptions of the King's bouts of insanity (1788–89), and was reluctantly allowed to resign her position in July 1791, with a pension of £100 a year. Her health improved and she moved to Mickleham, where she met Alexandre D'Arblay, exiled adjutant-general of the Marquis de Lafayette. Married 31 July 1793, first in a Protestant and then, on the following day, in a Catholic ceremony (the latter at the Sardinian embassy). A son, Alexandre, born in 1794. Fanny tries a tragedy, *Edwy and Elgiva*, performed at Drury Lane, 21 March 1795, with Mrs Siddons and Kemble in the lead, but the play fails and is taken off after the first night. Publishes *Camilla, or a Picture of Youth* (1796), by subscription (Jane Austen was one of the subscribers), but the novel was not an artistic success. In 1802 she joins her husband in Paris, where he finds employment, and the next ten years are spent at Passy (during which time she is operated on for cancer, 1811). In 1812 she returns to England with her son, now old enough to be conscripted to fight in the war. Her last novel, *The Wanderer, or Female*

Difficulties, published in 1814, and Dr Burney dies in April. Fanny returns to Paris, and on Napoleon's return she goes to Belgium (she is in Brussels during the Battle of Waterloo). Her husband is pensioned after an injury and both return to England. Fanny is visited by Sir Walter Scott in 1826, and she prepares the *Memoirs of Dr. Burney* for the press (1832). She dies on 6 January. Jane Austen takes the title for *Pride and Prejudice* from the last pages of *Cecilia* (Book X, Ch. 10).

> Ellis, A. R., *The Early Diary of Frances Burney, 1768–1778* (1907).
> Tinker, C. B., *Dr. Johnson and Fanny Burney* (New York, 1911).
> Balderston, K. C., ed., *Thraliana: The Diary of Mrs. Hester Lynch Thrale (Later Mrs. Piozzi)*, 2 vols (Oxford, 1951).
> Hahn, E., *A Degree of Prudery* (New York, 1950). (A hostile biography.)
> Hemlow, J., *The History of Fanny Burney* (Oxford, 1958). (The standard biography.)
> Adelstein, M. E., *Fanny Burney* (New York, 1968). (Good general introduction, examining the combination of life and novels.)
> Hemlow, J. and others, eds, *The Journal and Letters of Fanny Burney* (Mme D'Arblay), 12 vols (Oxford, 1972–84). (The standard edition.)

See: Horner, J. M., *The English Women Novelists and their Connection with the Feminist Movement (1688–1797)* (Northampton, Mass.: Smith College Studies in Modern Languages, 11, nos 1–3, 1929–30, 1930). (An early recognition of Burney as the first important woman novelist.)

> Leavis, Q. D., 'A Critical Theory of Jane Austen's Writing', *Scrutiny*, 10 (1941), 61–87. (Discusses Austen's indebtedness to Burney's *Evelina* and *Cecilia*.)
> White, E., *Fanny Burney, Novelist: A Study in Technique* (Hamden, Connecticut, 1960). (Detailed treatment of *Evelina*, *Cecilia*, *Camilla*, and *The Wanderer*.)
> Spacks, P. M., *Imagining a Self: Autobiography and Novel in Eighteenth-Century England* (Cambridge, Mass., and London, 1976). (Chs. 3 and 6 on Burney.)
> Bloom, L. D. and E. A. Bloom, 'Fanny Burney's Novels: The Retreat from Wonder', *Novel: A Forum on Fiction*, 12 (1978–79), 215–35.

CLELAND, John (1710–89), educated at Westminster School until 1723. He joined the East India Company in 1728 and in 1736–40 served in Bombay, latterly as secretary of the Bombay Council. Little is known of his wandering life between then and the publication of his *Memoirs of a Woman of Pleasure* (1748–49), which he later abridged as *Fanny Hill* (1750). From 23 February 1748 to 6 March 1749 he was an inmate of the Fleet (debtors') prison, where he worked on the novel, published before his release. Griffiths employed him as a founding contributor to the *Monthly Review*. A sequel, *Memoirs of a Coxcomb*, was published in 1751 (anonymously), and three more examples of erotic fiction: *Memoirs Illustrating the Manners of the Present Age* (1752); four erotic romances, *The Surprizes of Love* (1764); and a three-volume novel *The Woman of Honour* (1768). None were successful. His plays – *Titus Vespasian* (1755), *The Ladies Subscription* (1755), and *Tombo-Chiqui, or the American Savage* (1758) – were not performed. He translated an Italian work on transvestism, wrote a bizarre pamphlet speculating on the parallels between semen and saliva (1765), translated du Radier's *Dictionary of Love* (1753; reprinted in 1776), and wrote his linguistic speculations on the Celtic language in *The Way to Things by Words and to Words by Things* (1766), and *Specimen of an Etimological Vocabulary.*

> Epstein, W. H., *John Cleland: Images of a Life* (New York and London, 1974). (Standard biography.)

See: Foxon, D., *Libertine Literature in England, 1660–1745* (New York, 1965).

> Thomas, D., *A Long Time Burning: The History of Literary Censorship in England* (New York, 1969). (On the mid-eighteenth-century urge for purity and moral reformation in literature.)
>
> Naumann, Peter, *Keyhole and Candle: John Cleland's Memoirs of a Woman of Pleasure und die Entstehung des Pornographischen Roman in England* (Heidelberg, 1976). (The most detailed single study of the novel and its background.)
>
> Brooks-Davies, D., 'The Mythology of Love; Venerean (and Related) Iconography in Pope, Fielding, Cleland and Sterne', in *Sexuality in Eighteenth-Century Britain*, ed. by Paul-Gabriel Boucé (Manchester, 1982), pp. 176–97.
>
> Wagner, Peter, *Eros Revived: A Study of Erotica in Eighteenth-Century England and America* (London, 1985). (French influence and political/literary significance of pornography.)

DEFOE, Daniel (1660–1731), born in the year of the Restoration of Charles II, in Cripplegate, where he also died. The son of James Foe, a tallow-chandler and City liveryman, of Flemish descent, and raised in a dissenting family. At five years of age he was evacuated from London because of the Great Plague (the subject of the *Journal of the Plague Year*, pseudonymously written by 'H. F.', 1722), and later attended the dissenting academy of Newington Green run by Charles Morton. He took part in Monmouth's Rebellion in 1685 after his marriage to Mary Tuffley in 1684 (she brought him a substantial dowry of £3700). Fighting on the Protestant side against the Catholic James II, he was captured, imprisoned, and pardoned by the King. His various subsequent business ventures included breeding civet-cats for perfume, marine insurance, brick and tile manufacturing, wool-, oyster-, and linen-merchandising. Business failure led to imprisonment in the Fleet debtors' prison. His first important literary work, *An Essay upon Projects*, appeared in 1697. *The True Born Englishman* (1701) was an enormously popular poem satirizing the xenophobia of his day, written in the reign of William III. The intolerant High Churchmen under Queen Anne were for a time hoodwinked by his ironical *Shortest Way with the Dissenters*, which proposed execution of Dissenters as a 'final solution'. He was imprisoned in Newgate and in 1703 stood in the pillory for three days. As Pope incorrectly stated in *The Dunciad*, 'Earless on high, stood unabash'd De Foe'. His second bankruptcy followed the failure of his brickworks, but he was patronized and rehabilitated by Robert Harley. Defoe then began a ten-year period of work for the Tory administration as an intelligence gatherer and pamphleteer. From this period dates *A Review*. The Tory party collapsed in 1714 at the death of Queen Anne. Of the sixteen publications for the year 1719, *Robinson Crusoe* is one. In his fifty-ninth year Defoe commenced his career as a novelist. *Memoirs of a*

Cavalier, Captain Singleton, came out in 1720; *Moll Flanders, A Journal of the Plague Year*, and *Colonel Jacque* (1722); *Roxana* in 1724. The non-fictional work included his *Tour through the Whole Island of Great Britain* (Volume I, 1724; II, 1725; III, 1728). He died in April 1731, in debt, the author of more than 500 titles.

Dottin, P., *The Life and Strange Surprising Adventures of Daniel De Foe* (New York, 1929: translated by Louis Ragan).

Moore, J. R., *Daniel Defoe: Citizen of the Modern World* (Chicago, 1958). (Biographical and critical, but not a chronological structure.)

Sutherland, J., *Daniel Defoe* (1937). (The authoritative biography.)

Healy, G. H., ed., *The Letters of Daniel Defoe* (Oxford, 1955).

See: Secord, A. W., *Studies in the Narrative Method of Defoe* (Urbana, 1924). (Sources of *Robinson Crusoe, Captain Singleton*, and methods of *Journal of the Plague Year*.)

Novak, M. E., *Economics and the Fiction of Defoe* (Berkeley, 1962). (Defoe's novels in the light of contemporary mercantile economic theories.)

Novak, M. E., *Defoe and the Nature of Man* (Oxford, 1963). (The themes of necessity, love, marriage.)

Hunter, J. P., *The Reluctant Pilgrim: Defoe's Emblematic Method and Quest for Form* (Baltimore, 1966). (Chiefly on *Robinson Crusoe* and Puritan modes of thought.)

Shinagel, M., *Daniel Defoe and Middle Class Gentility* (Cambridge, Mass., 1968). (Detailed study of *The Complete English Tradesman*.)

Starr, G. A., *Defoe and Casuistry* (Princeton, 1971). (Influence of seventeenth-century casuistry on structure of novels and characters' psychology.)

Starr, G. A., *Defoe and Spiritual Autobiography* (Princeton, 1971). (Chiefly on *Robinson Crusoe, Moll*, and *Roxana*.)

Rogers, P., ed., *Defoe: The Critical Heritage* (London and Boston, 1972). (Collects contemporary critical responses to Defoe, 1703–1879.)

Richetti, J. J., *Defoe's Narratives: Situations and Structures* (Oxford, 1975). (Close reading of major novels.)

Zimmerman, E., *Defoe and the Novel* (Berkeley, 1975). (Clear exposition of Defoe's growing confidence in handling irony: one chapter on each of the major novels.)

Rogers, P., *Robinson Crusoe* (1980). (Extremely useful and detailed account of sources, background, criticism, structure, etc.)

FIELDING, Henry (1707–54), born at Sharpham Park, near Glastonbury, Somerset, on 22 April, the son of Edmund Fielding (1676–1741), an army officer, and of Sarah, daughter of Sir Henry Gould of Sharpham Park, a judge of the King's Bench. He was the second cousin of Lady Mary Wortley Montagu. After Gould's death (1710), the family moved to East Stour. Educated at Eton, and with contemporaries such as Pitt, Lyttelton, and Fox. A stormy love affair with Sarah Andrew preceded move to London, where he began writing plays (*Love in Several Masques*, 1728). He studied law at the university of Leyden (1728–29), and returned to the London theatre with *The Modern Husband* (1732, dedicated to Sir Robert Walpole), *The Mock Doctor* (1732), and *The Miser* (1733), the two latter being adaptations from Molière. His most popular play was the farce *Tom Thumb* (1730), followed by *The Author's Farce* in the same year. *Don*

Quixote in England was produced in 1734. He married his first wife, Charlotte Cradock, 28 November 1734, one of three Salisbury sisters, and the model for the heroine of *Amelia* (1751). Fielding returned to the London stage with *Pasquin: a Dramatick Satire on the Times*, which ran for fifty nights on the topic of political corruption, and with *The Historical Register* (1736: another attack on Walpole). Fielding's political satire of Walpole was partly responsible for the Theatrical Licensing Act of 1737 (June), which effectively imposed censorship on the stage and terminated Fielding's dramatic career. He entered the Middle Temple on 1 November 1737, and was called to the bar in June 1740. He joined the western circuit as a magistrate. While at the bar, he started *The Champion*, with James Ralph. Richardson's *Pamela* appeared in 1740, and Fielding pursued it with *Shamela* (4 April 1741) and *Joseph Andrews* (February 1742). In 1743 he published *Miscellanies* (including *A Journey from This World to the Next*, and *Jonathan Wild*). The preface he wrote to Sarah Fielding's *David Simple* (1744) suggests that he had now given up all literary ambitions, but *The True Patriot* is published, a weekly pro-government newspaper, starting in the year of the Jacobite Rebellion (1745), and *The Jacobite's Journal* follows (December 1747–November 1748). After his first wife's death, Fielding remarries, to Mary Daniel, his first wife's maid. In December 1748 he is appointed Justice of the Peace for Westminster and moves to Bow Street, through the influence of Lyttelton and the Duke of Bedford. His other major patron was Ralph Allen of Prior Park. *Tom Jones* appears on 3–10 February 1749, dedicated to Lyttelton, and *Amelia* on 19 December 1751, dedicated to Ralph Allen. His last literary production was *The Covent-Garden Journal*, a bi-weekly newspaper from January to November 1752. His *Enquiry into the Causes of the Late Increase of Robbers* had been published in 1751, and backbreaking work as a magistrate was to ruin his health. His attention turned to crime prevention and reform of the Poor Laws. Ordered to Bath by his doctor. His rapidly declining health (graphically described in *A Voyage to Lisbon*, 1755) drove him to try a warmer climate: he died at Lisbon after two months there, on 8 October 1754, and was buried in the English cemetery. Fielding's surviving children were brought up by their uncle, Sir John Fielding, and by Ralph Allen.

Cross, W. L., *The History of Henry Fielding*, 3 vols (1918; reprinted New York, 1963). (Remains an authoritative source, with Dudden below, until Martin Battestin's biography appears.)

Dudden, F. H., *Henry Fielding: His Life, Works, and Times*, 2 vols (Oxford, 1952). (Standard life, with Cross above.)

Rogers, P., *Henry Fielding: A Biography* (1979). (Short, popular style, and includes material from previously unpublished letters.)

See: Blanchard, F. T., *Fielding the Novelist: A Study in Historical Criticism* (1926; reprinted New York, 1966). (Fielding's contribution to the realism of the novel as a genre.)

Thornbury, E. M., *Henry Fielding's Theory of the Comic Prose Epic* (Madison, 1931). (Includes an account of books in Fielding's library.)

Bissell, F. O., *Fielding's Theory of the Novel* (1933; reprinted New York, 1966). (Particularly useful for *Joseph Andrews* and *Tom Jones*.)

Irwin, W. R., *The Making of Jonathan Wild: A Study in the Literary Method of Henry Fielding* (New York, 1941). (Biographical, critical and historical materials.)

Battestin, M. C., *The Moral Basis of Fielding's Art: A Study of Joseph*

Andrews (Middletown, Connecticut, 1959). (On the latitudinarian Christian background.)

Ehrenpreis, I., *Fielding: Tom Jones* (Studies in English Literature Series, 1964). (Brief and incisive study of doctrine, meaning, form, and comedy.)

Sacks, S., *Fiction and the Shape of Belief* (Berkeley, 1964). (On Fielding's formal representation of moral beliefs.)

Wright, A., *Henry Fielding: Mask and Feast (1965)*. (Fielding's comedy as a celebration of life and the novel's series playfulness.)

Irwin, M., *Henry Fielding: The Tentative Realist* (Oxford, 1967). (Moral and ethical themes in the three major novels.)

Alter, R., *Fielding and the Nature of the Novel* (Cambridge, Mass., 1968). (On symmetry of form with meaning: a useful critical introduction.)

Hatfield, G. W., *Henry Fielding and the Language of Irony* (Chicago, 1968). (Fielding's attitude towards and means of exposing corruptions in language.)

Rawson, C., *Henry Fielding and the Augustan Ideal Under Stress* (1972). (Centrally, *Jonathan Wild* and *Amelia* as transitional works: a stylish analysis of literary changes.)

Brooks, D., *Number and Pattern in the Eighteenth-Century Novel* (1973). (Numerological patterns related to meaning in *Tom Jones*, *Joseph Andrews*, and *Amelia*.)

Harrison, B., *Henry Fielding's Tom Jones: The Novelist as Moral Philosopher* (1975). (An important philosophical defence of Fielding as a moral thinker.)

Miller, H. K., *Henry Fielding's Tom Jones and the Romance Tradition* (Victoria, Canada, 1976). (*Tom Jones* and the epic romance tradition: discussion of narrative options chosen by Fielding.)

FIELDING, Sarah (1710–68), born at East Stour, Dorset, the third sister of Henry Fielding. Raised in Salisbury under the care of maternal grandmother, Lady Sarah Gould. Little is known of her life, but Sarah was in London during the early 1740s, where she became a friend and disciple of Samuel Richardson, among others, at North End. When Henry died she moved to Bath, under the protection of Ralph Allen of Prior Park, the dedicatee of *Amelia* (1751). She knew French, and enough Greek to translate Xenophon's *Memoirs of Socrates* (with some help from James Harris acknowledged in the footnotes), in 1762. Richardson praised her first novel, *The Adventures of David Simple* (1744, 'By a Lady'), and remarked (quoting Johnson on Henry Fielding): 'What a knowledge of the human heart! Well might a critical judge of writing say, as he did to me, that your late brother's knowledge of it was not (fine writer as he was) comparable to yours. His was but as the knowledge of the outside of a clockwork machine, while your's was that of all the finer springs and movements of the inside' (letter to Sarah, 7 December 1756). Henry wrote a Preface to the second edition of *David Simple*. *Familiar Letters Between the Principal Characters in David Simple, and Some Others* (3 vols in all, 1747–53) was followed by 'romance-novels': *The Cry: A New Dramatic Fable* (1754); *The Lives of Cleopatra and Octavia* (1957). *The History of the Countess of Dellwyn* (1759), contains a forty-page preface which argues that all imaginative fiction should have a moral purpose, and that her characters (like Henry's) are 'universal and not pointed at individuals'.

Biographical details on Sarah may be found in W. L. Cross, *The History of Henry Fielding*, and in A. L. Barbauld, ed., *The Correspondence of Samuel Richardson*, 6 vols (1804). There are no critical studies of Sarah Fielding published in English, but *David Simple* has been edited by Malcolm Kelsall (Oxford, 1969).

GOLDSMITH, Oliver (1730?–74), second son of the Rev. Charles Goldsmith, master of the diocesan school at Elphin, probably born at Pallas, County Longford, Ireland, on 10 November. Educated at a succession of schools in Lissoy, Elphin, Athlone, and Edgeworthstown and at Trinity College, Dublin (1745–49), a contemporary of Edmund Burke. Received his BA in 1749 and left with the intention of studying medicine at Edinburgh (1752–54), but goes on to Paris and Leyden (1754–55). Having visited Italy, France, and Switzerland on foot he returned to England in February 1756, and settles in London, where he tried acting, then became a chemist's assistant before setting up as a physician in Southwark. He began to write for Griffiths, publisher of the *Monthly Review* (1757), still looking for employment as a physician, but failing his examination at Surgeon's Hall in December 1758. Wrote a catchpenny Life of Voltaire (not published until 1761), but in 1759 his *Enquiry into the Present State of Polite Learning in Europe* appeared, which at least brought him the friendship of Percy. He started writing for Smollett's *Critical Review* (1757–59) and *The British Magazine* (1760). He served as a literary factotum on three other periodicals, *The Lady's Magazine, The Bee,* and *The Busybody*. Friendship with John Newbery led Goldsmith to write for *The Public Ledger* on a salary. Goldsmith's 'Chinese Letters' appeared there (ninety-eight in all, starting on 24 January 1760), later to be collected as *The Citizen of the World*. Meets Dr Johnson on 31 May 1761, publishes a Life of Richard Nash (the master of ceremonies at Bath), and sells a third share of *The Vicar of Wakefield* in October to the Salisbury printer Collins. Becomes one of the original members of Johnson's The Club, meeting at the Turk's Head, Soho. *The Vicar of Wakefield* published, 27 March 1766, probably through Johnson's agency and as a means of alleviating Goldsmith's almost constant penury. In 1768 *The Good Natur'd Man* was acted and published, and in the following year the *Roman History*, followed by lives of Parnell and Bolingbroke. In 1770 he is appointed Professor of Ancient History in the Royal Academy, publishes *The Deserted Village*, and writes a *History of England* derived from Hume (1771). His best play, *She Stoops to Conquer*, was acted and published in 1773, though written in 1771, with a dedication to Johnson. Died 4 April 1774, and his posthumous works include *An History of the Earth, and Animated Nature* (1774).

Wardle, R. M., *Oliver Goldsmith* (Lawrence, Kansas, 1957). (The definitive life.)

Ginger, J., *The Notable Man: The Life and Times of Oliver Goldsmith* (1977). (More detailed in some respects than Wardle, e.g. on the composition of *The Vicar of Wakefield*.)

Balderston, K. C., *The Collected Letters of Oliver Goldsmith* (1928; reprinted New York, 1969). (The standard text.)

See: Smith, H. J., *The Citizen of the World: A Study* (New Haven, 1926). (Bibliographical, source, and background material on Goldsmith's oriental tale.)

Emslie, M., *Goldsmith: The Vicar of Wakefield* (1963; Studies in

English Literature series). (Brief, systematic analysis, a good
introduction.)

Quintana, R., *Oliver Goldsmith: A Georgian Study* (New York,
1967). (A clear, partly biographical and partly critical study, if
unadventurous.)

Hopkins, R. M., *The True Genius of Oliver Goldsmith* (Baltimore,
1969). (Sees Goldsmith as a master of irony: close reading of *The
Vicar*.)

Bäckman, S., *'This Singular Tale': A Study of The Vicar of Wakefield
and its Literary Background* (Lund, 1971). (Sources and antecedents
of the novel.)

GRAVES, Richard (1715–1804), born in Mickleton, Gloucestershire, educated
privately, then at Abingdon Grammar School before taking up a
scholarship at Pembroke College, Oxford, where his circle included
Blackstone, Hawkins, Jago, and William Shenstone. He studied medicine
in London, and was ordained, becoming rector of Claverton, near Bath, in
1749. Ralph Allen was one of his patrons. Graves established a private
school, and among his pupils there was Malthus, the political economist,
and the painter Prince Hoare. His early poems appeared in Dodsley's
collections and a collection of epigrams, *The Festoon*, appeared in 1766.
Graves's first book, *The Spiritual Quixote, or the Summer's Ramble of Mr
Geoffrey Wildgoose, a Comic Romance*, 3 vols, 1773, was written between
1757 and 1773. Its literary model is Fielding's comic epic in prose, with
some additional satire on pedantry derived from Sterne. Geoffrey
Wildgoose is the Quixotic figure to Jerry Tugwell's Sancho Panza, and the
topographical ramblings take place around Bath, Bristol, William
Shenstone's estate (the Leasowes), and the Peak District. It satirizes George
Whitefield's brand of Methodism, Wesley himself making only one
appearance. Graves produced numerous miscellaneous pieces in prose and
verse, and *The Sorrows of Werter* (published anonymously) is attributed to
him in the British Museum catalogue.

> Hill, C. J., *The Literary Career of Richard Graves* (Northampton,
> Mass., 1935). (The only systematic and book-length study of the
> life and work.)

See: Tracy, Clarence, ed., *The Spiritual Quixote* (London, 1967). (The
standard edition of the novel, with brief introduction, chronology,
and notes.)

There is no modern edition of *Werter* in Graves's translation. This is a pity,
since it is an elegant, clear, and significant contribution to the literature of
sensibility and to Anglo–German relations.

For a list of Graves's publications, including editions of *Werter*, see *NCBEL*,
II, *1660–1800*, columns 1174–75.

HAYWOOD, Eliza (1693?–1756), the subject of social gossip, perhaps based on
an early and injudicious marriage and confirmed by the scandalous element
in her novels, especially her use of thinly veiled allusions to prominent
contemporaries. Like Charlotte Lennox, she first attempted a stage career,
before settling in London. Employed by the theatre manager Rich as a
hack writer, her own play *A Wife to be Lett* was produced in 1723,
followed by a tragedy in 1729. Her novels typically deal with the maiden
in distress and in some cases are supplied with 'keys' to the intended

contemporary scene. Her novels include: *Love in Excess* (1717: into its ninth edition by 1750), *A Spy upon the Conjurer* (1724–25), *The Injur'd Husband, or Mistaken Resentment* (1724), *Memoirs of a certain Island adjacent to Utopia* (1725), and *The Secret History of the Present Intrigues of the Court of Carmania* (1727), which provoked Pope's attack on her in *The Dunciad* (1728), where she is the prize for which the infamous Curll competes ('yon Juno of majestic size', Book II, 165). Between 1744 and 1746 she collaborated in the production of *The Female Spectator* (moral tales and reflections), and her later novels include *The History of Jemmy and Jenny Jessamy* (1753), *Mary Stuart, Queen of Scots, being the Secret History of her Life* (1725), *Love Letters on all Occasions Lately passed between Persons of Distinction* (1730). A collection of her *Secret Histories, Novels, and Poems* was published in 1725.

See: Whicher, G. F., *The Life and Romances of Mrs. Eliza Haywood* (New York, 1915).

Elwood, J. R., 'The Stage Career of Eliza Haywood', *Theatre Survey*, 5 (1964), 107–16.

LENNOX, Charlotte (1720–1804), the daughter of Colonel James Ramsay, lieutenant-governor of New York, was sent to England in 1735 for adoption. But the aunt chosen seems to have been insane. She first tried the stage, and then turned to writing. She married in 1748. The publisher of her first book, a collection of poems (1747), Samuel Paterson, introduced her to Dr Johnson, through whom she also met Richardson. Johnson cites her under 'Talent' in his *Dictionary*. Her most popular book, *The Female Quixote; or the Adventures of Arabella*, was published in 1752, and reprinted in 1783 and 1810. Fielding praises this novel in *A Voyage to Lisbon*, and Johnson reviewed it for *The Gentleman's Magazine*, 22, 146. *Shakespeare Illustrated* (1753–54) was less successful, and concerned Shakespeare's alleged mishandling of literary sources, although Johnson wrote a dedication for it. In 1760–61 she ran a magazine, *The Ladies Museum*, and had her comedy unsuccessfully performed at Covent Garden (*The Sister*, 1769). She died in poor health and poverty, the beneficiary of a pension from the Royal Literary Fund. Her novels include: *The Life of Harriot Stuart* (1751 – to celebrate its publication, Johnson organized an all-night party); *Henrietta* (1758); *Sophia* (1762); and *Euphemia* (1790). She also translated works from French, on occasion assisted by Johnson and Lord Orrery, and had her portrait painted by Reynolds.

Miriam Rossiter Small, *Charlotte Ramsay Lennox: An Eighteenth Century Lady of Letters* (1935; reprinted New York, 1969). (A biography, including bibliographical details, and some of Lennox's poetry.) Ernest Baker surveys her novels in *The History of the English Novel*, Volume V, pp. 37–43, and Patricia Meyer Spacks has some trenchant remarks in *Imagining a Self*, pp. 57–65.

MACKENZIE, Henry (1745–1831), was born on the day Prince Charles landed in Scotland (26 July, Old Style). He was the son of one of Edinburgh's leading physicians, educated at the High School and Edinburgh University. His biographer (H. W. Thompson, see below) regards the dates of Harley's life as the 'Golden Age of Scotland', the period of Hume, Burns, Scott, Boswell, the portrait-painter Raeburn, the architect Robert Adam, the political economist Adam Smith, and the engineer Watt. Mackenzie spent his professional life in the law, becoming an articled clerk to the

King's Attorney in Exchequer, George Inglis, before proceeding to London for two years in 1765. His first publications were poems in the *Scots Magazine* (1764–65), including 'Melancholy', 'To Night, An Ode', 'To the Lyric Muse', and 'Landscape'. Later poems such as 'The Pursuit of Happiness' were influenced by Thomas Gray and Goldsmith's *The Deserted Village*. Of his first novel, Mackenzie writes: 'Of *The Man of Feeling*, my first novel, the idea was first adopted in London . . . In London I not only conceived the plan of this novel, . . . some of the incidents I had a certain degree of share in myself. I was often the martyr of that shyness which Harley is stated as being affected by in his intercourse with mankind.' In 1768 he returned to Edinburgh, and in April 1771 the novel appeared, to be followed by a second edition within four months. A tragedy, *The Prince of Tunis*, was performed in 1773, and in the same year (February) *The Man of the World* (the villainous baronet Sir Thomas Sindall is the antithesis of the benevolent and sentimental Harley). His third novel, *Julia de Roubigné*, in the epistolary form, appeared in 1777 (eight editions by 1800), and between January 1779 and May 1780 Mackenzie published *The Mirror* periodical, succeeded by *The Lounger* (February 1785–January 1787, including no. 97, the *Extraordinary Account of Robert Burns, the Ayrshire plowman*, the first substantial critical account of Burns). Sir Walter Scott dedicated *Waverley* (1814) to Mackenzie, and credited him with the introduction of German Romantic literature into Edinburgh intellectual circles, through his paper *An Account of the German Theatre*, read to the Royal Society of Edinburgh in April 1788. His sentimental comedy, *False Shame, or the White Hypocrite* (1789), was a failure. Made Comptroller of Taxes for Scotland in 1799, probably through the friendship of William Pitt the younger. Mackenzie's close friendship with Scott included co-direction of the Edinburgh Theatre. His *Life of J. Home* was published in 1822, and from 1824 until his death he compiled his *Anecdotes and Egotisms*.

> Thompson, H. W., ed., *The Anecdotes and Egotisms of Henry Mackenzie, 1745–1831* (1927). (Mackenzie's autobiographical and literary remarks.)
> Thompson, H. W., *A Scottish Man of Feeling: Some Account of Henry Mackenzie, Esq. of Edinburgh, and of the Golden Age of Burns and Scott* (London and New York, 1931). (Somewhat whimsical, but the only full-length biography, and which includes some of Mackenzie's poetry, pp. 68–76.)
> Drescher, Horst W., ed., *Henry Mackenzie's Letters to Elizabeth Rose of Kilravock: On Literary Events and People, 1768–1815* (Edinburgh, Münster, and London, 1967). (Full of biographical interest, details of Mackenzie's literary opinions, etc.)

See: Tompkins, J. M. S., *The Popular Novel in England, 1770–1800* (1932; reprinted 1962).
Crane, R. S., 'Suggestions toward a Genealogy of the "Man of Feeling"', *ELH*, 1 (1935), 205–30.
Humphreys, A. R., 'The Friend of Mankind', *Review of English Studies*, 24 (1948), 203–18.

MANLEY, Mary de la Rivière (1663–1724), the daughter of a Cavalier soldier and historian, Sir Roger Manley, and born at sea between Jersey and Guernsey. Tricked into a bigamous marriage with her cousin, John Manley, a Whig politician, she was then deserted by him and went to live with the Duchess of Cleveland. She began writing plays with *The Lost*

Lover (1696), a comedy, and with *The Royal Mischief* (1696), a heroic tragedy. Her novel, *The Secret History of Queen Zarah and the Zarazians* (1705), is a 'key' novel about the politics and scandalous lives of Sarah, Duchess of Marlborough, and the court circles (e.g. Young Volpone is Walpole, Foeski is Defoe). When she published *Secret Memoirs and Manners of Several Persons of Quality, of both Sexes. From the New Atalantis* (1709) she was arrested, interrogated for the sources of her inside information, and then bailed, before being discharged in 13 February 1710. In May of the same year she published *Memoirs of Europe towards the close of the Eighth Century*. This and a further volume were added as the third and fourth volumes of *The New Atalantis*. Attacked by Swift in *Tatler* 63, but in 1711 she succeeded Swift as editor of the Tory journal *The Examiner*. Also in 1711 she produced *Court Intrigues from the Island of New Atalantis*, and in 1720 produced *The Power of Love, in Seven Novels*. She lived as the mistress of Alderman Barber, the Tory Lord Mayor of London, and Swift described her as a woman of 'generous principles . . . a great deal of good sense and invention . . . about forty, very homely, and very fat'. She was the first eighteenth-century English novelist to be translated into French (*Queen Zarah*, 1708), and she fictionalized her own autobiography in *The Adventures of Rivella; or, the History of the Author of the Atalantis* (1714). Her preface 'To the Reader' in *Queen Zarah* is neither an early nor an original argument for psychological probability in characterization and for verisimilitude in setting and historical context. It is a literal translation from Bellegarde's *Lettres curieuses* (1702), itself a paraphrase of du Plaisir's *Sentiments sur les lettres* (1683).

The *New Atalantis*, her best-known compilation of novels, is essentially a series of lengthy stories strung together by a dialogue and allegory: its intrigue, sexual seductions, theme of incest and lesbianism, moralizing on the perils of a careless education, predatory males and passive maidens, last-minute deliverances, etc., are perfunctorily held together with a conventional homily on the dangers of appearance. But Manley also attacks the 'double standard' which allowed male promiscuity but demanded female chastity, and as for the sexual language, the following is perhaps typical, from the second volume of the 1709 edition, pp. 228–29:

> she suffer'd all the glowing pressures of his *roving* Hand, that Hand, which with a Luxury of Joy, wander'd through all the rich *Meanders* of her Bosom; she suffer'd him to *drink* her dazling naked Beauties at his Eyes! to *gaze*! to *burn*! to press her with *unbounded Rapture*! taking by intervals a thousand *eager short-breath'd* Kisses. Whilst Diana, lull'd by the enchanting Poison Love had diffus'd throughout her form, lay *still*, and *charm'd* as he! she *thought* no more! – she *could not* think! – let *Love* and *Nature* plead the weighty Cause! – let *them* excuse the beauteous Frailty! – Diana was become a *Votary* to Venus! – obedient to the Dictates of the Goddess! –

See: Richetti, J. B., *Popular Fiction Before Richardson: Narrative Patterns 1700–1739* (Oxford, 1969), pp. 119–53.
     Köster, P., ed., *The Novels of Mary Delarivière Manley*, 2 vols (Gainesville, 1971). (A facsimile reprint, with critical and biographical introduction, of *The Secret History of Queen Zarah, The New Atalantis, Memoirs of Europe*, and *The Adventures of Rivella*.)
     Sutton, J. L., 'The Source of Mrs Manley's Preface to *Queen Zarah*', *MP*, 81 (November 1984), 167–72.

REEVE, Clara (1729–1807), born at Ipswich, the daughter of a Suffolk rector. One of eight children, and educated by her father. Her first attempt at authorship was a translation of Barclay's romance *Argenis* (published in 1772 as *The Phoenix*). In 1777 she produced her best work, *The Champion of Virtue, a Gothic Story* (which earned her ten pounds). The second edition was retitled *The Old English Baron* (1778), reprinted thirteen times between 1778 and 1886, the 'literary offspring' of Walpole's *The Castle of Otranto*, and dedicated to Richardson's daughter, Mrs Brigden. Walpole denounced it as a reduction of the Gothic genre 'to reason and probability'. *The Progress of Romance* (1785) was followed by *The Exiles, or Memoirs of the Count de Cronstadt* (1788), a historical novel. She also wrote two contemporary novels, *The Two Mentors* (1783), and *The School for Widows* (1791). *Fatherless Fanny, or the Little Mendicant* was posthumously published in 1839.
   Not listed in *NCBEL* as a separate entry.

RICHARDSON, Samuel (1689–1761). Probably born in the Derbyshire village of Mackworth, the son of a joiner and apparently intended 'for the Cloth'. Apprenticed to a printer, then a compositor, wrote prefaces and compiled indexes. At thirteen was employed by a group of young women to provide models for their love-letters: nicknamed 'Serious and Gravity' at school. Official printer to the House of Commons. Friends included Aaron Hill, Lewis Theobald, Dr George Cheyne, Arthur 'Speaker' Onslow, and, later, Joseph Spence. Printed several books sponsored by the Society for the Encouragement of Learning (formed in 1736); printer of the House of Commons parliamentary *Journals* (26 folio volumes, 1742–55); partner in the office of Law Printer to the King (1760) and for a time printed the pro-Walpole newspapers *The Daily Journal* (1736–37) and *Daily Gazetteer* (1738); printed two of Defoe's conduct-books. In 1738 he bought a suburban retreat, The Grange, Fulham. Invited by the printers Rivington and Osborn to write 'a little Volume of Letters' (written November 1739–January 1740; published January 1741, as *Familiar Letters*), based on popular seventeenth-century letter-writing manuals, intended for 'country readers' but set in the city. *Pamela*, with 'some slight Foundation in Truth', appeared in two vols, 6 November 1740, second edition in February 1741, third in March, fourth in May, fifth in October: a bestseller. Admired by Pope, and Fielding's patron Ralph Allen, *Pamela* was copied, spuriously continued, dramatized. Richardson produced his own continuation (Volume III and IV) on 7 December 1741, generally reckoned an artistic failure but anticipating *Clarissa* in its use of two-sided correspondence (*Pamela* being generally composed of letters out rather than letters received), and in its use of character-types. *Pamela* I was dramatized by Henry Gifford (1741: Garrick taking a role), by a Mr Edge (1742), and versified by George Bennett (1741). Joseph Highmore painted twelve scenes from the novel, and there were prints by Philip Mercier (1750), and a waxworks (1745). One of the earliest 'anti Pamelae' was Henry Fielding's *Shamela* (April 1741), followed by *Pamela Censured* (1741), *Pamela's Conduct in High Life*, Charles Povey's *Virgin in Eden*, etc. Pirated by Dublin printer Faulkner, and reprinted in America (1744, New York, Philadelphia, Boston), and translated into French, Italian, Dutch, German, and eventually into Swedish, Russian, Spanish, and Portuguese.
   Before the end of 1744 Richardson had a précis of *Clarissa*. By June, Edward Young knew the whole story. (*Grandison* had no such prior plan.)

First two volumes of *Clarissa* published in December 1747; three and four, April 1748; last three in December 1748 (the change to smaller type was made in Volume VI – otherwise there are eight volumes). Second edition, June 1749, and translated quickly into German (1748–52), Dutch (1752–55), French (abbreviated and translated by Abbé Prévost, 1751–62), Russian (1791–92), Italian (1783–89), and Portuguese (1804–18). Third edition, 1751. Many of Clarissa's decorative literary allusions are taken from Dryden, Otway, Lee, and Rowe (serious tragic drama), and may be found in contemporary collections of Bysshe and Gildon, providing the high tragic tone Richardson was seeking. Fielding, among many others, urged a happy ending on Richardson. Richardson was mortified at the success of Fielding's *Tom Jones*, and gratified by the critical failure of the latter's *Amelia* (1751). Johnson remarked: 'There was as great a difference between them as between a man who knew how a watch was made, and a man who could tell the hour by looking on the dial-plate.' Richardson preferred the company of intelligent women, including Lady Bradshaigh, Sarah Fielding, Charlotte Lennox, Mary Granville, Mrs Donellan, Mrs Chapone, and Elizabeth Carter. *Sir Charles Grandison*, Volumes I–IV, published on 13 November 1753, V–VI on 11 December 1753, VII on 14 March 1754 (third edition like the second has over 900 revisions, on 19 March 1754). Other works are: *Aesop's Fables. With Instructive Morals and Reflection, Abstracted from all Party Considerations* (1740); the above-mentioned *Familiar Letters on Important Occasions* (1741); and *Collection of the Moral and Instructive Sentiments . . . Contained in . . . Pamela, Clarissa, and Sir Charles Grandison* (1755).

McKillop, A. D., *Samuel Richardson: Printer and Novelist* (1936; reprinted New York, 1960). (The standard biography until the following.)

Eaves, T. D. and B. D. Kimpel, *Samuel Richardson: A Biography* (Oxford, 1971). (Definitive.)

Barbauld, A. L., ed., *The Correspondence of Samuel Richardson*, 6 vols (1804).

Carroll, J., ed., *Selected Letters of Samuel Richardson* (Oxford, 1964). (A modern annotated edition.)

See: Sale, W. M., Jr, *Samuel Richardson, Master Printer* (Ithaca, New York, 1950). (Identifies all the works from Richardson's press.)

Van Ghent, D., 'On Clarissa Harlowe', in *The English Novel: Form and Function* (1953), pp. 45–63. (On the novel's imagery and power as mythology.)

Watt, I., 'Clarissa and Lovelace', in *The Rise of the Novel* (1957), pp. 225–38. (On the sexual stereotypes and unconscious symbolism.)

Kreissman, B., *Pamela-Shamela* (Lincoln, 1960). (The parodies, adaptations, and critical responses to *Pamela*.)

Kearney, A., *Samuel Richardson: Clarissa* (1968: Profiles in Literature series). (Brief and systematic commentary on setting and techniques.)

Konigsberg, I., *Samuel Richardson and the Dramatic Novel* (Lexington, 1968). (Influence of sentimental drama on the novels.)

Ball, D. L., *Samuel Richardson's Theory of Fiction* (The Hague, 1971). (Systematic analysis of the novels in terms of Richardson's own theories of fiction.)

Kinkead-Weekes, M., *Samuel Richardson: Dramatic Novelist* (1973). (Close critical commentary.)

Doody, M. A., *A Natural Passion: A Study of the Novels of Samuel Richardson* (Oxford, 1974). (Literary background, sources, analogues, and ideas: the best single critical book on Richardson.)

Eagleton, T., *The Rape of Clarissa: Writing, Sexuality and Class Struggle in Samuel Richardson* (Oxford, 1982). (Very brief, controversial analysis using feminist, Marxist, and post-structuralist critical methods.)

Goldberg, R., *Sex and Enlightenment: Women in Richardson and Diderot* (Oxford, 1984). (Chiefly on *Clarissa*, with some pages on *La Religieuse*: excellent on feminist themes in former.)

SMOLLETT, Tobias (1721–71), born in Dumbartonshire, Scotland, and educated at Dumbarton Grammar School and Glasgow University, where he read medicine. In 1736 he began a five-year apprenticeship to Dr John Gordon before going to London (1739) with a play in his pocket. He gained a post as surgeon and sailed to the West Indies, witnessing the battle at Cartagena (1741). Lived for a time in Jamaica, met and later married the creole heiress Nancy Lascelles on his return to England in 1747. Sets up medical practice in Downing Street, Westminster, and writes *The Tears of Scotland* in response to the crushing of the Jacobites after the 1745 rebellion. *Roderick Random* was published in 1748, anonymously, and Lady Mary Wortley Montagu attributed it to Henry Fielding. In London Smollett was at the centre of a group of expatriate Scots, including the medical men Hunter, Armstrong, and Smellie. He gained his MD from Marischal College, Aberdeen, in 1750 and embarked on Continental travels. *Peregrine Pickle* was published in 1751, including splenetic personal attacks on Garrick, Akenside, Cibber, and Fielding. These were deleted from the second edition. After a visit to Bath, with the intention of setting up medical practice, he published *An Essay on the External Use of Water* (1752), deflating the medical claims made for spa water. In London he is visited by Johnson, Goldsmith, Sterne, Garrick, Wilkes, and John Hunter. *Ferdinand Count Fathom* appeared in 1753, and his translation of *Don Quixote* two years later. In 1756 he revisits Scotland and on his return to London helps to found *The Critical Review* (February 1756) and begins writing his *History of England* (intended to compete with Hume's *History*). In 1756 he published his *Compendium of Authentic and Entertaining Voyages*, and in January 1757 his nautical farce *The Reprisal, or The Tears of Old England* was performed at Drury Lane. As a result of his remarks in the *Critical Review* he was tried for defamation of Admiral Sir Charles Knowles, and jailed for three months. *Launcelot Greaves* appears serially in *The British Magazine* (monthly chapters, January 1760–December 1761). Joint editor, and manager of a collaborative team of translators, on a thirty-eight-volume translation of Voltaire's works (1761–65). Asthma attacks prompt journey to France after the death of his daughter (1763) and then to Italy (1763–65). His *Travels through France and Italy* published in 1766, and he returns to Scotland, where he is visited by the Edinburgh illuminati (Hume, Home, Robertson, Adam Smith, Blair, Carlyle). Back in London in late 1766 he publishes *The Present State of all Nations* (1768; begun in 1760), and leaves for Italy, his health poor, settling at Leghorn, where he finishes *Humphry Clinker* (1771). He dies at his villa on 17 September 1771, and is buried at the English cemetery.

Melville, L., *The Life and Letters of Tobias Smollett* (1926; reprinted New York, 1966). (A biography; but see Knapp below.)

Knapp, L. M., *Tobias Smollett: Doctor of Men and Manners* (Princeton, 1949). (The definitive biography.)

Bruce, D., *Radical Doctor Smollett* (1964). (Partly biographical; on Smollett's voice of social and political protest.)

Knapp, L. M., ed., *The Letters of Tobias Smollett* (Oxford, 1970). (Standard edition.)

See: Martz, L. L., *The Later Career of Tobias Smollett* (New Haven, 1942). (Smollett's historical work, compiling and editing.)

Kahrl, G., *Tobias Smollett, Traveler-Novelist* (1945; reprinted New York, 1968). (Analysis of each of the novels in the travel context.)

Boege, F. W., *Smollett's Reputation as a Novelist* (Princeton, 1947). (Reputation, from 1748 to 1940.)

Goldberg, M. A., *Smollett and the Scottish School: Studies in Eighteenth-Century Thought* (New Mexico, 1959). (On the Primitivism and Progress theme in *Humphry Clinker*; Smollett's context in the Scottish Common-Sense School.)

Giddings, R., *The Tradition of Smollett* (1967). (The picaresque tradition.)

Spector, R. D., *Tobias Smollett* (New York, 1968). (Detailed analysis of the novels within the picaresque tradition.)

Price, J. V., *Tobias Smollett: The Expedition of Humphry Clinker* (1973, Studies in English Literature series). (Brief, detailed analysis of characters, structure, meaning.)

Boucé, P. G., *The Novels of Tobias Smollett*, translated by Antonia White and the author (1976). (Partly biographical; the standard critical work.)

Grant, D., *Tobias Smollett: A Study in Style* (Manchester, 1977). (Close analysis of Smollett's prose style, and a vigorous defence of Smollett as a literary artist.)

STERNE, Laurence (1713–68), son of an army officer and great-grandson of an Archbishop of York, born in Clonmel, Tipperary, Ireland, on 24 November. Early experience was of barrack life, following the postings of his father in Ireland, the Isle of Wight, in Dublin, and Halifax (1723). His father was wounded at the siege of Gibraltar (1727), and died in Jamaica in 1731, having achieved the rank of lieutenant, and leaving his widow and children a pension of £20 a year. Sterne's cousin Richard supervised his education and he was sent to Jesus College, Cambridge, at the late age of almost twenty. Locke's *Essay Concerning Human Understanding* (1690) intellectually excited him, but not much else in the curriculum. At college he formed a close friendship with John Hall-Stevenson (1735–36), and graduated BA in 1736, MA in 1740, in debt and showing early signs of the tuberculosis that would eventually kill him. His uncle, Jaques, precentor and canon of York, helped him to take holy orders and acquire the vicarage of Sutton-in-the-Forest (about 12 km from York) in 1739. Sterne preached occasionally in the Minster. He courted Eliza Lumley for two years before marrying her in 1741, improved his ecclesiastical income up to £200 a year, supplemented by some dairy farming (1738–39). A proficient musician on the bass-viol, an amateur artist, and a voracious reader of Cervantes and Rabelais in particular, he socialized with Hall-

Stevenson's 'Demoniack' drinking friends. One surviving daughter, Lydia, born in 1747. Sterne's first publication was a sermon, 'The Case of Elijah and the Widow Zerepath consider'd' (York, 1747), and his second, 'The Abuses of Conscience' (1750) was later incorporated into the second volume of *Tristram Shandy* (Ch. 17). The manuscript of what was later to become *A Political Romance* (York, 1759) circulated in the late 1740s, satirizing a local ecclesiastical dispute featuring a character called Trim. In 1758 Sterne's wife was committed to a private mental asylum in York, and by 26 March 1759 he had reached the twenty-first chapter of *Tristram Shandy*. He begins a flirtation with a young French lady, Mme Fourmantelle ('dear, dear Kitty'), who becomes Jenny in *Tristram Shandy*. Two volumes of the novel completed by end of 1759. Dodsley declines the offer of publication and the volumes are privately printed at York in an edition of 200–300 copies by John Hinxham, written 'not to be fed but to be famous'. London reaction was immediately enthusiastic (Walpole, Garrick, and Bishop Warburton, in particular, although Johnson maintained a strong disapproval). The Sterne family visit London (Mrs Sterne having recovered) and Dodsley publishes *Sermons of Mr Yorick* (Volumes I–II) in 1760, with 500 subscribers. Sterne becomes a literary and social celebrity (*Tristram* having appeared 29 March 1760, Volumes I–II). Returning to York, Sterne moves to Coxwold and calls his house Shandy Hall. By August he finished the third volume, a fourth by October (published 1761), fifth and sixth completed by December and published. Illness necessitated a journey to France (January 1762), financed by a loan from Garrick (never repaid); joined by his family in July. In Toulouse for twelve months, and attempts to complete a seventh volume set in the courts of Europe. Visits to Aix, Marseilles, Montpellier, and back to England in March 1764, leaving his wife and daughter in Montauban. Volumes VII and VIII completed in December at Coxwold and published 26 January 1765. In October makes a seven-month tour of France and Italy. *The Sermons of Mr Yorick* (Volumes III–IV) published in January 1766, and completes the final, ninth volume of *Tristram Shandy* (published January 1767). In December 1766, Sterne meets Elizabeth Draper in London, and during a brief but intense romantic flirtation on his part she is summoned back to her husband in Bombay (April 1767). Sterne writes *The Journal to Eliza* between April and November (as 'The Bramine's Journal'). Mrs Sterne and Lydia return to him in August, but only to arrange separation, Mrs Sterne to return to France on an allowance. *A Sentimental Journey* appears, February 1768 (Volumes I–II), and Sterne dies 18 March, in London. In 1904 Wilbur L. Cross first published *The Journal to Eliza*, and on 8 June 1969, Sterne's remains were reburied in Coxwold churchyard.

Cross, W. L., *The Life and Times of Laurence Sterne* (1925; revised and reprinted New York, 1929). (The standard biography.)

James, O. P., *The Relation of Tristram Shandy to the Life of Sterne* (The Hague, 1966). (Argues that Yorick and Sterne are distinguishable, the latter being Sterne's persona.)

Cash, A. H., *Laurence Sterne: The Early and Middle Years* (1975).

Curtis, L. P., ed., *Letters of Laurence Sterne* (Oxford, 1935). (Standard edition.)

See: Hammond, L. van der H., *Laurence Sterne's Sermons of Yorick* (New Haven, 1948, reprinted New York, 1970). (The originality and indebtedness of Sterne's sermons.)

Traugott, J., *Tristram Shandy's World: Sterne's Philosophical Rhetoric* (Berkeley and Los Angeles, 1954). (Sterne subverts Locke, transcending rationalism by wit.)

Howes, A. B., *Yorick and the Critics: Sterne's Reputation in England, 1760–1868* (New Haven, 1958). (Critical reputation.)

Fluchère, H., *Laurence Sterne: From Tristram to Yorick: An Interpretation of Tristram Shandy*, translated and abridged by Barbara Bray (1965). (Omits the biographical section of the original; a detailed analysis of *Tristram Shandy*.)

Cash, A. H., *Sterne's Comedy of Moral Sentiments: The Ethical Dimension of the Journey* (Pittsburgh, 1966). (On *A Sentimental Journey*.)

Hartley, L., *Laurence Sterne in the Twentieth Century: An Essay and a Bibliography of Sternean Studies 1900–1965* (1966; revised edn, 1900–68, Chapel Hill, 1968). (Annotated bibliography, with discussion of the novels, sermons, and letters.)

Stedmond, J. M., *The Comic Art of Laurence Sterne: Convention and Innovation in Tristram Shandy and A Sentimental Journey* (Toronto, 1967). (The comic use of narrative conventions, and the purpose of Sterne's comedy.)

New, M., *Laurence Sterne as Satirist: A Reading of Tristram Shandy* (Gainesville, 1969). (*Tristram Shandy* in the tradition of satires on human pride.)

Lanham, R. A., *Tristram Shandy: The Games of Pleasure* (Berkeley, 1973). (Sterne's comedy in the context of traditional narrative forms.)

Moglen, H., *The Philosophical Irony of Laurence Sterne* (Gainesville, 1975). (An important study of the elaborate ironic strategies in *Tristram Shandy*.)

Swearingen, J. E., *Reflexivity in Tristram Shandy: An Essay in Phenomenological Criticism* (New Haven, 1977). (A complex investigation of Sterne's novel and the destiny of modern life.)

Conrad, P., *Shandyism: The Character of Romantic Irony* (New York, 1978). (On Sterne's 'rearrangement' of comedy and tragedy.)

Byrd, M., *Tristram Shandy* (1985, Unwin Critical Library series). (Detailed discussion and commentary on background, themes, structure, and critical history.)

WALPOLE, Horatio (Horace), fourth Earl of Orford (1717–97), born in London on 24 September, the fourth and third surviving son of Sir Robert Walpole by his first wife, Catherine Shorter. Horace (the version which he himself preferred) was by eleven years the youngest of the children. Privately educated, then to Eton (1727–34), where his contemporaries included the poet Thomas Gray, Richard West (the painter), and Charles Hanbury-Williams. Then to King's College, Cambridge (March 1735). In 1737, through his father's influence, he was appointed to several lucrative posts, including one in the Custom-House. He left Cambridge in March 1739, and set off on the Grand Tour with Gray – Paris, Rheims, Dijon, Lyons, Geneva, and across the Alps to Turin, Genoa, and Florence, where they were welcomed by Sir Horace Mann (Minister-Plenipotentiary, and soon to become one of the recipients of Walpole's indefatigable epistolary energy). He visited Rome, and shortly thereafter separated from Gray, returning to England (having been elected to Parliament in his absence) on

12 September 1741. Sir Robert Walpole had resigned from the Commons
and been elevated to the Peerage in 1742 as Lord Orford. Horace now set
about writing up the family art treasures at the Norfolk seat of Houghton:
Aedes Walpolianae (1747), and publishes some minor journalism. In 1747 he
moves to Twickenham, and eventually buys a house once occupied by
Colley Cibber, Strawberry-Hill-Shot, which he renames. In January 1750,
he writes: 'I am going to build a little Gothic castle at Strawberry Hill.'
This occupied his time until beyond 1770, and in 1774 he published a
Description of the Villa of Horace Walpole (reprinted in 1784, with
engravings). He was also working on his *Memoirs*. The *Description* was
printed on his own press at Strawberry Hill, Officina Arbuteana, as were
the *Odes* of Gray, works by several others, and his own *Anecdotes of
Painting in England* (5 vols, 1762–80), *The Mysterious Mother* (a tragedy,
1768), and *An Essay on Gardening* (1785). In December 1764 *The Castle of
Otranto* appeared (printed by Lownds, London). Walpole travels to Paris
(September 1765), meets the blind Mme du Deffand, and on his return is
unsuccessfully approached for patronage by Thomas Chatterton. *Historic
Doubts on the Life and Reign of King Richard the Third* appeared in 1768, and
Walpole retires from Parliament, succeeding his nephew as fourth Earl of
Orford. He died in London in his eightieth year. His *Memoirs of the Reign
of George II and George III* published posthumously.

> Lewis, W. S. and others, eds, *The Yale Edition of Horace Walpole's
> Correspondence*, 48 vols (New Haven, 1937–83). (A monumental
> edition, with four index volumes.)

See: Mehrotra, K. K., *Horace Walpole and the English Novel: A Study of
      the Influence of 'The Castle of Otranto', 1764–1820* (1934; reprinted
      New York, 1970). (Appendix B lists 195 'romantic' novels
      published between 1762 and 1797.)
      Lewis, W. S., *Horace Walpole* (The A. W. Mellon Lectures in the
      Fine Arts, 1960; 1961). (Richly illustrated section on Strawberry
      Hill, pp. 97–136.)
      Smith, W. H., *Horace Walpole: Writer, Politician, and
      Connoisseur: Essays on the 250th Anniversary of Wadpole's Birth* (New
      Haven and London, 1967). (Nineteen essays on many aspects,
      including the editor's piece on Walpole and the French Revolution,
      pp. 91–114.)
      Kallich, M., *Horace Walpole* (New York, 1971). (Critical–analytical
      study: a good general introduction.)

Index